Teaching and Researching Language and Culture

APPLIED LINGUISTICS IN ACTION

General Editors:

Christopher N. Candlin and David R. Hall

Books published in this series include:

Teaching and Researching Motivation	Zoltán Dörnyei
Teaching and Researching Lexicography	R.R.K. Hartmann
Teaching and Researching Autonomy in Language Learning	Phil Benson
Teaching and Researching Translation	Basil Hatim
Teaching and Researching Writing	Ken Hyland
Teaching and Researching Listening	Michael Rost
Teaching and Researching Speaking	Rebecca Hughes
Teaching and Researching Computer-assisted Language Learning	Ken Beatty

Teaching and Researching Language and Culture

Joan Kelly Hall

An imprint of **Pearson Education**

London · New York · Toronto · Sydney · Tokyo · Singapore · Hong Kong · Cape Town
Madrid · Paris · Amsterdam · Munich · Milan

PEARSON EDUCATION LIMITED

Head Office:
Edinburgh Gate
Harlow CM20 2JE
Tel: +44 (0)1279 623623
Fax: +44 (0)1279 431059

London Office:
128 Long Acre
London WC2E 9AN
Tel: +44 (0)20 7447 2000
Fax: +44 (0)20 7447 2170
Website: www.pearsoneduc.com/linguistics

First edition published in Great Britain in 2002

© Pearson Education Limited 2002

The right of Joan Kelly Hall to be identified as Author
of this Work has been asserted by her in accordance
with the Copyright, Designs and Patents Act 1988.

ISBN 0 582 42337 6

British Library Cataloguing in Publication Data
A CIP catalogue record for this book can be obtained from the British Library

Library of Congress Cataloging in Publication Data
A CIP catalog record for this book can be obtained from the Library of Congress

10 9 8 7 6 5 4 3 2 1

Set in 11/13pt Janson by Graphicraft Limited, Hong Kong
Printed in Malaysia, LSP

The Publishers' policy is to use paper manufactured from sustainable forests.

Contents

General Editor's Preface   ix
Acknowledgements   xi

Introduction   1

Section I   Defining language and culture   5

   1   A sociocultural perspective on language and culture   7

1.1   Introduction   7
1.2   Language as sociocultural resource   8
1.3   Culture as sociocultural practice   17
1.4   Linguistic relativity   19
1.5   A socially constituted linguistics   21
1.6   Systemic functional linguistics   25
1.7   Summary   28

   2   Language and identity   31

2.1   Introduction   31
2.2   Social identity   32
2.3   Agency, identity and language use   35
2.4   Research on language use and identity   38
2.5   Summary   45

3   Language-and-culture learning   48

3.1   Introduction   48
3.2   A sociocultural perspective on language and
      culture learning   49
3.3   Language socialisation   53
3.4   Learning how to mean   56
3.5   Social activity and language development   57
3.6   Social activity and cognitive development   60
3.7   Language classrooms as fundamental sites of learning   62
3.8   Summary   66

Section II   Teaching language and culture   69

4   The sociocultural worlds of learners   71

4.1   Introduction   71
4.2   Language socialisation practices: Home and school
      connections   72
4.3   Language variation   74
4.4   Redesigning curriculum and instruction   75
4.5   Summary   82

5   Language and culture of the classroom   85

5.1   Introduction   85
5.2   Schools and classrooms as communicative
      environments   86
5.3   The role of classroom discourse   89
5.4   Redesigning curriculum and instruction   94
5.5   Summary   100

6   Language and culture as curricular content   104

6.1   Introduction   104
6.2   Defining knowledge of language and culture   105
6.3   Pedagogical approaches for redesigning language
      classrooms   112
6.4   Summary   123

Section III   Researching language and culture   125

7   The research enterprise   127

7.1   Introduction   127
7.2   Methodological foundations of research on language
       and culture from a sociocultural perspective   128
7.3   Research ethics   137
7.4   Summary   139

8   Approaches to research on language,
     culture and learning   141

8.1   Introduction   141
8.2   Ethnography of communication   142
8.3   Interactional sociolinguistics   146
8.4   Conversation analysis   148
8.5   Discourse analysis   151
8.6   Critical discourse analysis   154
8.7   Microgenetic approach   155
8.8   Summary   159

9   Guidelines for doing research   160

9.1   Introduction: The research cycle   160
9.2   Identify concerns and develop research questions   160
9.3   Identify research approach and sources of data   162
9.4   Collect data   166
9.5   Analyse the data   166
9.6   Reflect on the findings   168
9.7   Share findings and take action where appropriate   168
9.8   Summary   170

10   Contexts of research   172

10.1   Introduction   172
10.2   Contexts of research   173
10.3   Summary   198

Section IV   Resources for teaching and researching language and culture   199

11   Resources for teaching and researching language and culture   201

11.1   Introduction   201
11.2   Journals   202
11.3   Professional organisations   206
11.4   Web-based resources for teaching and researching language and culture   208

Glossary   212
References   219
Author Index   237
Subject Index   241

General Editor's Preface

Applied Linguistics in Action, as its name suggests, is a Series which focuses on the issues and challenges to practitioners and researchers in a range of fields in Applied Linguistics and provides readers and users with the tools they need to carry out their own practice-related research.

The books in the Series provide readers with clear, up-to-date, accessible and authoritative accounts of their chosen field within Applied Linguistics. Using the metaphor of a map of the landscape of the field, each book provides information on its main ideas and concepts, its scope, its competing issues, solved and unsolved questions. Armed with this authoritative but critical account, readers can explore for themselves a range of exemplary practical applications of research into these issues and questions, before taking up the challenge of undertaking their own research, guided by the detailed and explicit research guides provided. Finally, each book has a section which is concurrently on the Series *website* www.booksites.net/alia and which provides a rich array of chosen resources, information sources, further reading and commentary, as well as a key to the principal concepts of the field.

Questions the books in this innovative Series ask are those familiar to all practitioners and researchers, whether very experienced, or new to the fields of Applied Linguistics.

- What does research tell us, what doesn't it tell us, and what should it tell us about the field? What is its geography? How is the field mapped and landscaped?

- How has research been carried out and applied and what interesting research possibilities does practice raise? What are the issues we need to explore and explain?

- What are the key researchable topics that practitioners can undertake? How can the research be turned into practical action?

- Where are the important resources that practitioners and researchers need? Who has the information? How can it be accessed?

Each book in the Series has been carefully designed to be as accessible as possible, with built-in features to enable readers to find what they want quickly and to home in on the key issues and themes that concern them. The structure is to move from practice to theory and research, and back to practice, in a cycle of development of understanding of the field in question. Books in the Series will be usable for the individual reader but also can serve as a basis for course design, or seminar discussion.

Each of the authors of books in the Series is an acknowledged authority, able to bring broad knowledge and experience to engage practitioners and researchers in following up their own ideas, working with them to build further on their own experience.

Applied Linguistics in Action is an **in action** Series. Its *website* will keep you updated and regularly re-informed about the topics, fields and themes in which you are involved.

We hope that you will like and find useful the design, the content, and, above all, the support the books will give to your own practice and research!

Christopher N. Candlin & David R. Hall
General Editors

Acknowledgements

I owe a great debt of thanks to many individuals whose models of scholarship, collegiality and friendship have given shape to my own intellectual and personal pursuits. The late Alan Purves was most responsible for setting my direction in the early years of graduate school by drawing me into work by and about such intellectual luminaries as Vygotsky, Wittgenstein and Bakhtin. I have also benefited immensely from discussions with Bob Sanders and Rose-Marie Weber. They provided enormous intellectual and emotional support during my time as a graduate student, and they continue to play a significant role in my life. Special thanks must also go to Jim Lantolf, who has been for me the embodiment of congenial scholar and friend. I also extend my appreciation to many colleagues, students and friends who, over the last several years, have provided invaluable assistance in the development of this text by affording me numerous opportunities to cultivate my ideas in extended discussions with them in classrooms, at conferences, in restaurants and over coffee.

I am equally grateful to series editors, Chris Candlin and David Hall, whose patient assistance has been extraordinary. Their thorough attention to both substance and form has greatly enhanced the text, and me. Thanks to Hyun-woo Lim and Becky Hendren for their editorial and other assistance in attending to the details needed to bring the project to completion. Finally, I offer my deepest gratitude to my husband Bill and daughters Kate and Kelly. In their inimitable ways, they continue to enrich my efforts with their endless affection and good humour.

Introduction

Applied Linguistics is, and has always been, centrally concerned with language use. Although originally conceived as an applied branch of the field of linguistics, as a site for discussions on the practicalities of using language, Applied Linguistics has come into its own as an internationally recognised and recognisable field. It has its own conferences and its own academic degree programmes. It also has its own journals and, as the series of which this text is a part illustrates, its own disciplinary base.

This transformation has come about largely from explorations taken by those interested in the practicalities of language use into an assortment of scholarly territories including communication, cultural psychology, linguistic anthropology, linguistic philosophy and social theory in search of new ways to understand language use. The many theoretical insights and empirical findings gleaned from these quests have led to new ways of understanding and engaging in applied linguistics activity.

The aim of *Teaching and Researching Language and Culture* is to lay out some of the major underpinnings of contemporary thought on two concepts considered to be at the heart of applied linguistics activity: language and culture. The book is organised into four sections. Section I contains three chapters in which I present some of the more significant assumptions on the nature of language and culture, and the nature of language-and-culture learning embodied in a sociocultural perspective of human action. In Chapter 1, I describe and trace the lineage of current perspectives on language and culture. In Chapter 2 I examine and trace the sources of current perspectives on the notion of identity and language use. In Chapter 3 I present current understandings on the nature of language-and-culture learning, tie them to recent findings from research on language development and discuss their implications for the development of an integrated theory of language teaching and learning.

The task of Section II, also containing three chapters, is to examine how current understandings of language, culture and learning inform pedagogical practices. In Chapter 4 I provide an overview of current research revealing the vitality and richness of the culturally and linguistically diverse worlds that learners bring with them to school, and discuss some pedagogical innovations arising from this research. Chapter 5 is concerned with the sociocultural worlds of schools and classrooms. Here I present some recent research on these worlds and describe some pedagogical innovations for creating particular kinds of sociocultural communities in the classroom. In Chapter 6 I examine recent conceptualisations of language and culture as curricular content, and describe some current pedagogical approaches to teaching language and culture that have sprung from these discussions.

The purpose of the four chapters in Section III is to familiarise readers with current research interests in and approaches to the study of language and culture. In Chapter 7 I discuss some issues and concerns with doing 'good' research. In Chapter 8 I summarise six approaches currently used by applied linguists to research language, culture and learning from a sociocultural perspective, and in Chapter 9 I present a set of guidelines for planning, conducting and evaluating research projects. I present a framework for conceptualising research contexts to give readers a sense of how current undertakings in the field are connected in Chapter 10. In the discussion I include plans or blueprints for several research projects, using the framework set out in Chapter 9, that readers can try by themselves. It is hoped that the discussion of possibilities will help readers to develop and carry out their own ideas for doing research.

Section IV (Chapter 11) provides additional sources and resources to help readers in their explorations. The chapter contains an annotated list of some of the main journals in the field that publish studies on language and culture. It also includes a short list of some of the major professional organisations for applied linguists. Finally, it includes an annotated listing of web-based resources for doing research and provides a link with others around the globe who are doing work of a similar nature. Following Chapter 11 is a glossary of the terms used in the text that readers may find of assistance.

Postscript

The task of mapping current thought on two such crucial concepts as language and culture in such a broad field was daunting, to say the least. This was not only because of the breadth of the field but also because of the significant implications embodied in the act of writing. On one hand, writing is facilitative in that it helps to fix and preserve ideas across time and space. In this regard, written words function like a map. They provide us with a specific location from which to view the surrounding territory and get a sense of where we are in the larger landscape of ideas. On the other hand, written words constrain us. In completing our thoughts, they limit us to particular ways of making sense, and thus only partially represent the worlds in which we live.

The written world I have created here is intentionally broad in that I have attempted to give shape to some of the major sites of contemporary activity in applied linguistics, to chart some of the more well-travelled routes that have led to these sites, and to point out some of the more well-known expedition leaders. It is also partial. There are connecting routes and related activities that are surely a part of this larger landscape but are not included here. There are also alternative routes and different sorts of activities taking place in the field that, while different from the world presented here, are worth exploring. What I hope, then, is that the conceptual charts on the nature of language, culture and learning provided in this text are useful to the readers in orienting them to some current theoretical and practical activities taking place in applied linguistics. At the same time, I hope readers' travels through this text engender enough curiosity in them to begin charting their own explorations in the teaching and researching of language and culture.

I Defining language and culture

A sociocultural perspective on language and culture

This chapter will...

- describe current perspectives on the nature of language and culture in the field of applied linguistics;
- trace the lineage of some of the more significant assumptions on which current understandings are based.

1.1 Introduction

Few would disagree that the study of language use is the central concern of applied linguistics, but opinions differ in how such study is to be conceptualised. Some have argued (see, for example, Pennycook, 2001, and Widdowson, 2000), that much of what has taken place in applied linguistics is better understood as 'linguistics applied', a subset of the field of linguistics in which knowledge about language is used to address language-related concerns such as language teaching and language policy decisions. From the 'linguistics applied' perspective, language is considered to be a set of abstract systems whose meanings reside in the forms themselves rather than in the uses to which they are put. The contexts from which data are taken are considered useful places from which to locate and extract linguistic elements. But, at the same time, they are treated as ancillary to the analysis.

Investigations taking a 'linguistics applied' approach involve overlaying linguistic forms on instances of language use and interpreting their meanings in light of the structural frameworks. That is, concern is not with the concrete act of using language but rather with the forms themselves as objects of analysis in their own right. As Widdowson notes, 'The process whereby these forms inter-relate co-textually with each other and contextually with the circumstances of their use is left largely unexplored' (2000: 22).

> **Quote1.1**   Henry Widdowson on the nature of *linguistics applied*
>
> So long as linguistics was defined along traditional and formal lines, as the study of abstract systems of knowledge idealized out of language as actually experienced, the task of applied linguistics seemed relatively straightforward. It was to refer such abstract analysis of idealized internalized I-language back to the real world to find ways in which externalized E-language could be reformulated so as to make it amenable to benevolent intervention.
>
> Widdowson (2000: 4)

In recent years, as concerns with the limitations of this approach for understanding language experiences have grown, applied linguistics has begun to loosen its ties to mainstream linguistics. At the same time, it has begun to explore other disciplines, extending its reach to fields such as communication, cultural psychology, linguistic anthropology, linguistic philosophy and social theory in search of new ways to address concerns with language use. These explorations have been fruitful, yielding theoretical and methodological insights into the nature of applied linguistics activity that differ fairly substantially from those embodied in the more traditional 'linguistics applied' approach typical of earlier applied linguistics research.

Current views consider the fundamental concern to be the study of social action – the use of language in real-world circumstances – with the goal of understanding how language is used to construct our sociocultural worlds. Analytic primacy is not language per se, but the ways in which language is used in the accomplishment of social life. Central to the transformation of applied linguistics activity is the reconceptualisation of two concepts, *language* and *culture*, considered fundamental to the task. While current understandings of these concepts derive from an assortment of scholarly interests, they are bound together by a sociocultural perspective on human action (Cole, 1996; Wertsch et al., 1995). We look more closely at some of the more significant assumptions embodied in this perspective in the following sections.

1.2   Language as sociocultural resource

A sociocultural perspective on human action locates the essence of social life in communication. Through our use of linguistic symbols with others, we establish goals, negotiate the means to reach them, and reconceptualise those we have set. At the same time, we articulate and manage our individual identities, our interpersonal relationships, and memberships in our social groups and communities.

A great deal of research on communication makes it apparent that much of what we do when we communicate is conventionalised (Gumperz, 1981, 1982a, 1992; Hymes, 1972a; Tomasello, 1998). That is to say, in going about our everyday business, we participate in a multiplicity of recurring communicative activities in which the goals, our roles, and the language we use as we play these roles and attempt to accomplish the goals, are familiar to us. On a daily basis, we give and take orders, request help, commiserate, chat with friends, deliberate, negotiate, gossip, seek advice and so on. We participate in such routine activities with relative ease and can easily distinguish one activity from other. For example, we can usually tell when the utterance 'What are you doing?' is meant as a prelude to an invitation and when it is meant as a reproach. Likewise, if we hear the utterance 'That's a great pair of shoes'. We can anticipate with some accuracy the communicative event that is taking place, and construct an appropriate response.

The knowledge we use to help us navigate through our communicative activities comprises sets of communicative plans, that is to say, 'socially constructed models for solutions of communicative problems' (Luckmann, 1995: 181). These plans lay out for us the expected or typical goals of an activity, and the typical trajectories of linguistic actions by which such goals are realised. They also lay out the role relationships that are likely to obtain among those involved in the activity. The plans are constructed within and by the sociocultural groups of which we are members, and are maintained and modified in our uses of them as we participate in the activities constituting our daily lives. Because we share the plans with other members of our sociocultural groups and communities, they provide some common ground for knowing what we can each appropriately, or conventionally, say and do. In other words, the plans help us to synchronise our actions and interpretations and reach a mutually identifiable idea of what is going on (Edwards, 1995; Luckmann, 1995). It is through such everyday, conventionalised communicative activities, or *language games* (Wittgenstein, 1963), by which we experience the world. Thus, they constitute dynamic, vital forms of life (Shotter, 1993, 1996).

In this view of language as social action, language is considered to be first and foremost a sociocultural resource constituted by 'a range of possibilities, an open-ended set of options in behaviour that are available to the individual in his existence as social man' (Halliday, 1973: 49). Options for taking action in our communicative activities include a wide array of linguistic resources such as lexical and grammatical elements, speech acts and rhetorical structures, and in the case of oral language use, structured

---

Concept 1.1   Ludwig Wittgenstein's notion of *language games*

The term *language games* is commonly attributed to the Austrian philosopher, Ludwig Wittgenstein, whose views on language are best captured in *Philosophical Investigations* (1963). According to Wittgenstein, language games are established, conventionalised patterns of communicative action. These patterns, which are agreed upon and shared by members of a culture group, embody particular definitions of the situation and meanings of possible actions and, more generally, particular ways of knowing, valuing and experiencing the world.

---

patterns for taking turns and phonological, prosodic and paralinguistic resources such as intonation, stress, tempo and pausing.

More formalist views of language consider these resources to be fixed, invariant forms that we take from stable, bounded structural systems. In contrast, a sociocultural perspective considers them to be fundamentally social, their essence tied to their habits of use. That is, rather than a prerequisite to actual individual use, the shape or structure of our resources is an emergent property of it, developing from their locally situated uses in activity. Structures, then, do not precede use, but, in their use, develop their shape (Ochs and Schieffelin, 1995).

This view is captured most clearly in Hopper's (1987, 1998) and Hopper and Thompson's (1993) notion of *emergent grammar*. According to Hopper, rather than being the source of communication, language structures are more appropriately understood as by-products of it. It is through their frequent, routinised uses in specific sociocultural contexts that the symbolic means by which we take action develop into 'a collection of largely prefabricated particulars, available for use in appropriate contexts and language games' (Hopper, 1998: 164).

At the same time, while the various shapes of our linguistic resources develop from past uses, the specific forms they take at particular points in time are open to negotiation. However, the degree of negotiation that is possible at any communicative moment is dependent on two factors: the frequency of the resources' past uses and the amount of institutional force behind them. The more frequently the linguistic resources are used, or the more institutional force there is behind their use, the more systematised or codified their shapes become. The more systematised the resources are, in turn, the more invisible their sociohistorical roots are. This system is then treated as if it has a life of its own, existing apart from any context of use, and from its users. Any individual language use becomes measured against this universal yardstick with the assumption that there is an inherent correctness to the shape the forms take.

> **Quote 1.2** Paul Hopper on the notion of *Emergent Grammar*
>
> The notion of *Emergent Grammar* is meant to suggest that structure, or regularity, comes out of discourse and is shaped by discourse as much as it shapes discourse in an on-going process. Grammar is hence not to be understood as a pre-requisite for discourse, a prior possession attributable in identical form to both speaker and hearer. Its forms are not fixed templates, but are negotiable in face-to-face interaction in ways that reflect the individual speaker's past experience of these forms, and their assessment of the present context, including especially their interlocutors, whose experiences and assessments may be quite different.
>
> Hopper (1987: 142)

1.2.1 Dialogue as the essence of language use

As the structures of our linguistic resources emerge from their real-world uses, so do their meanings. That is, the linguistic resources we choose to use do not come to us as empty forms ready to be filled with our personal intentions; rather, they come to us with meanings already embedded within them. These meanings, however, are not derived from some universal, logical set of principles; rather, as with their shapes, they are built up over time from their past uses in particular contexts by particular groups of participants in the accomplishment of particular goals that, in turn, are shaped by myriad cultural, historical and institutional forces.

The linguistic resources we choose to use at particular communicative moments come to these moments with their conventionalised histories of meaning. It is their conventionality that binds us to some degree to particular ways of realising our collective history. However, while our resources come with histories of meanings, *how they come to mean* at a particular communicative moment is always open to negotiation.

Thus, in our individual uses of our linguistic resources we accomplish two actions simultaneously. We create their typical – historical – contexts of use and at the same time we position ourselves in relation to these contexts. Our locally situated uses of our linguistic resources are what Bakhtin (1981, 1986) calls *utterances*, concrete responses to the conditions of the moment. It is in our utterances that we fill the linguistic resources with our own voices, negotiating their conventional – historical – meanings in light of the communicative task at hand. Together their conventional meanings and our uses of them exist as inseparable parts of a *dialogue*, and are in a continually negotiated state of 'intense and essential axiological interaction' (Bakhtin, 1990: 10).

Concepts 1.2 and 1.3   **Mikhail Bakhtin's notions of *dialogue* and *translinguistics***

The concepts of *dialogue* and *translinguistics* are central to the linguistic philosophy of the Russian linguist, Mikhail Bakhtin. According to Bakhtin, meaning is located neither solely in our linguistic resources nor in each individual's mind. Rather, it resides in between these two interdependent spheres, in the interaction, the *dialogue*, that is realised in our lived moments of social action. *Translinguistics* is the name Bakhtin gives to the study of the dialogue obtaining between our linguistic resources and the ways in which we use them to respond to real-world circumstances. Of particular significance in *translinguistics*, Bakhtin argues, is the study of our everyday, mundane communicative actions, since they are the source of individual innovation and social change.

From this perspective, then, the meaning of language does not reside in the system of linguistic resources removed from their contexts of use and communities of users. Nor does it reside in our individual use of them as we engage in activities particular to our sociocultural worlds. Rather, language meaning is located in the dialogic relationship between the historical and the present, between the social and the individual. We come to understand the conventional meanings of the resources only in terms of how they are used at particular moments of time. Conversely, our understandings of the concrete, here and now uses of language are developed only in terms of the positioning of the resources against their conventional, i.e. historical, meanings. Bakhtin's (1981, 1986) notion of *dialogicality* captures well this relational character of meaning.

Quote 1.3   **Mikhail Bakhtin on the relation between language use and meaning, between meaning and culture**

There are no 'neutral' words and forms – words and forms that belong to 'no one'; language has been completely taken over, shot through with intentions and accents. For any individual consciousness living in it, language is not an abstract system of normative forms but rather a concrete heteroglot conception of the world. All words have the 'taste' of a profession, a genre, a tendency, a party, a particular work, a particular person, a generation, an age group, the day and hour. Each word tastes of the context and contexts in which it has lived its socially charged life; all words and forms are populated by intentions.

Bakhtin (1981: 293)

The excerpt below, taken from Hall (1993a: 209), illustrates the dialogic, or relational, nature of meaning.

Husband: Take these shirts to the cleaners tomorrow, will you?
Wife: (*stands and gives military salute by raising hand to forehead*) Yes, sir.

As noted by Hall, the military salute and verbal utterance used by the wife to respond to her husband's request are typically used together in a military context by someone in a subordinate position to mark the other as a superior. If we bring their expected meanings to this context, we may conclude that the woman is using them to create a similar military-style, hierarchical relationship with her husband and thereby mark or index her understanding of this subordinate position. Alternatively, she can be using the conventional meaning of the salute and verbal utterance not to recreate their conventional context of use, and her role in it, but to mark her stance towards an utterance that she considers inappropriate. It might be, for example, that she hears the utterance as a directive instead of a request. She may regard a request as more suitable to the situation, and so uses the salute and verbal response to convey at the same time both her interpretation of her husband's utterance and her offense towards it.

Either way, there is a dialogue between the meaning conventionally associated with the salute and verbal response and their use by the woman in this particular communicative moment. Only by examining the dialogue obtaining between the conventional meanings of the linguistic resources used by the husband and wife, and their uses of them at this particular time, can we derive a full understanding of the activity – of the shapes and meanings deriving from the locally situated uses of the resources, of the participants and their relationships to each other, and of how each views his or her place within that particular communicative moment – and of the role that language plays in constructing one's social worlds.

In positing dialogue as the core of language study and the utterance as the fundamental unit of analysis, Bakhtin erases any *a priori* distinction between form and function, between individual and social uses of language. Just as no linguistic resource can be understood apart from its contexts of use, no single utterance can be considered a purely individual act, 'a completely free combination of forms of language' (Bakhtin, 1986: 81), whose meanings are created on the spot. Rather, it can only be understood fully by considering its history of use by other people, in other places, for other reasons. Thus, rather than being considered extraneous to the study of language, dialogue in its encounter between historical meaning and individual motivations at a particular moment of action is considered its essence (Williams, 1977).

1.2.2   Single- and double-voiced utterances

Important to understanding this dialogic relationship obtaining between the personal and social meanings embodied in our language use is the degree of authority attached to the conventional meanings of our linguistic resources. As we noted previously, our linguistic resources come to us already laden with meanings that have been developed in their histories of use. These histories of meanings determine in part the degree of force that our voices will have in using the resources towards our own ends.

Useful for understanding the links between the historical meanings of our resources and our individual uses of them are Bakhtin's concepts of *single-voiced utterances* and *double-voiced utterances* (Bakhtin, 1981; Morson and Emerson, 1990; Schultz, 1990). According to Bakhtin, single-voiced utterances consist of resources whose meanings are unquestioned, non-negotiable and thus resistant to change. The more institutionalised the meanings of the resources, the more authoritative their voices are likely to be. The more authoritative their voices, the more invisible their histories become, and the more resistant they are to individually motivated innovations. Instead, the resources take on a life of their own, and become defined as a distinct, internally coherent, logical system of meanings and values. When we use the resources to take action in our worlds, they come not only with their authoritative, decontextualised meanings, but their values as well. As their users, we become defined by the values thought to be inherent within them.

For example, the one-speaker-at-a-time turn-taking pattern usually associated with mainstream westernised social institutions such as schools and places of work, is often considered the predominant means by which turns are taken. Because its use is thought to facilitate the orderly and logical progression of talk, those who use it are considered orderly, well mannered, logical and even intelligent. Variations to this pattern, such as simultaneous turn-taking (Reisman, 1974), or the call-response turn (Sims-Holt, 1972) – and their users – are judged against this unquestioned norm, and thus framed as 'disorderly', 'irrational', 'rude' and 'uneducated'. Similar stigmatised judgements are made against users of equally reified grammatical, semantic and prosodic features considered different from mainstream use.

What is invisible is the fact that such institutionalised versions of linguistic resources are social facts, 'not inherent and universal, but local, secondary, and projected' (Hymes, 1980: 112). In other words, mainstream uses of linguistic resources, and the values associated with them, are the construction of particular groups who historically have had a considerable amount of sociopolitical authority behind them. It is their unquestioned, authoritative use over time by groups with such authority by which resource meanings are given authority and institutionalised. In addition to propagation of the resources through their continued and unquestioned use by such groups, written documents such as dictionaries, grammar books, style manuals and etiquette guides serve as primary means for institutionalising resource meanings (Hopper, 1998).

Concepts 1.4 and 1.5   Single- and double-voiced utterances

According to Bakhtin, *single-voiced utterances* are those with authority, those whose sociohistorical meanings are invisible to the speaker. The individual speaks as if the words she uses have a life of their own apart from any context of use. In contrast, in *double-voiced utterances* the sociohistorical meanings of words are visible to the speaker, and she can choose to use the words in two ways. In *passive double-voiced utterances*, the individual chooses to use the words as others before her have used them, that is, with their conventional meanings. In *active double-voiced utterances*, the individual uses the words not as they are meant to be used, but for her own purposes. That is, she uses the conventional meanings in such a way as to assert her own voice in their use.

It is not the case, however, that the meanings of our resources always go unquestioned. Rather, we often make conscious choices about the language we use and, in so doing, we decide on 'a particular way of entering the world and a particular way of sustaining relationships with others' (Duranti, 1997: 46). Utterances in which we acknowledge the conventional meanings of our resources, and use them with volition to respond to the conditions of the moment, are what Bakhtin calls *double-voiced utterances*. On the one hand, we can consciously choose to use the conventional meanings associated with the resources in predictable ways; that is, we use our resources in such a way as to create their typical contexts of use. If we come across an individual in a public area, for example, and we wish to establish some kind of interpersonal contact with that person, we can create such a context with the utterance 'Hi, how are you today?' This utterance is typically associated with a greeting among friends or acquaintances and its use at that time with that person helps to create such a context. Bakhtin calls these *passive double-voiced utterances*.

We can also choose to use our resources in unexpected ways. Bakhtin calls these *active double-voiced utterances*. In such utterances, we use our resources not so much to create the particular set of conditions typical of them, but more to use their histories of meaning to create our unique positioning towards a particular communicative moment. The following, taken from a public billboard displayed shortly after the acts of terrorism experienced by the USA in New York City and Washington DC in the fall of 2001, is an example of an active double-voiced utterance.

> Don't make me have to come down there
> – God

For many social groups, the utterance 'Don't make me have to come down there' evokes a typical role-relationship between a parent and a child, and a typical situation in which one or some children are misbehaving. The utterance by the parent serves to admonish the children for their behaviour. While the consequences for ignoring the warning are not stated, it is implied that they will be dire if the actions do not stop. In the billboard message, the attribution of the utterance to a divine being, believed by many to be the supreme protector of all humanity, evokes a similar context of use. In this case, the utterance ascribes to God the role of scolding parent to a world filled with badly behaved children. One does not have to be a believer in the existence of a higher presence to appreciate how the conventional meanings embedded in language can be used to create a unique stance towards any locally situated communicative moment. It is important to note that what makes an utterance passive or active depends not just on the user's intentions. It also includes the response it engenders, the relationships existing among the particular participants and the history of intentions embedded in the resources themselves.

Quote 1.4 Mikhail Bakhtin on the nature of voice

Each large and creative verbal whole is a very complex and multifaceted system of relations ... there are no voiceless words that belong to no one. Each word contains voices that are sometimes infinitely distant, unnamed, almost impersonal, almost undetectable, and voices resounding nearby and simultaneously.

Bakhtin (1986: 124)

In sum, in a sociocultural perspective on human action, language is viewed at one and the same time as both an individual tool and a sociocultural resource, whose use on a day-to-day basis is conventionalised, shaped by the myriad intellectual and practical communicative activities that constitute our daily lives. In using language to participate in our activities, we reflect our understanding of them and their larger cultural contexts and, at the same time, create spaces for ourselves as individuals within them. The meanings that our individual uses of language assume at those moments draw from their historical, conventional meanings in relation to their situated, immediate contexts of use. Hence, different uses of language embody different meanings.

This perspective rejects the idea that literal or decontextualised meaning exists apart from the use of a linguistic resource. There is no word, no use of a resource that can be considered unprejudiced, independent of its users or contexts of use. Instead, our words come to us already used, filled with the evaluations and perceptions of others. Their meanings emerge from the juxtaposition of their past uses with our locally situated uses of them in the present. Thus, when we use language to act in our social worlds, it cannot be said that we 'use our own words'. Rather, in our actions we make use of available meaning-laden resources to construct our worlds as we would have them be at that moment.

Wittgenstein (1963: 12) captures the contextualised character of our linguistic resources when he states, 'If you do not keep the multiplicity of language-games in view you will perhaps be inclined to ask questions like: "What is a question?" – Is it the statement that I do not know such-and-such, or the statement that I wish the other person would tell me . . . ? Or is it the description of my mental state of uncertainty?'. Here, in linking language meaning to its contexts of use, Wittgenstein makes apparent the interdependence of meaning in the here-and-now and historical meaning, of individual meaning and meaning based in community. 'Not what one is doing now, but the whole hurly-burly, is the background against which we see an action, and it determines our judgment, our concepts and our reactions' (Wittgenstein, 1980, no. 629).

One final point needs to be made. As noted earlier, there is nothing essential to our linguistic resources themselves that makes their meanings more privileged or authoritative. Rather, their authority develops from their past uses. It follows then that language is inherently ideological. As Bakhtin (1981, 1986, 1990) argues, in the language we choose to use at any particular moment we make visible our attitudes and beliefs towards the communicative moment, towards those with whom we are communicating, and towards what we believe our social positioning is within our sociocultural worlds. Only by examining our language use at particular moments of time in relation to its history can we reveal the varied ways in which we create our voices in response to the larger social and political forces shaping our worlds.

1.3 Culture as sociocultural practice

The notion of culture has always been considered an important concept in applied linguistics. However, in studies taking a more traditional 'linguistics applied' approach it is often treated as its own logical system of representational knowledge, located in the individual mind, and existing independent of language, when it is treated at all. The basis of the system is assumed to be an abstract, universal structure for organising and generating the knowledge. When exposed to culture-specific data, provided by the physical world, the mind is thought to generate systems of knowledge that are specific to a particular culture group. Hence, while the underlying formal structures of culture are assumed to be universal, the actual substance generated by the formal structures is considered to be fairly homogeneous static bodies of knowledge consisting of accumulated and classifiable sets of thoughts, feelings, values and beliefs. By virtue of their group membership, and their innate possession of the formal structures needed to process culture-specific data, individual members are assumed to have full and equal possession of these sets of knowledge. Thus, any pattern detected across individuals is automatically assumed to reflect their cultural affiliations (cf. Sarangi, 1994).

In addition to an assumption of cultural homogeneity, the more traditional perspective assumes knowledge acquisition to be unidirectional, transmitted by, but fundamentally unrelated to, language. That is, while language may be used as a way to uncover the culture-specific bodies of knowledge, it is not deemed to have any influence on their development or, more generally, on the abstract structures by which the information is organised. Thus, the primary, if not only, role that language is thought to play is representational. In other words, language can only *reflect* cultural understandings; it can not *affect* them (Goodenough, 1964; Lévi-Strauss, 1963; cf. Williams, 1992).

A sociocultural perspective of culture stands in marked contrast to this more traditional view. Rather than viewing culture as systems of fixed bodies of knowledge possessed equally by all members of well-defined culture groups, current understandings view it as 'recurrent and habitual systems of dispositions and expectations' (Duranti, 1997: 45), and, on a more concrete level, the meanings our linguistic resources have accumulated from their past uses, with which we approach and work through our communicative activities. As noted earlier, in our activities with others, we rely on these expectations for making sense of the moment, and working towards the accomplishment of our social lives.

Because we are members of multiple groups and communities, we take on and negotiate multiple cultural identities, and in our roles, participate in myriad cultural activities. At any communicative moment, through our linguistic actions, we choose particular ways to construe our worlds, to induce others to see our worlds in these ways, as we create and sustain particular kinds of relationships with them and thus make relevant some as opposed to other identities.

> **Quote 1.5** Brian Street on the notion of culture as embodied action
>
> In fact, there is not much point in trying to say what culture is. What can be done, however, is to say what culture does. For what culture does is precisely the work of defining words, ideas, things and groups. We all live our lives in terms of definition, names and categories that culture creates. The job of studying culture is not of finding and then accepting its definitions but of discovering how and what definitions are made, under what circumstances and for what reasons ... Culture is an active process of meaning making and contest over definition, including its own definition. This, then, is what I mean by arguing that *Culture is a verb*.
>
> Street (1993b: 25; emphasis in the original)

To locate culture one must look not in individual mind, as an accumulated body of unchanging knowledge, but in the dialogue, the embodied actions, 'discursively rearticulated' (Bhabha, 1994: 177) between individuals in particular sociocultural contexts at particular moments of time. This perspective of culture as a dynamic, vital and emergent process located in the discursive spaces *between* individuals links it inextricably to language. That is to say, language is at the same time a repository of culture and a tool by which culture is created. In making visible the mutual dependency of language and culture, current understandings overcome the analytic separation of the 'linguistics applied' approach. Because culture is located not in individual mind but in activity, any study of language is by necessity a study of culture.

1.4   Linguistic relativity

Current views of language and culture as mutually shaping forms of social life owe a great deal to ideas found in linguistic anthropology, and in particular, to the idea of linguistic relativity as found in the work of American linguistic anthropologist Edward Sapir (1929/1949), and, more prominently, in that of his student Benjamin Whorf (1940/1956). Sapir's ideas came mainly from his study of different American indigenous languages, which led him to posit a dynamic relation between language and culture.

Whorf also studied Native American languages, in particular Hopi. Influenced by Sapir's work as well by his experiences as a claims agent for an insurance company in the first half of the twentieth century, Whorf's work on language, and his ideas on linguistic relativity, are encapsulated in what has come to be called the Sapir–Whorf hypothesis. This hypothesis

Quote 1.6 Edward Sapir on the relationship between language and culture

Human beings do not live in the objective world alone, nor alone in the world of social activity as ordinarily understood, but are very much at the mercy of the particular language which has become the medium of expression for their society. It is quite an illusion to imagine that one adjusts to reality essentially without the use of language and that language is merely an incidental means of solving specific problems of communication or reflection. The fact of the matter is the 'real world' is to a large extent unconsciously built up on the language habits of the group. No two languages are ever sufficiently similar to be considered as representing the same social reality. The worlds in which different societies lie are distinct worlds, not merely the same world with different labels attached.

Sapir (1929/1949: 162)

proposes that patterned, structural components of specific languages regularly or habitually used by members of culture groups contain particular meanings that are systematically linked to the worldviews of the groups whose languages they are. Thus, they influence the way group members view, categorise, and in other ways think about their world. Since different culture groups speak different languages, individual worldviews are tied to the language groups to which individuals belong. To state this another way, if individual thought is shaped by language, individuals with different languages are likely to have different understandings of the world. A significant contribution of the Sapir–Whorf hypothesis is that it links individual thought to larger, culturally based patterns of language and thus posits an interdependent relationship between language and culture (Lee, 1996).

Quote 1.7 Benjamin Whorf's view on linguistic relativity

We dissect nature along lines laid down by our native languages. The categories and types that we isolate from the world of phenomena we do not find there because they stare every observer in the face; on the contrary, the world is presented in a kaleidoscopic flux of impressions which has to be organized by our minds – and this means largely by the linguistic systems in our minds. We cut nature up, organize it into concepts, and ascribe significance as we do, largely because we are parties to an agreement to organize it in this way – an agreement that holds throughout our speech community and is codified in the patterns of our language.

Whorf (1940/1956: 213)

1.5   A socially constituted linguistics

A similar connection between language and culture can be found in the more recent work of Dell Hymes (1962, 1964, 1971, 1972a, 1974), another linguistic anthropologist. Hymes developed a conceptualisation of language as context-embedded social action in response to linguist Noam Chomsky's (1957, 1965) theory of language. In keeping with a formalist perspective, Chomsky conceptualised language as a fixed, universal property of the human mind containing internalised sets of principles from which language-specific grammatical rules could be derived, and thus describable in context-free, invariant terms.

Hymes regarded this view of language as too restrictive in that it did not, in fact could not, account for the social knowledge we rely on to produce and interpret utterances appropriate to the particular contexts in which they occur. He noted, ' . . . it is not enough for the child to be able to produce any grammatical utterance. It would have to remain speechless if it could not decide which grammatical utterance here and now, if it could not connect utterances to their contexts of use' (Hymes, 1964: 110). It is this social knowledge, Hymes argued, that shapes and gives meaning to linguistic forms. Because involvement in the communicative activities of our everyday lives is usually with others who share our expectations, these links are often difficult to see. However, although it may be difficult to perceive their vitality, they cannot be considered insignificant to the accomplishment of our everyday lives. Thus, Hymes called for a more adequate theory of language that could account for the knowledge that we as individuals require to use our linguistic resources so that they are considered structurally sound, referentially accurate and contextually appropriate within the different groups and communities to which we belong.

> **Quote 1.8**   Dell Hymes on the nature of a socially constituted linguistics
>
> The phrase 'socially constituted' is intended to express the view that social function gives form to the ways in which linguistic features are encountered in actual life. This being so, an adequate approach must begin by identifying social functions, and discovering the ways in which linguistic features are selected and grouped together to serve them.
>
> Hymes (1974: 196)

1.5.1   A socially constituted approach to the study of language and culture

Arguing for a *socially constituted linguistics* (Hymes, 1974) in which social function is treated as the source from which linguistic features are formed,

Hymes developed an approach to the study of language he called the *ethnography of speaking*. In response to more formal descriptions of language as inherently coherent systems, the focus of Hymes's approach is on capturing patterns of language use as used by members of particular sociocultural groups to reflect and create their social worlds.

A great deal of recent research, particularly in the fields of linguistic anthropology, communication and education, has used this approach to investigate a wide range of communicative events and activities of many different groups and communities. These have included descriptions of oral events such as storytelling (e.g. Sherzer, 1983), preaching (Abrahams, 1976), classroom teaching (e.g. Duff, 1995; Foster, 1989), gossiping (Hall, 1993b; Haviland, 1977), and even ritual treat sharing among children (Katriel, 1987).

Quote 1.9   Dell Hymes on the conceptual base of an ethnography of speaking

Now it is desirable . . . to take as a working framework: 1. the speech of a group constitutes a system; 2. speech and language vary cross-culturally in function; 3. the speech activity of a community is the primary object of attention. A descriptive grammar deals with this speech activity in one frame of reference, an ethnography of speaking in another. So (what amounts to a corollary, 3b), the latter must in fact include the former.

Hymes (1962: 42)

Concept 1.6   **Ethnography of speaking**

As proposed by Hymes, an *ethnography of speaking* is both a conceptual framework and a method for conducting language study. Presuming a systematic link between language use and context, this approach considers the communicative activity, or what Hymes termed the communicative event, a central unit of analysis. Analytic attention is given to describing the components of communicative events and the relations among them that participants make use of to engage in and make sense of their social worlds and, in turn, to link their use to the larger social, cultural, political and other institutional forces giving shape to them. More recent formulations of this approach to the study of language refer to it as ethnography of *communication* to capture a more encompassing understanding of the variety of resources, in addition to language, that are used in communication. Leeds-Hurwitz (1984) provides a useful summary of the history of both terms.

In addition to oral communicative events, literacy activities of various groups and communities have been the subject of ethnographies of communication. Ahearn (2000), for example, studied the literacy practices of young Nepali women, focusing in particular on their use of love letters in courtship. Radway (1984) explored the role that reading romance novels played in the lives of a group of women. Taking more of a wide-angle ethnographic approach, McCarty and Watahomigie (1998) studied both home and school literacy activities in American Indian and Alaskan native communities. Similarly, Torres-Guzman (1998) investigated literacy activities in Puerto Rican communities, Dien (1998) looked at similar activities in Vietnamese American communities, and Barton and Hamilton (1998) explored the activities constituted in the everyday lives of a group of adults in England. Findings from these and other studies have shown that literacy activities do indeed vary, in some cases considerably, from community to community. As these groups differ – and as the social identities of the readers and writers differ within the groups – so does the value that is placed on literacy activities and the communicative conventions used to engage in them.

The differences in literacy practices notwithstanding, the principal assumption of literacy underlying the ethnographies remains the same. Literacy is defined not as 'a technology made up of a set of transferable cognitive skills, but [as] a constellation of practices' (Ivanic, 1998: 65), made up of particular arrangements of skills and ways of reading and writing that are tied to their contexts of use. Likewise, they share the goal of making visible the linguistic resources and communicative plans shared by group members and used to engage in their socioculturally important communicative activities. In addition to adding to our knowledge of cultural groups, studies taking an ethnography of communication approach to the study of language and culture have contributed a great deal to current educational practices. Their pedagogical significance is discussed in Chapter 4.

1.5.2 The recent turn in ethnographic studies of communicative activities

Lately, studies of communicative events, particularly those realised through face-to-face interaction, have moved beyond general descriptions of the resources needed to engage in them to more detailed descriptions that show the moment-to-moment coordination by which the communicative context is created. This move has come about in part by the development of techniques for analysing conversation by the more recently developed discipline of conversation analysis (CA). The assumption on which CA is based is that orderliness in conversation is a local achievement, mutually produced by the participants, using resources whose structures can be discovered only through the sequential analysis of talk-in-interaction (Psathas, 1995). Thus, the analytic focus is on uncovering and describing the particular resources used in the joint achievement of local order. More details on this particular approach to language study are given in Chapter 8.

For our purposes, it is sufficient to note that the analytic techniques and findings on conversation regularities such as turn-taking patterns, self-repair strategies, and turn projections have been usefully incorporated into ethnographies of communication. This, in turn, has allowed us to see the multitude of methods in addition to the more traditional syntactic, semantic and prosodic means we have at our disposal for sense-making in our communicative activities (Jacoby and Ochs, 1995). Studies incorporating a close analysis of talk-in-interaction with an ethnography of communication include, for example, Michael Moerman's (1988) study of Thai conversations, Marjorie Harness Goodwin's (1990, 1995) studies of conversational techniques that African American children use for establishing and managing social interaction and relationships in their peer group activities, and He's (1995) examination of the conversational strategies employed by university student counsellors and their advisees to construct their institutional role relationships.

In addition to drawing out the shared understandings that members rely on to make sense of each other's actions in talk-in-interaction activities, interest has developed in uncovering the *variability* of resource use. A criticism of early ethnographies of communication noted that ethnographic descriptions of communicative events often gave the impression that individual members' participation was always consensual, always orderly. Assuming a more dynamic understanding of community and language use, more recent studies have begun to examine how individual members use the resources of their communicative activities to challenge the status quo. As one example, Hall (1993c) revealed how one Dominican woman was able to manipulate the conventional opening to the activity of gossiping as practised among her peers in such a way as to positively transform the nature of her involvement in the activity. Typically, the opening of the gossiping event was signalled with the utterance 'tengo una bomba' [I have a bomb], the purpose of which was to alert the others that a story about the scandalous behaviour of another was about to be told. When this particular woman used it, however, what often followed was not a story about someone's impropriety, but a humorous anecdote, in which she was the central figure. Her unconventional use of the utterance to take the stage, so to speak, generated a great deal of humour among the other participants, and thus helped to raise her status within the group. At the same time, it solidified her allegiance as a knowledgeable insider to her peers.

1.5.3   From *linguistic* relativity to *sociolinguistic* relativity

Without a doubt, Hymes's theory of language and his approach to the study of language use have made significant contributions to our understanding of the pragmatically based, mutually constitutive nature of language and culture. A less visible but equally significant contribution of his work is the advancement of our understanding of the concept of linguistic relativity. Like Whorf, Hymes sees language and culture as inextricably linked. However, by giving primacy to language use and function rather than linguistic code and form, Hymes transforms Whorf's notion of linguistic relativity in a subtle but significant way. More to the point, in asserting the primacy of language as human action, the source of relativity becomes located in language *use*, not language *structure*.

Quote 1.10   Dell Hymes on the priority of *sociolinguistic relativity* relative to the notion of *linguistic relativity*

With particular regard to the Sapir–Whorf hypothesis, it is essential to notice that Whorf's sort of linguistic relativity is secondary, and dependent upon a primary sociolinguistic relativity, that of differential engagement of languages in social life. For example, description of a language may show that it expresses certain cognitive style, perhaps implicit metaphysical assumptions. But what chances the language has to make an impress upon individuals and behavior will depend upon the degree and pattern of its admission into communicative events . . . Peoples do not all everywhere use language to the same degree, in the same situations, or for the same things; some peoples focus upon language more than others. Such differences in the place of a language in the communicative system of a people cannot be assumed to be without influence on the depth of a language's influence on such things as world view.

Hymes (1974: 18)

1.6   Systemic functional linguistics

One last source to note from which a notion of language as context-embedded social action draws is the work of British-Australian linguist Michael Halliday (1973, 1975, 1978, 1985). Like Hymes, Halliday views language as fundamentally social, and thus locates the meanings of language forms in their systematic connections between the functions they play and their contexts of use. Also like Hymes, Halliday considers that the essential role of a theory of language is to explain the social foundations of the language system. Thus, his work has been concerned primarily with the development of a systemic functional theory of language, the specific aim of which is the articulation of 'the functionally organised meaning potential of the linguistic system' (1975: 6). That is, it seeks to describe the linguistic options that are available to individuals to construct meanings in particular contexts or situations for particular purpose (Christie and Unsworth, 2000).

To make these connections between language use and context visible, Halliday proposed an analytic framework consisting of a set of three inter-related functions. The first function is the *ideational*, which is concerned with the propositional or representational dimensions of language. The second is the *interpersonal*, which is concerned with the social dimensions of language, i.e. how interpersonal connections are made and sustained. The third function is the *textual*, which is concerned with the construction of coherent and cohesive discourse. According to Halliday, all languages manage all three functions. Also part of the framework is a set of three components for describing situation types. The first component, *field*, refers to the setting and purpose. *Tenor*, the second component, pertains to the participants' roles and the key or tone of the situation. The third component, *mode*, refers to the symbolic or rhetorical means by which the situation is realised, and the genre to which it is most appropriately related.

According to Halliday's theory, meanings of the linguistic resources used by individuals in particular situations can be linked to the conventionalised, or systematic interactions between the three components of the situation and the three language functions: field interacts with ideational, tenor with interpersonal, and mode with textual. This knowledge comprises the communicative plans with which individuals approach their communicative activities, and they use their shared understandings of a situation in terms of field, tenor and mode to anticipate the language forms and meanings likely to be used (Chapelle, 1998).

Quote 1.11 Michael Halliday on the explanatory value of systemic functional linguistics

Given an adequate specification of the situation in terms of field, tenor and mode, we ought to be able to make certain predictions about the linguistic properties of the text that is associated with it: that is, about the register, the configurations of semantic options that typically feature in this environment, and hence also about the grammar and vocabulary, which are the realizations of the semantic options.

Halliday (1975: 131)

Like Hymes's approach to the study of language, systemic functional linguistics has engendered much empirical research. The tacks taken, however, differ somewhat in that the focus of studies from Halliday's perspective is on describing functions of particular linguistic features as they are realised in a variety of texts. Moreover, although there has been some consideration of oral communicative activities (e.g. Eggins and Slade, 1997), a primary focus of attention has been on the analysis of written genres. However, although the analytic approaches differ, findings from myriad investigations using the theoretical frameworks of both Hymes and Halliday make apparent in empirically interesting and compelling ways the socially constituted nature of language.

It is probably worth noting that claiming a fundamentally social base to language does not mean turning one's focus from competence to performance, as the terms have been used in traditional linguistics, since to do so assumes acceptance of the assumptions on which these concepts are based (cf. Crowley, 1996). One of the more fundamental assumptions of the traditional perspective on language treats competence and performance as two distinct systems: the formal and the functional. In contrast, a theory of language as socially constituted makes no such distinction. Rather it takes as fundamental the existence of one system, a system of action, in which knowledge and use are two mutually constituted components.

Quote 1.12 Tony Crowley addresses the fundamental differences in assumptions embodied in more traditional 'ahistorical' approaches to the study of language and more recent, sociocultural approaches

... it is clear that the decontextualised, ahistorical approach to language must be called into question by a method which does not seek for an abstract structure but looks instead for the uses, and their significance, to which language is put at the micro- and macro-social levels. And this is not just a question of turning away from *langue* to *parole*, or from competence to performance, since that would be to accept the misleading alternatives on offer in the established models. The new approach would seek and analyse precisely neither abstract linguistic structure nor individual use but the institutional, political and ideological relationships between language and history ... In short, it would consider the modes in which language becomes important for its users not as a faculty which they all share at an abstract level, but as a practice in which they all participate in very different ways, to very different effects, under very different pressures, in their everyday lives.

Crowley (1996: 28)

1. 7 Summary

Incorporation of recent developments in fields historically considered outside the main purview of applied linguistics has helped the field to reconceptualise two essential concepts: language and culture. In contrast to traditional views, which consider language to comprise structural and propositional systems transcending their users and contexts of use, sociocultural conceptualisations see language as dynamic, living collections of resources for the accomplishment of our social lives. These collections are considered central forms of life in that we use them not only to refer to, or represent, the world in our communicative activities. They are also forms of action by which we bring our cultural worlds into existence, maintain them, and shape them for our own purposes.

Current understandings have also transformed the way we view language meaning. While we can and do use our resources to realise personal intentions, our intentions alone do not give them their meaning. Nor is meaning inherent in the forms themselves. That is to say, we cannot pull resources from their contexts, dust off any contextual residue, and then claim to know their meaning. Doing so only renders them lifeless. Rather, meaning is dynamic, emerging from the dialogic interaction between our uses of particular linguistic resources at particular moments in time, and their conventional meanings, determined by their prior uses by other individuals, in other communicative activities, and at other times. The specific components of language then are considered to be fundamentally communicative, their shapes arising from their uses by individuals to construct and enact certain social identities as they engage in activities particular to their sociocultural worlds.

In this view, then, language is not an individual phenomenon but a social one, comprising linguistic resources whose meanings are both embodied in and constitutive of people's everyday practices, and, more generally, their social, cultural and political contexts. Residing in these linguistic resources are structures of expectations for using and interpreting their uses. Through our individual use of them at any particular moment we attempt to shape how others see the world and each other as participants in it.

Also transformed is our understanding of what it means to know language. From a sociocultural perspective, to know language does not mean to know something *about* it. It is not a body of information about forms and functions that we first accumulate and then use in our communicative activities. Rather, to know a language means 'knowing how to go on, and so is an ability' (Shotter, 1996: 299). Tying language knowledge to social action in this way makes visible its mutually dependent, inextricable link to culture. It is through the ways we live our lives, and through our social actions, that culture is made and remade.

Quote 1.13 John Shotter on a sociocultural understanding of what constitutes the study of language use

We must study how, by interweaving our talk with our other actions and activities, we can first develop and sustain between us different, particular *ways* of relating ourselves to each other...And then, once we have a grasp of the general character of our (normative) relations both with each other and to our surroundings...we should turn to a study of how, as distinct individuals, we can 'reach out' *from within* these forms of life, so to speak, to make the myriad different kinds of contact with our surroundings *through* the various ways of making sense of such contacts our forms of life provide. Where some of the contacts we make, perhaps, can elicit new or previously unnoticed reactions and responses from us, to function as the origins of entirely new language games. And it is these fleeting, often unremarked responses that occur in the momentary gaps between people as they react to each other – from within an established form of life – that must become the primary focus for our studies here, for it is in these reactions that people reveal to each other what *their world* (their 'inner life') is like for them; and can also, perhaps, initiate a new practice.

Shotter (1996: 299–300; emphasis in the original)

Ultimately, then, from a sociocultural perspective on language and culture, what we pursue in our research endeavours is not a theory of linguistic systems. Neither is it a theory of universal culture. Rather, the aim is the development of a theory of social action that is centrally concerned with how we live our lives through our everyday communicative activities, through our language games. To do this requires our attention to the explication of 'the relationships between human action, on the one hand, and the cultural, institutional, and historical situations in which this action occurs on the other' (Wertsch et al., 1995: 11). A discussion on research possibilities made possible by this perspective is taken up more fully in Section III. In the next chapter, we examine current understandings of the concept of identity and its link to language use, and in Chapter 3 we review current theoretical insights and empirical findings on language and culture learning.

Further reading

Agar, M. (1996) *Language shock: Understanding the culture of conversation*. New York: William Morrow & Company. Drawing on his own experiences as linguistic anthropologist and world traveller, Agar presents a range of evidence on the inextricable links between language and culture. Because language and culture are so deeply intertwined, Agar proposes that we refer to the communicative means by which we take action as languaculture. His account of a sociocultural perspective on language and culture is very accessible even to the most novice reader.

Duranti, A. and Goodwin, C. (eds) (1992) *Rethinking context: Language as an interactive phenomenon*. Cambridge, England: Cambridge University Press. Drawing on assumptions about the sociocultural nature of language found in fields such as linguistic anthropology, sociology and communication, the essays in this volume re-examine empirically the concept of context from a variety of different vantage points, including face-to-face interactions, radio talk, and political encounters. Each essay argues ultimately for an understanding of context as a locally situated, interactional achievement rather than a predetermined set of features detached and detachable from the interactions themselves.

Lucy, J. (1992) *Language diversity and thought*. Cambridge, MA: Cambridge University Press. Lucy re-examines the Sapir–Whorf linguistic relativity hypothesis by reviewing various strands of empirical research. Based on findings from his review, he proposes a more comprehensive approach to researching the links between language and thought.

Shotter, J. (1993) *Conversational realities: Constructing life through language*. Thousand Oaks, CA: Sage. This book provides a provocative exploration of what Shotter calls a rhetorical-responsive account of social constructionism. Drawing on the linguistic philosophy of Bakhtin and Wittgenstein, Shotter lays out a theoretical framework for understanding how we constitute our interpersonal relationships, and, more generally, our social worlds in our interactions with others.

Shotter, J. (1993) *Cultural politics of everyday life: Social constructionism, rhetoric and knowing of the third kind*. Toronto: University of Toronto Press. In this text, Shotter explores the significance of our social interactions, and the cultural tools we use to interact with others, to the development of mental representations. He draws a distinction between two kinds of knowing – knowing that and knowing how – and introduces what he calls 'a third kind of knowing', which he argues emerges in the dialogue between interactants. Here, too, he draws on the work of Bakhtin and Wittgenstein in addition to many others.

Thompson, G. (1996) *Introducing functional grammar*. London: Arnold. This book offers an accessible introduction to systemic functional linguistics by providing a clear explanation of how grammar is used as a resource for making meaning, and the kinds of meanings conventionally associated with different grammatical systems.

Voloshinov, V.N. (1986) *Marxism and the philosophy of language*. New York: Seminar Press. Although there is some dispute over the author of this text – some claim that the book was written by Bakhtin, others claim it was constructed as part of the 'Bakhtin Circle', a group of contemporaries of Bakhtin that included P.N. Medvedev and V.N. Voloshinov – the ideas presented here form a large part of the core assumptions on language and mind from a sociocultural perspective.

Chapter 2

Language and identity

This chapter will...

- describe current perspectives on the concept of identity and its connection to culture and language use;
- explore some of the more relevant theoretical insights and empirical findings on which current understandings are based.

2.1 Introduction

In the more traditional 'linguistics applied' approach to the study of language use, individuals are usually given consideration as significant sources of data on language. In keeping with the assumption of language as universal, abstract systems, individual language users are typically treated as stable, internally homogeneous, fixed entities in whose heads these systems reside. Because of their universal nature, the systems themselves are considered self-contained, independent entities, extractable from individual minds. That is, while they reside in individual minds they have a separate existence. Consequently, even though individuals are considered to be fundamental sources of the systems, they are assumed to play no role in shaping them.

Individuals, however, can make whatever use they want of their language systems since the more traditional view considers individuals to be agents of free will, and thus, autonomous decision-makers. It considers the systems themselves to be the central means for the expression of personal meaning. Consequently, since all individual action is driven by internally motivated states, individual language use is seen as involving a high degree of unpredictability and creativity in both form and message as individuals strive to make personal connections to their surrounding contexts.

Moreover, although the more traditional perspective considers culture to be an important construct, it is treated separately from language. That is, culture is assumed to be *in* individuals but not *of* them. Individual language users can *display* their cultural norms, but they do not *inhabit* them and thus cannot *affect* them in any way. From this perspective, then, individuals are assumed to play no role in defining cultural norms, only reflecting them. Furthermore, because agency is assumed to lie solely in their power, individuals can use language to realise personal intentions that are not necessarily related to their culture group. From this view, cultural identities are like cloaks that individuals can put on or take off, as they choose.

Language use and identity are conceptualised rather differently in a sociocultural perspective on human action. Here, identity is not seen as singular and unitary, but rather as socially constituted, a reflexive product of the social, historical and political contexts of an individual's lived experiences. This view has helped to set new directions for current research in applied linguistics. The purpose of this chapter is to lay out some of the more significant assumptions embodied in contemporary understandings of identity and its connection to culture and language use. Included is a discussion of some of the routes in the broad arena of applied linguistics that research on language, culture and identity is taking.

2.2 Social identity

When we use language, we do so as individuals with social histories. Our histories are defined in part by our membership in a range of social groups into which we are born such as gender, social class, religion and race. For example, we are born as female or male and into a distinct income level that defines us as poor, middle class or well-to-do. Likewise, we are born as Christians, Jews, Muslims or with some other religious affiliation, and take on particular individual identities ascribed to us by our particular religious association. Even the geographical region in which we are born provides us with a particular group membership and upon our birth we assume specific identities such as Italian, Chinese, Canadian, or South African, etc. Within national boundaries, we are defined by membership in regional groups, and we take on identities as, for example, northerners or southerners.

In addition to the assorted group memberships we acquire by virtue of our birth, we appropriate a second layer of group memberships developed through our involvement in the various activities of the social institutions that comprise our communities, such as school, church, family and the workplace. These institutions give shape to the kinds of groups to which we have access and to the role-relationships we can establish with others. When we approach activities associated with the family for example, we take on roles as parents, children, siblings or cousins and through these roles fashion particular relationships with others such as mother and daughter, brother and sister, and husband and wife. Likewise, in our workplace, we assume roles as supervisors, managers, subordinates or colleagues. These roles afford us access to particular activities and to particular role-defined relationships. As company executives, for example, we have access to and can participate in board meetings, business deals, and job interviews that are closed to other company employees, and thus are able to establish role-relationships that are unique to these positions.

Our various group memberships, along with the values, beliefs and attitudes associated with them, are significant to the development of our social identities (Gee, 1996; Ochs, 1993; Tajfel and Turner, 1986) as they define in part the kinds of communicative activities and the particular linguistic resources for realising them to which we have access. That is to say, as with the linguistic resources we use in our activities, our various social identities are not simply labels that we fill with our own intentions. Rather, they embody particular histories that have been developed over time by other group members enacting similar roles. In their histories of enactments, these identities become associated with particular sets of linguistic actions, beliefs, attitudes and norms.

> **Quote 2.1** Elinor Ochs defines social identity
>
> Social identity encompasses participant roles, positions, relationships, reputations, and other dimensions of social personae, which are conventionally linked to epistemic and affective stances.
>
> Ochs (1996: 424)

The sociocultural activities constituting the public world of a white female born into a working-class family in a rural area in northeastern United States, for example, will present different opportunities for group identification and language use from those constituting the community of a white female born into an affluent family residing in the same geographical region. The knowledge, skills, beliefs and attitudes comprising our various social identities – predisposing us to act, think and feel in particular ways and to perceive the involvement of others in certain ways – constitute what social theorist Pierre Bourdieu calls our *habitus* (Bourdieu, 1977). It develops through the process of social categorisation in which we learn to sort the world and the people within it into groups made meaningful by larger sociocultural forces (Hewstone and Jaspers, 1984; Tajfel and Turner, 1986).

We approach our communicative activities with the perceptions and evaluations we have come to associate with both our ascribed and appropriated social identities and those of our interlocutors, and we use them to make sense of each other's involvement in our communicative encounters. That is to say, when we come together in a communicative event we perceive ourselves and others in the manner in which we have been socialised. We carry expectations, built up over time through socialisation into our own social groups, about what we can and cannot do as members of our various groups. We hold similar expectations of what others are likely to do and not do as members of their particular groups. The linguistic resources we use to communicate, and our interpretations of those used by others, are shaped by these mutually held perceptions. In short, who we are, who we think others are, and who others think we are, mediate in important ways our individual uses and evaluations of our linguistic actions in any communicative encounter.

2.2.1   Contextual relevancy of social identity

Even though we each have multiple, intersecting social identities, it is not the case that all of our identities are always relevant. As with the meanings of our linguistic resources, their relevance is dynamic and responsive to contextual conditions. That is to say, while we approach our communicative encounters as constellations of various identities, the particular identity or set of identities that becomes significant depends on the activity itself, our goals, and the identities of the other participants. Let us assume, for example, that we are travelling abroad as tourists. In communicative activities with others from different geographical regions it is likely that our national identity will be more relevant than, say, our gender or social class. Thus, we are likely to interact with each other as, for example, Americans, Spaniards, Australians or Italians. On the other hand, if we were to interact with these same individuals in schooling events such as parent–teacher conferences, we are likely to find that certain social roles take on more relevance than our nationalities, and we will interact with each other as parents, teachers and school administrators. Likewise, in events whose purpose is to provide opportunities to socialise with others, we are likely to orient to each other's gender identity, and interact as males and females rather than as parents and teachers, or Americans and Canadians.

How we enact any particular identity is also responsive to contextual conditions. Phillipsen's (1975) study of the ways in which a group of men enacted their identities as 'men' in a town he called Teamsterville is a compelling illustration of the fluid nature of identity. When members of the group of men considered their relationships with other men symmetrical in terms of age, ethnicity or occupational status, Phillipsen revealed that they considered it highly appropriate to engage in a good deal of talk with each other. However, when they considered the relationship asymmetrical, that is, when the event included men of different ages, ethnic groups or occupations, they spoke little to each other, as they regarded a high quantity of talk between men of unequal status to be inappropriate.

It is important to remember that our perceptions and evaluations of our own and each other's identities are tied to the groups and communities of which we are members. Expectations for what we, in our role as parent, can say to a child, for example, are shaped by what our social groups consider acceptable and appropriate parental actions. Some groups, for example, do not consider it appropriate for a parent to tell a child how to do something. Instead, the child is expected to observe and then take action (Heath, 1983). Other groups consider it important to discuss the task with the child before the child is allowed to attempt it (Harkness et al., 1992). Use of our linguistic resources then can perform an action in a communicative event only to the extent to which their expected meanings are shared among the participants. Given the diversity of group memberships we hold, we can expect our linguistic actions and the values attached to them to be equally varied.

2.3 Agency, identity and language use

While our social identities and roles are to a great extent shaped by the groups and communities to which we belong, we as individual agents also play a role in shaping them. However, unlike the more traditional view, which views agency as an inherent motivation of individuals, a sociocultural perspective views it as the 'socioculturally mediated capacity to act' (Ahearn, 2001: 112), and thus locates it in the discursive spaces between individual users and the conditions of the moment. In our use of language we represent a particular identity at the same time that we construct it. The degree of individual effort we can exert in shaping our identities, however, is not always equal. Rather, it is 'an aspect of the action' (Altieri, 1994: 4) negotiable in and arising from specific social and cultural circumstances constituting local contexts of action.

Quote 2.2 Richard Bauman defines individual identity from a sociocultural perspective

[Individual identity is] the situated outcome of a rhetorical and interpretive process in which interactants make situationally motivated selections from socially constituted repertoires of identificational and affiliational resources and craft these semiotic resources into identity claims for presentation to others.

Bauman (2000: 1)

From this perspective, then, individual identity is always in production, an outcome of agentive moves rather than a given. When we enter a communicative event, we do so as individuals with particular constellations of historically laden social identities. While these social identities influence our linguistic actions, they do not determine them. Rather, they predispose us to participate in our activities and perceive the involvement of others in certain ways. At any communicative moment there exists the possibility of taking up a unique stance towards our own identity and those of others, of using language in unexpected ways towards unexpected goals.

As with the meanings of our linguistic actions, however, how linguistically pliable our identities are depends to a large extent on the historical and sociopolitical forces embodied in them. Thus, while we have some choice in the ways we choose to create ourselves, our every action always takes place with a social context, and thus can never be understood apart from it (Altieri, 1994). Therefore individual agency is neither inherent in nor separate from individual action. Rather 'it exists through routinized action that includes the material (and physical) conditions as well as the social actors' experience in using their bodies while moving through a familiar space' (Duranti, 1997: 45).

> **Quote 2.3**   Chris Weedon articulates the dynamic relationship between individual identity and language use
>
> The individual is both the site for a range of possible forms of subjectivity and, at any particular moment of thought or speech, a subject, subjected to the regime of meaning of a particular discourse and enabled to act accordingly ... Language and the range of subject positions which it offers always exist in historically specific discourses which inhere in social institutions and practices and can be organized analytically in discursive fields.
>
> Weedon (1997: 34)

2.3.1 Giddens' theory of structuration

While current conceptualisations of agency and language use in applied linguistics draw from several sources, one of the more significant is Anthony Giddens' (1984) *theory of structuration*. According to Giddens, individual agency is a semiotic activity, a social construction, 'something that has to be routinely created and sustained in the reflexive activities of the individual' (Giddens, 1991: 52). In our locally occasioned social actions, we, as individual agents, shape and at the same time are given shape by what Giddens refers to as social structures – conventionalised, established ways of doing things. In our actions we draw on these structures and in so doing recreate them and ourselves as social actors. Our social structures do not, indeed cannot, exist outside action but rather can only exist in their continued reproduction across time and space. Their repeated use in recurring social practices, in turn, leads to the development of larger social systems, 'patterns of relations in groupings of all kinds, from small, intimate groups, to social networks, to large organizations' (ibid.). The mutually constituted act of 'going on' in the contexts of our everyday experiences – the process of creating and being created by our social structures – is what Giddens refers to as the process of structuration.

While Giddens is not particularly concerned with identity and language use per se, his ideas are useful in that, by locating individual action in the mutually constituted, continual production of our everyday lives – the dialogue (Bakhtin, 1986) between structure and action – Giddens' social theory provides us with a framework for understanding the inextricable link between human agency and social institutions.

Quote 2.4 Anthony Giddens on his theory of structuration

The basic domain of study of the social sciences, according to the theory of structuration, is neither the experience of the individual actor, nor the existence of any form of social totality, but social practices ordered across space and time. Human social activities, like some self-reproducing items in nature, are recursive. That is to say, they are not brought into being by social actors but continually recreated by them via the very means whereby they express themselves *as* actors. In and through their activities agents reproduce the conditions that make these activities possible.

Giddens (1984: 2; emphasis in the original)

2.3.2   Bourdieu's notion of habitus

Also influential to current understandings is the notion of *habitus*, as popularised by social theorist Pierre Bourdieu. According to Bourdieu (1977, 2000), habitus is a set of bodily dispositions acquired through extended engagement in our everyday activities that dispose us to act in certain ways. We bring them with us to our social experiences, and are inclined to make sense of our experiences, and coordinate our actions with others in particular ways. It is through our lived experiences as individual actors by which our habitus is continually being reconstituted.

> **Quote 2.5** Pierre Bourdieu's definition of habitus
>
> Habitus as a system of dispositions to be and to do is a potentiality, a desire to be which, in a certain way, seeks to create the conditions most favourable to what it is. In the absence of any major upheaval (a change of position, for example), the conditions of its formation are also the conditions of its realisation.
>
> Bourdieu (2000: 150)

For both Giddens and Bourdieu, individual identity is not a precondition of social action but rather arises from it. Moreover, in the recursive process of identity production individuals are constituted 'neither free agents nor completely socially determined products' (Ahearn, 2000: 120). How free or constrained we are by our habitus depends on 'the historically and socially situated conditions of its production' (Bourdieu, 1977: 95). The empirical concern is then to identify the actions that individual actors take in their lived experiences that lead, on the one hand, to the reproduction of their larger social worlds and, on the other, to their transformation.

> **Quote 2.6** Pierre Bourdieu on the mutually constituted relationship between individual agency and habitus
>
> The notion of habitus restores to the agent a generating, unifying, constructing, classifying power, while recalling that this capacity to construct social reality, itself socially constructed, is not that of a transcendental subject but of a socialised body, investing in its practice socially constructed organising principles that are acquired in the course of a situated and dated social experience.
>
> Bourdieu (2000: 136–7)

2.4 Research on language use and identity

2.4.1 Interactional sociolinguistics

One approach to the study of language use and identity that has had great impact on much research in applied linguistics is *interactional sociolinguistics* (IS), an approach that, to a large extent, is based on the work of linguistic anthropologist John Gumperz (1981, 1982a, 1982b). At the heart of IS is the notion of *contextualisation cues*. Gumperz (1999: 461) defines these cues as 'any verbal sign which when processed in co-occurrence with symbolic grammatical and lexical signs serves to construct the contextual ground for situated interpretations, and thereby affects how constituent messages are understood'. The cues encompass various forms of speech production including the lexical, syntactic, pragmatic and paralinguistic. They also include turn-taking patterns, and even the language code itself. The cues provide individual interlocutors with recognisable markers for signalling and interpreting contextual presuppositions. Such signals, in turn, allow for the mutual adjustment of perspectives as the communicative event unfolds.

Quote 2.7 John Gumperz explains the function of contextualisation cues

How do contextualization cues work communicatively? They serve to high-light, foregound or make salient certain phonological or lexical strings *vis-à-vis* other similar units, that is, they function relationally and cannot be assigned context-independent, stable, core lexical meanings. Foregrounding processes, moreover, do not rest on any one single cue. Rather, assessments depend on cooccurrence judgments that simultaneously evaluate a variety of different cues. When interpreted with reference to lexical and grammatical knowledge, structural position within a clause and sequential location within a stretch of discourse, foregrounding becomes an input to implicatures, yielding situated interpretations. Situated interpretations are intrinsically context-bound and cannot be analyzed apart from the verbal sequences in which they are embedded.

Gumperz (1992: 232)

This approach to the study of language use assumes that individuals enter into communicative activities with others as *cooperative agents*, that is, as individuals interested in working towards a common end. The specific analytic focus is on the particular cues these individuals use to index or signal an aspect of the situational context in which the sign is being used. Any misuse or misinterpretation of cues is assumed to be due to a lack of shared knowledge of specific cue meanings.

Early studies investigated intercultural and interethnic communicative events, with the aim of uncovering differences in use of cues to signal and interpret meaning and revealing the subtle but significant communicative outcomes resulting from these differences. Gumperz (1982b), for example, examined the misunderstanding resulting from the particular use of cues by a Filipino English-speaking doctor while being interrogated by FBI agents. While the cues the doctor used were familiar to Filipino English speakers, they were not familiar to the American English-speaking FBI agents and thus, Gumperz argued, their use by the doctor led to the agents' misreading of his motives. Similarly, Erickson and Shultz (1982) looked at how differences in the rhythmic organisation of discourse, including, for example, the timing of turns, between counsellors and individual students in advising interviews affected the counsellors' evaluation of the students' abilities.

In a more recent study, Field (1998, 2001) examined the miscues arising from classroom interactions between Navajo children and their teachers. According to Field, in Navajo communities it is not expected that responses will immediately follow their questions. This contrasts with more mainstream communities, whose practices are mirrored in schools, where it is assumed that replies will be immediately forthcoming. In her analyses of teacher–student interaction, Field reveals how such differences in participation structures led to the misjudging of the children's language abilities by the teacher, a member of the mainstream schooling community, who often interpreted the children's silence as deficiencies in their abilities to communicate in English. These and other studies (e.g. Scollon and Scollon, 1981; Tyler and Davies, 1990) reveal similar findings about the lack of shared knowledge on cue use between interlocutors.

As noted earlier, a basic assumption of much of this early research is that participants are mutually interested in the successful accomplishment of the interaction and that their success is basically a matter of shared understandings on the use of cues. Thus, any miscommunication occurring in interactions is assumed to be explainable in terms of differences in this knowledge. Recent critiques (e.g. Kandiah, 1991; Pratt, 1987; Sarangi, 1994), however, have raised some concerns about this assumption.

Kandiah (1991), for example, noted that such a view could not account fully for those cases of miscommunication between participants who share in knowledge of the use and interpretation of cues. Nor could it account for those interactions occurring between participants who do not share cue knowledge but do not break down. He argued that something other than shared knowledge of cues must account for these kinds of communicative interactions.

To make his case, Kandiah (1991) examined a job interview from the film *Crosstalk*, developed by Gumperz and his colleagues (1979) to illustrate difficulties in cross-cultural communication. In the film, communication difficulties arising between an English interviewer and the interviewee, an Indian immigrant to England, were attributed to differences in the individuals' communicative styles. One difference, for example, was found in the individuals' use of prosodic cues used to draw attention to particular bits of information in their presentation of the information. Kandiah argues that attributing the difficulties to a lack of shared knowledge ignores several crucial factors such as the length of time and experience the interviewee had had in the country before the interview and thus is inadequate in explaining the miscommunication. Instead, Kandiah argues, there are other possible explanations not accounted for in an analysis of cue use such as each participant's degree of willingness to accommodate to the other. For example, individuals can knowingly use different cues or misunderstand those used by others to *create* a lack of shared knowledge and thereby distance themselves from each other.

Shea's (1994) study of interactions between one university student and two academic advisers is a compelling example of how the lack of inter-actional cooperation rather than lack of shared knowledge led to communication difficulties. In the interactions, a non-native English-speaking student requested a letter of recommendation from two native English-speaking academic advisers. With one, his request was successful; with the other it was not. In looking closely at the interactional unfolding of each advising session, Shea makes a strong case that the different outcomes resulted not from a difference in shared knowledge of contextualisation cue use, but rather from the advisers' use of different structuring strategies. In the successful session, the adviser attempted to move past their communicative differences to construct a shared understanding of what the student was requesting by using affiliating strategies like amplification, requests for clarification, and agreement markers. In the unsuccessful interaction, the adviser treated the different cues as obstacles to achieving understanding, using distancing strategies such as interruptions, and exclusions to control the interaction and thereby position the student as 'a disfluent, inappropriate outsider' (p. 25). This adviser ended her session with the student by directing him to get more information, making it clear that she 'want[s] it *written down*! Because you struggle too hard to tell me what they [those to whom the letter will be directed] need' (emphasis in the original, p. 34).

The different strategies used by the advisers, Shea argues, are rooted not in communicative styles, but in ideological orientations towards the non-native speaker of English. By not taking such factors into consideration and focusing only on differences in cue use, interactional sociolinguistics runs the risk of 'divert[ing] attention away from the real, underlying issues that often render communicative exchanges at these points of contact unsuccessful in a fundamental sense to surface issues . . . the diversion of attention from the real issues has the unwelcome effect of legitimizing the behavior that is so destructive of real communicative interaction' (Kandiah, 1991: 372). Thus, as Shea concludes, regardless of the degree to which knowledge of cue meanings is shared, communicative cooperation cannot be assumed. Rather, it is an empirical matter, and one that goes beyond the moment-to-moment unfoldings of interaction to encompass larger social, political and historical discourse orders. In any study of inter-cultural communication, then, 'it is not enough simply to mention these very important matters; it is necessary to draw out with care and sophistication the highly complex issues they involve and to examine their close and integral interaction with the communicative behavior under investigation' (Kandiah, 1991: 371).

A related criticism has to do with the view of culture embodied in many of the earlier studies in IS. It has been argued (e.g. Pratt, 1987; Sarangi, 1994; Spack, 1998; Verschueren, 1999; Williams, 1992) that locating communication difficulties in cultural norms ascribes a deterministic role to culture, and thus renders invisible the role of individual agency in shaping social action. Rather, individuals are treated as if they reside in well-defined communicative worlds separated by immutable, clear boundaries, and within which they are compelled to act in particular ways. They approach interactions with culturally different others as representatives of a particular culture group – say, as American, Japanese, Chinese or Russian – and the group label functions as the sole interpretive lens through which their communicative behaviour is analysed and explained.

Alongside this deterministic view of culture is the assumption of culture as a one-dimensional, stable, homogeneous and consensual entity, with easily identifiable markers, and whose members share equally in the knowledge of and ability to use its norms. Such a monolithic view, it is argued, renders invisible the varied lived experiences of individuals *within* groups. We can only see in our analyses how culture is reflected in communicative encounters. What we cannot see is how it can also be a 'site of social struggle or producer of social relations' (Pratt, 1987: 56).

These criticisms notwithstanding, most agree that IS approaches to the study of language use have made significant contributions to a sociocultural perspective on human action. The concept of contextualisation cues, for example, draws our attention to detailed ways in which language use is tied to individual identities and provides a window onto the microprocesses by which such cues are used in the accomplishment of communicative events. Relatedly, in focusing on the moment-to-moment unfolding of interaction this approach draws our attention to the reflexive nature of context. Context is not a prior condition of interaction, but it is something that is 'both *brought along* and *brought about* in a situated encounter' (Sarangi and Roberts, 1999: 30; emphasis in the original).

2.4.2   Co-construction of identity

Drawing on the strengths of interactional sociolinguistics and incorporating insights from such social theorists as Bourdieu (1977, 1980, 2000), Giddens (1984, 1991) and others (e.g. de Certeau, 1984; Foucault, 1972; Weedon, 1997, 1999), much current research on language, culture and identity is concerned with the ways in which individuals use language to both index and construct their everyday worlds and, in particular, their own social roles and cultural identities and those of others within them. The studies assume that identity is multiple and varied, individual representations of which embody particular social histories that are built up through and continually recreated in one's everyday experiences (Sarangi,

1994). Moreover, it is acknowledged that individuals belong to varied groups and so take on a variety of identities defined by their memberships in these groups. These identities, however, are not fixed but 'multifaceted in complex and contradictory ways; tied to social practice and interaction as flexible and contextually contingent resources; and tied to processes of differentiation from other identified groups' (Miller, 2000: 72).

While operating from within the same theoretical framework, specific research interests have moved in two general directions. In the first, the specific concern is with demonstrating in micro-analytic detail how identities are constructed in the moment-to-moment unfoldings of social interaction. This strand draws from a larger interest in *co-construction* defined by Jacoby and Ochs (1995: 171) as 'the joint creation of a form, interpretation, stance, action, activity, identity, institution, skill, ideology, emotion or other culturally meaningful reality'. A primary concern of these studies is with identifying the specific cues or resources that index or mark individuals as particular kinds of social actors in particular inter-actional contexts. While not denying the significant role that verbal cues play, analytic interests cover a range of semiotic means including eye gaze, body posture, and even physical space arrangements by which individuals coordinate the process of identity construction in their interactions.

A study by Jacoby and Gonzáles (1991), for example, focused on the locally situated, mutually constituted achievement of the institutional roles of 'expert' and 'novice' in conversations occurring among members of a physics research team that included both faculty and students. Their analysis revealed that faculty members constructed themselves as experts through the use of such strategies as issuing directives, disagreeing and evaluating the assertions and performance of the others – strategies which are often associated with those with high institutional status and expertise. Their use, however, was not limited to faculty members as students also used them at particular moments to construct themselves as experts.

A study by Capps and Ochs (1995) is another example of how institutional identity is co-constructed. Here, the interest was in uncovering the ways that a woman diagnosed with agoraphobia used language in stories about herself and with others. In one particular analysis based on the woman's interactions with family members, Capps and Ochs reveal how her identity as an agoraphobic was constructed across space and time in the stories that she and her husband related at the dinner table. More specifically, they show how the husband's minimal responses to the woman in their conversations, rather than calming the woman's expressed fears and concerns as he apparently hoped to do, served to perpetuate them and at the same time help him to maintain an identity as a source of rational behaviour. These and other recent studies exemplify in rather compelling ways the dynamic, contingent and socially constructed nature of such identities as gender (e.g. Bergvall et al., 1996; Bucholtz et al., 1999; Livia and Hall, 1997), ethnicity (e.g. Field, 2001), non-native-speaking status (e.g. Wong, 2000a, 2000b), and interpersonal associations such as friends, siblings, parents, peers and so on (e.g. Hopper and Chen, 1996; Taylor, 1995).

A second direction taken by current scholarship on language and identity is similar to the first but its analytic lens is substantially wider in that it incorporates a variety of other data sources such as field notes, interviews, written documents and observations in the analysis in addition to taped versions of naturally occurring talk. Interest is not solely or even primarily in the sequential unfoldings of identity development in interaction, but rather includes more macro patterns of identity construction via language, including individual self-perceptions and beliefs. Moreover, many of the studies draw on constructs from social theory to help to explain their findings.

One example is the study of Wodak and colleagues (1999) on the construction of Austrian national identity. They based their study on Bourdieu's concept of habitus, and thus began with the assumption that because national identity is constructed in and through discourse, it is 'malleable, fragile, and frequently, ambivalent and diffuse' (p. 4). In addition to publicly available texts such as political commemorative speeches and poster campaigns, the researchers included group and individual interviews with Austrian individuals from different occupations and geographical regions as sources of data. Their analysis focused on the topics, discursive strategies and linguistic devices that were used to construct an in-group national identity, and out-group differences with respect to other national groups.

Included here, too, is recent work on the construction of language learner identities. Norton's study of immigrant women learning English in Canada (Norton, 2000; Pierce, 1995) is one example of such a study. Using data sources such as personal diaries and interviews, Norton illustrates how these women's identities were differentially constructed in their interactions with others in and out of the classroom. She argues that these different constructions had a significant influence on the women's interest in language learning, making some more willing than others to invest the time and effort needed to learn English.

Similar findings emerged from the study by McKay and Wong (1996), in which they examined the identity construction of four Mandarin-speaking adolescents in the contexts of their schools. Their specific focus was on documenting the many ways in which the learners attempted to negotiate the shaping of their identities as English language learners and users, and the consequences of their attempts relative to the development of their academic skills in English. They concluded that 'learners' historically specific needs, desires, and negotiations are not simply distractions from the proper task of language learning or accidental deviations from a "pure" or "ideal" language learning situation. Rather, they must be regarded as constituting the very fabric of students' lives and as determining their investment in learning the target language' (p. 603). Findings from these and other studies (e.g. Canagarajah, 1993; Day, 1999; Harklau, 1999; Ibrahim, 1999; Toohey, 2000) reveal how individuals are discursively categorised by their learning environments according to particular identities, how particular learning conditions reinforce or react against these identities, and how individuals linguistically position themselves in relation to the various forms of identity construction.

A related focus of attention in research on language use and identity is on the creative formation and dissolution of social identities as they are formed and reformed in zones of contact between persons of multiple and different languages, and different cultural identities (Pratt, 1987). The study by Rampton (1995) on language crossing is a compelling example of the permeability of social identities. His central concern was with the ways in which youths from mixed-race peer groups in Britain used language to construct hybrid identities. The groups were ethnically mixed, and consisted not only of Anglos but also of youths from Caribbean, Indian and Pakistani descent.

Using observations and interviews in addition to audio-tapes as his primary sources of data, Rampton found that the youngsters often used the languages associated with each other's ethnic and racial identities in creative, unexpected ways. For example, Afro-Caribbean youths often made use of Punjabi in their interactions with others. Rampton calls such uses 'crossing' and found that they occurred most often when individuals wanted to mark their stances towards particular social relationships. Asian adolescents, for example, often used stylised Asian English with teachers in their schools to feign a minimal level of English language competence and thus playfully resist teacher attempts to involve them in class activities. The youths also 'crossed' when playing games with their peers, or when they interacted with members of the opposite sex.

In documenting the myriad ways in which these youngsters used each other's languages to create social identities that were unique to their multi-ethnic communities, Rampton's study demonstrates how identities are not just *reproduced*, but, as significantly, *are transformed* in 'the slippages in reproduction, the erosions of long-standing patterns' (Ortner, 1996: 17) resulting from the zones of contacts when crossing language borders.

2.5 Summary

As we have discussed in this chapter, a sociocultural perspective on identity and language use is based on several key premises. One of the more significant replaces the traditional understanding of unitary, unique and internally motivated individuals with a view of language users as social actors whose identities are multiple, varied and emergent from their everyday lived experiences. Through involvement in their socioculturally significant communicative activities, individuals take on or inhabit particular social identity configurations, and use their understandings of their social roles and relationships to others to mediate their involvement and the involvement of others in their practices. These identities are not stable or held constant across contexts, but rather are emergent, locally situated and at the same time historically constituted, and thus are 'precarious, contradictory and in process, constantly being reconstituted in discourse each time we think or speak' (Weedon, 1997: 32).

In the contexts of our experience, then, we use language not as solitary, isolated individuals giving voice to personal intentions. Rather, we 'take up a position in a social field in which all positions are moving and defined relative to one another' (Hanks, 1996: 201). Social action becomes a site of dialogue, in some cases of consensus, in others of struggle, where, in choosing among the various linguistic resources available (and not so available) to us in our roles, we attempt to mould them for our own purposes, and thereby become authors of those moments.

Finally, this view recognises that culture does not exist apart from language or apart from us, as language users. It sees culture, instead, as reflexive, made and remade in our language games, our lived experiences, and 'exist[ing] through routinized action that includes the material (and physical) conditions as well as the social actors' experience in using their bodies while moving through a familiar space' (Duranti, 1997: 45). On this view, no use of language, no individual language user is considered to be 'culture-free'. Rather, in our every communicative encounter we are always at the same time carriers and agents of culture.

Quote 2.8 Elinor Ochs on the dialogic relationship between language, culture and identity

In this view as well, while language is a socio-historical product, language is also an instrument for forming and transforming social order. Interlocutors actively use language as a semiotic tool (Vygotsky, 1978) to either reproduce social forms and meanings or produce novel ones. In reproducing historically accomplished structures, interlocutors may use conventional forms in conventional ways to constitute the local social situation. For example, they may use a conventional form in a conventional way to call into play a particular gender identity. In other cases, interlocutors may bring novel forms to this end or use existing forms in innovative ways. In both cases, interlocutors wield language to (re)constitute their interlocutory environment. Every social interaction in this sense has the potential for both cultural persistence and change, and past and future are manifest in the interactional present.

Ochs (1996: 416)

Such a view of language, culture and identity leads to concerns with articulating 'the relationship between the structures of society and culture on the one hand and the nature of human action on the other' (Ortner, 1989: 11); a central focus of research becomes the identification of ways we as individuals use the cues available to us in our communicative encounters in the (re)constitution of our social identities and those of others.

Further reading

Bryant, C. and Jary, D. (eds) (2001) *The contemporary Giddens: Social theory in a globalizing age*. New York: Palgrave. The essays in this volume introduce the social theory of Anthony Giddens to both academic and general readers. Topics include Giddens' structuration theory and his views on the relation of the personal self to the social. The text concludes with a transcribed interview with Giddens conducted by the volume's editors.

Cameron, D. (ed.) (1998) *The feminist critique of language: A reader* (2nd edn). New York: Routledge. The chapters in this volume explicate the many layered connections between language and gender. The text includes essays examining the historical development of feminist thinking on language and identity, as well as current developments in research on the varied ways in which the social category of woman is both reflected in and shaped by language use.

Collier, M.J. (ed.) (2001) *Constituting cultural difference through discourse*. Thousand Oaks, CA: Sage Publications. The essays in this text examine the myriad ways in which culture and discourse are related through communication. Of particular interest are the linguistic means by which individuals create their cultural identities in communication with one another. A variety of cultural groups and perspectives on discourse analysis is represented in the chapters.

Duranti, A. (1994) *From grammar to politics: Linguistic anthropology in a Western Samoan Village*. Berkeley: University of California Press. Alessandro Duranti explores the way that language is used in traditional oratory in a Samoan village to shape the political process. Beginning with a view of language as social action, Duranti examines the specific grammatical means by which individual agency is created and how such creations serve the political processes in the community. It is a particularly useful illustration of how individual agency and social identity are both reflected in and shaped by the varied uses of a community's linguistic resources.

Jordan, G. and Weedon, C. (1995) *Cultural politics: Class, gender, race, and the postmodern world*. Oxford: Basil Blackwell. Using concepts from current social and cultural theories, the authors examine the role of culture in shaping social identities and relations of class, gender and race. They focus in particular on relationships between culture, subjectivity, and power.

Tannen, D. (1984) *Conversational style: Analyzing talk among friends*. Norwood, NJ: Ablex. Taking an interactional sociolinguistic approach and drawing on Gumperz's notion of contextualisation cues, Tannen presents a study of conversational style and the misunderstandings that can arise from different use of cues. The analysis is based on a taped conversation occurring among friends during a Thanksgiving dinner. Among the cues examined are tone of voice, speed, tempo, and the timing and taking of turns.

Chapter 3

Language-and-culture learning

This chapter will ...

- describe current thinking on the nature of language and culture learning;
- examine current research on language development;
- discuss the implications of a sociocultural perspective on learning for an integrated theory of teaching and learning.

3.1 Introduction

Language and culture learning has long been considered an important area of study in applied linguistics. However, as our understandings of the notions of language and culture have changed, so have the concerns on which such study is based. Research relying on understandings embodied in a more traditional 'linguistics applied' approach has rested on rationalist assumptions of learning. These assumptions consider language acquisition to be a process by which the human mind, with its innate, coherent and abstract systems, imposes order on incoming linguistic and non-linguistic data.

Studies of language learning from a 'linguistics applied' approach have ranged from attempts to uncover the universal properties of an innate language capacity to concerns with the roles played by particular cognitive processes and various external factors in the developmental sequence by which particular aspects of language and culture systems are acquired. Of concern, too, has been the examination of various forms of pedagogical interventions to determine the most effective way to facilitate learners' assimilation of new systemic knowledge into known knowledge structures.

Current understandings stand in marked contrast to the more traditional view of language and culture learning. They draw from theoretical insights and findings from investigations of learning drawn from areas outside what has traditionally been considered the main theoretical territory of applied linguistics. A primary source is cultural psychologist Lev Vygotsky's (1981, 1986) sociocultural theory of development first proposed over fifty years ago, and the more recent formulations that have built on, and in some cases modified and extended this earlier work (see, for example, A.N. Leontiev, 1981; A.A. Leontiev, 1981; Scribner, 1997a, 1997b; Wertsch, 1991, 1994). Also contributing to current views is recent research on language development in the fields of linguistic anthropology, developmental psychology, and psycholinguistics. In this chapter we look more closely at some of the more significant assumptions and empirical findings providing direction to current studies of language and culture learning in applied linguistics.

3.2 A sociocultural perspective on language and culture learning

A major premise of a sociocultural perspective on language and culture learning locates the source of learning in the pursuit of action in our social worlds. As discussed in Chapter 1, our worlds are constituted by a varied mix of goal-directed regularly occurring, intellectual and practical activities comprising various linguistic and other symbolic resources for their accomplishment. We acquire the knowledge and skills needed to be full participating members in these activities through the assisted guidance of more capable members (Vygotsky, 1978, 1986; Wertsch, 1991, 1994). With time and experience in our activities with the more experienced members, we learn to recognise what is taking place and to anticipate the typical uses and consequences of the uses of the activities' resources. In addition to learning how to take action with our words, we also develop a shared base of knowledge about the world, including frameworks of expectations for what counts as knowledge and for what we can and cannot do as individuals and as group members in using the resources to build upon our understandings of this knowledge. Likewise, we develop an understanding of the sociocultural importance of the activity, its values and goals, and the roles we, and the other participants, are appropriated into playing (Vygotsky, 1978).

This process of appropriation, according to Vygotsky (1978), takes place in the *zone of proximal development* (ZPD). The ZPD is 'the distance between the actual development level as determined by independent problem solving and the level of potential development as determined through problem solving under adult guidance or in collaboration with more capable peers' (ibid.: 86). The specific means of assistance provided by the more capable members in the ZPD can take many forms and includes *scaffolding* in which the more capable members share responsibility with the less capable members in the doing of an act, gradually letting them assume greater responsibility; *modelling*, where the more experienced members provide models or examples of the expected behaviours for the novices to notice, observe and imitate; and *training*, in which the more expert members coach or directly instruct the learners in the realisation of the expected actions. Also considered significant to the process are the varied ways in which we, as learners, individually positions ourselves in relation to the different modes of assistance and to the role and relationships made available to us.

With such socially mediated assistance, our performances are raised to a level they could not have achieved on their own, and in the process of learning we transform the specific linguistic symbols and other means for realising these activities that were once conjointly enacted into individual knowledge and abilities. We also acquire the communicative intentions and specific perspectives on the world that are embedded in them (Tomasello, 1999). In this way, habits of language use become the tools with which we make sense of, and participate in, our communicative worlds. It is our eventual internalisation or self-regulation of the specific means for realising our activities, including the particular worldviews embodied in them, that characterises psychological growth.

On this view the essence of mind does not exist separately from the varied worlds it inhabits. That is, the communicative contexts in which we spend our time and the means we use to realise our activities and the relationships we form with others, do not simply enhance the development of mental processes that already exist. Rather, they fundamentally shape and transform them. As noted by Vygotsky (1981) and others (A.N. Leontiev, 1981; A.A. Leontiev, 1981), the inherited biological characteristics of language and our innate abilities to learn – including the cognitive means to perceive, categorise, take a perspective and make patterns and analogies – constitute only the necessary preconditions for the ability to learn language. In the process of interacting with others, our innate capacities dynamically merge with and are ultimately shaped by the sociocultural, constituted by the myriad communicative activities made available to us as social actors in our sociocultural worlds. Also helping to shape our inner capabilities are the actions we take and respond to as we learn to make sense of and take part in our activities. The linguistics signs arising from this process 'are living evidence of a continuing social process' into which we are born and thus 'are at once [our] socialization and individuation' (Williams, 1977: 37).

Quote 3.1 Lev Vygotsky captures the social nature of development

Any function in the child's cultural development appears twice, or on two planes. First it appears on the social plane, and then on the psychological plane. First it appears between people as an interpsychological category, and then within the child as an intrapsychological category...Social relations or relations among people genetically underlie all higher functions and their relationships.

Vygotsky (1981: 163)

3.2.1 Mediational means

A key concept to understanding learning from a sociocultural perspective is the notion of *mediational means*. Considered 'the "carriers" of sociocultural patterns and knowledge' (Wertsch, 1994: 204), these are the tools and resources with which more expert members assist less competent participants in noticing, ordering, representing and remembering their involvement in their communicative activities. The means can be visual or physical in addition to verbal. They can also include computational

---

Concept 3.1 **Mediated action and mediational means**

From a sociocultural perspective, almost all human action is *mediated action* whereby we use linguistic and other cultural tools and resources – *mediational means* – to move through, respond to and make sense of our worlds. Understanding the links between human action and development entails understanding the nature of these means. James Wertsch (1994) characterises mediated action and mediated means in the following ways:

(1) mediated action exists in the irreducible tension between agent and mediational means;

(2) mediational means are material, existing across time and space;

(3) mediated action typically serves multiple, concurrent goals;

(4) mediated action is situated on one or more developmental paths;

(5) mediational means both constrain and enable action;

(6) new mediational means transform mediated actions;

(7) the relationship of agents towards mediational means can be characterised in terms of appropriation and mastery;

(8) mediational means are often produced for reasons other than to facilitate mediated action;

(9) mediational means are associated with power and authority.

resources such as computers and calculators, graphic resources such as diagrams, maps and drawings, and writing systems. We use calendars, for example, to help us to remember when events will take place and to organise our commitments; we use maps to help us to get from one place to another; and we use diagrams and drawings to help us to visualise spatial and other kinds of arrangements.

In the ways we use them to carry on our lives, these meaning-making resources give shape to the environments within which development occurs, and, more specifically, to the paths that individual development takes via the specific actions we take as participants within these environments. In other words, the means themselves and the ways in which we use them in the pursuit of action with others in our activities do not simply enhance our individual development; rather, they give it its fundamental form. Thus, it is, as Vygotsky argues, that we 'grow into the intellectual world of those around us' (1978: 88).

> **Quote 3.2**   Lev Vygotsky explains the essential role of mediational means in development
>
> The greatest characteristic feature of child development is that this development is achieved under particular conditions of interactions with the environment, where the ideal and final form (ideal in the sense that it acts as a model for that which should be achieved at the end of the developmental period; and final in the sense that it represents what the child is supposed to attain at the end of its development) is not only already present and from the very start in contact with the child, but actually interacts and exerts a real influence on the primary form, on the first steps of the child's development. Something which is only supposed to take shape at the very end of development, somehow influences the very first steps in this development.
>
> Vygotsky (1994: 344)

On this view of development, language becomes a primary vehicle for creating human mind. It is at one and the same time the means by which our history is generalised and handed down to us, a significant condition for our individual appropriation of our experiences, the means by which we pursue our goals in our experiences, and its form of existence in our consciousness (A.N. Leontiev, 1981).

As noted earlier, the linguistic means we use to engage in our communicative contexts often vary, sometimes widely, across groups. Likewise, the uses to which we put similar appearing means can also vary. Given the fundamentally social nature of learning, our participation in different activities, different uses of means in similar activities, or even different opportunities and experiences with using similar resources, give shape to equally different developmental paths (Wertsch, 1991).

In defining language learning as a process of sociocultural transformation this view makes it impossible to consider it outside its specific contexts, that is, to consider the psychological conditions of learning apart from their social conditions. As Scribner (1997a: 268) suggests, 'neither mind as such nor behavior as such can be taken as the principal category of analysis . . . The starting point and primary object of analysis is the actual process of interaction in which humans engage the world and each other.' So, if individual development begins in one's goal-directed socioculturally significant and interpersonally realised activities, the key to understanding language development is to study the processes by which individual language use is linked to its external worlds. Such study must begin with an analysis of the cultural, historical and institutional language-based contexts in which individuals live their everyday lives and, more specifically, the mediational means or cultural tools that individuals use to take action in these contexts. As important is analysis of the linguistic and other developmental consequences that result from individuals' varied uses of these tools as they engage with others in their socioculturally significant settings (Wertsch, 1994; 2000).

3.3 Language socialisation

Recent research on language development among children in several different cultural communities, undertaken by linguistic anthropologist Elinor Ochs (1988) and her colleague Bambi Schieffelin (1990), lends empirical support to these theoretical insights on the intrinsic link between language activities and language development. In their investigations of Western Samoan and Kaluli communicative activities they reveal the connections between community beliefs about language use, the language activities into which children are regularly appropriated, and the specific kinds of linguistic resources children eventually acquire.

In her investigations of Western Samoan caregivers' communicative practices, for example, Ochs found evidence linking these practices to larger community beliefs about language use on the one hand, and to children's acquisition of language on the other. In her analysis of one particular communicative activity regularly engaged in by caregivers and children, she found that when some clarification of the children's utterances was needed, caregivers were reluctant to expand or guess their meaning. Instead, they preferred to use what Ochs calls minimal grasp strategies such as using statements of non-understanding (e.g. 'what?' and 'huh?'), issuing directives (e.g. 'Say it again'), and making quizzical face expressions. Such actions, Ochs argues, reflect a cultural dispreference or unwillingness to speculate on the mental states of others. These same strategies that were prevalent in caregiver interactions with children, were found in peer interactions as well, evidencing, Ochs argued, the children's developing proficiency in using such strategies.

These findings led Ochs to conclude that in their activities with caregivers children were not only being socialised into particular ways of using and interpreting linguistic means for clarifying speech. They were at the same time being socialised into local epistemologies on the appropriateness and value of such means for self- and other-expression. A comparison of findings on caregiver–child interactions from Samoan, Kaluli and white middle-class American communities (Ochs and Schieffelin, 1982) offers further evidence on the subtle but significant ways that language is used to socialise children into meaningful, appropriate and effective uses of language and at the same time into culturally specific ways of thinking and knowing.

This and other research on the language practices of communities (e.g. Eisenberg, 1986; Heath, 1983; Peters and Boggs, 1986; Phillips, 1983; Schieffelin and Ochs, 1986) has led to the development of an integrated approach to the study of language use and acquisition called *language socialisation*. A key premise of this approach views language as socialising others not only through its propositional content but also through its use. That is, it is not only *what* is encoded *in language forms*, but *how* meaning is constructed *in social action* that shapes language development. Moreover, Ochs (1988, 1996) argues that the process of language socialisation is not limited to early childhood but is a lifespan experience.

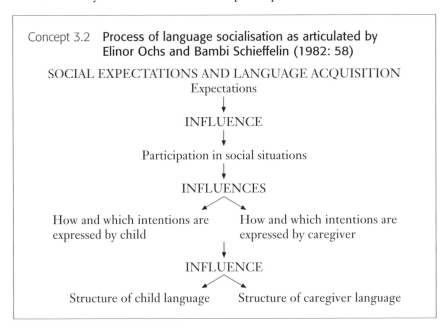

Concept 3.2   **Process of language socialisation as articulated by Elinor Ochs and Bambi Schieffelin (1982: 58)**

SOCIAL EXPECTATIONS AND LANGUAGE ACQUISITION
Expectations

↓

INFLUENCE

↓

Participation in social situations

↓

INFLUENCES

How and which intentions are   How and which intentions are
expressed by child   expressed by caregiver

↓

INFLUENCE

Structure of child language   Structure of caregiver language

At the heart of the language socialisation approach is the notion of *indexicality*. This is the process by which situational meanings (e.g. social identity, resource meaning, affective and epistemic stances) are assigned to forms (e.g. intonation patterns, speech acts, turn-taking patterns). Meanings of forms arise from their past uses in particular contexts by particular individuals in certain roles with certain goals, and from their relation to co-occurring forms at the time of their uses. Their uses at particular times in particular contexts *index* or invoke those meanings that are conventionally associated them.

The process of invoking meaning is what Ochs refers to as *linguistic indexing*, and the cues used in the process are called *linguistic indexes* or *indexicals*. These cues 'either alone or in sets, either directly or indirectly, and either retrospectively, prospectively or currently, establish contexts and as such are powerful socializing structures' (Ochs, 1988: 227). It is worth noting that the concept of indexicals in language socialisation research is similar to, if not the same as, Gumperz's notion of contextualisation cues as used in research taking an interactional sociolinguistics approach to the study of language use and identity (and discussed in Chapter 2).

Quote 3.3 Elinor Ochs explains the inextricable link between language and culture learning

The acquisition of language and the acquisition of social and cultural competence are not developmentally independent processes, nor is one process a developmental prerequisite of the other. Rather the two processes are intertwined from the moment a human being enters society (at birth, in the womb, or at whatever point local philosophy defines as 'entering society'). Each process facilitates the others, as children and other novices come to a perspective on social life in part through signs and come to understand signs in part through social experience.

Ochs (1996: 407)

According to Ochs (1988, 1996), knowledge of these cues is the basis for both linguistic and culture competence. Understanding language forms necessarily involves understanding their conventional social meanings, that is, their indexical potentials. Likewise, understanding social order involves knowing how such order is linguistically instantiated, that is, knowing which forms to use to point to and make relevant particular aspects of one's sociocultural worlds. A key challenge of research on language socialisation is to identify how language activities 'encode and socialize information about society and culture' (Ochs, 1996: 409). In showing how our communicative activities and world views are mutually constitutive, findings from such research offer compelling evidence for Hymes's (1974) notion of sociolinguistic relativity.

3.4 Learning how to mean

Much current research on child language development further corroborates this sociocultural perspective on language and culture learning. One early influential study was undertaken by the linguist Michael Halliday (1975). Using language data gathered from his own child during the period covering the child's growth from 9 to 18 months, Halliday demonstrated the intrinsic links between language learning and social context. He showed how adults, by interpreting the child's utterances in ways that made sense to them in their interactions with the child, influenced what the child eventually learned. In their interpretations, the adults afforded particular socially based meanings to the child's language. Eventually, his meanings – what the child ultimately took on as his own – became those meanings encoded in the adults' language. Halliday concluded that children learn language by 'learning how to behave in situations, not by learning rules about what to say' (Halliday et al., 1964: 179).

Like Vygotsky (1978, 1986), Ochs (1988, 1996) and others, Halliday understands the act of learning language and the act of learning culture to be mutually constitutive. Halliday considers language to be a quintessential cultural tool, an embodiment of the social system of meanings that enables its users to coordinate activities with others and, at the same time, learn the knowledge and practices, beliefs and values of their culture. In other words, as the child participates in communicative events of her daily life, she 'builds up a potential for exchanging the meanings that are engendered by the system' (Halliday, 1975: 121). Likewise, like Vygotsky, Halliday sees learning as an integration of both social and cognitive processes. He states (ibid: 140):

> In learning a language the child's task is to construct the system of meanings that represents his own model of social reality. This process takes place inside his own head; it is a cognitive process. But it takes place in contexts of social interaction, and there is no way it can take place except in these contexts. As well as being a cognitive process, the learning of the mother tongue is also an interactive process . . . The social context is therefore not so much an external condition of the learning of meanings as a generator of the meanings that are learnt.

Halliday's research on child language development forms the basis for his systemic functional theory of language (see Chapter 1).

Quote 3.4 Michael Halliday on language learning

In the development of the child as a social being, language has the central role. Language is the main channel through which the patterns of living are transmitted to him, through which he learns to act as a member of a 'society' – in and through the various social groups, the family, the neighbourhood, and so on – and to adopt its 'culture', its modes of thought and action, its beliefs and its values. This does not happen by instruction, at least not in the pre-school years; nobody teaches him the principles on which social groups are organized, or their systems of beliefs, nor would he understand it if they tried. It happens indirectly, through the accumulated experience of a number of small events, insignificant in themselves, in which his behaviour is guided and controlled, and in the course of which he contracts and develops personal relationships of all kinds. All this takes place through the medium of language.

Halliday (1978: 9)

3.5 Social activity and language development

Additional research on child language development from the fields of psychology and developmental psycholinguistics including the work of, for example, Berman and Slobin (1994), Ninio and Snow (1996), Pine (1994a, 1994b) and Tomasello and his colleagues (e.g. Tomasello et al., 1990; Tomasello and Barton, 1994) further substantiates the social nature of language learning. Findings from this research demonstrate the links between the development of language and children's participation in their socioculturally important communicative activities with their caregivers and other more competent participants. More specifically, it has been shown that children acquire both the forms and meanings of their linguistic resources from repeated experiences in regularly occurring communicative activities with their primary caregivers. In their joint interactions, the children are provided with a substantial amount of input in which the care-givers make salient the more important cues to the children. Children's attention is drawn to these cues through sociopragmatic actions including non-verbal cues such as gazing and gesturing, and verbal cues such as cue repetition and tone and pitch changes. They are also provided with verbal instructions that direct them to perceive or notice these cues and make connections between them and their contexts.

In their interactions with adults in the routines of their daily lives, even very young children play an active role by attempting to figure out the goals of their interlocutors' actions, and to reproduce the actions used by their interlocutors to reach those goals (Tomasello, 2000). For example, they observe and look for patterns of behaviour in their activities with others. Likewise, they actively select and attend to specific kinds of information, hypothesise about the meanings of their and others' actions, and continually try out their hunches in their interactions. Over time, and with help from more expert participants, young children and other novice participants learn to recognise the activity taking place and the goals embedded within it, and develop expectations about it and about the communicative values of the resources conventionally associated with the activity. Also facilitating the children's growing competence in taking part in their activities is the gradual increase in their working memory and attention span (Elman, 1999).

Eventually, their initial actions approximate the conventional forms used by the more expert participants, and thus serve as building blocks upon which their subsequent communicative development is based. As the children assume more responsibility in using language to accomplish their activities, they shape their context-specific patterns or habits of language use into prototypes for action and ultimately internalise them for their own use. Because different communicative activities comprise different arrangements of linguistic resources, different conditions for communicative development are created. In turn, these different conditions, the varied means of assistance in recognising and using the linguistic cues, and the children's individual responses to them give rise to distinct developmental outcomes.

Quote 3.5 Michael Tomasello on the role of structured, predictable and regularly occurring activities in the development of language

To acquire language the child must live in a world that has structured social activities she can understand . . . For children, this often involves the recurrence of the same general activity on a regular or routine basis so that they can come to discern how the activity works and how the various social roles in it function. And of course if we are interested in language acquisition it must be the case that the adult uses a novel linguistic symbol in a way that the child can comprehend as relevant to that shared activity. In general, if a child were born into a world in which the same event never recurred, the same object never appeared twice, and adults never used the same language in the same context, it is difficult to see how that child – whatever her cognitive capabilities – could acquire a natural language.

Tomasello (1999: 109)

Pine's (1994b) analysis of the different placements of syntactic elements in mothers' input to their children illustrates the contextually contingent nature of the process. His close analysis of their interactions reveals how the frequency of overall use of nouns and verbs in the mothers' talk, their functional saliency, and their connection to the children's interest and focus of attention created different patterns of language use. As a result of sustained interaction with their mothers using these patterns, the different patterns of language use were appropriated by the children.

In another study that looked at caregiver–child talk (Tomasello et al., 1990), it was shown how children developed different ways of communicating from their participation in different communicative contexts. In looking at the differences between mother–child and father–child interaction, the authors found, for example, that when conversational breakdowns occurred in interactions with their parents, children elaborated upon their utterances if their mothers did not initially acknowledge them. In contrast, the children repeated their utterances or abandoned talk if their fathers did not acknowledge them. The authors argue that the different communicative actions taken by the children in response to each parent's non-acknowledgements arose from their different communicative experiences with each parent. Because mothers usually followed up on their children's utterances when a breakdown in communication occurred, the children learned to interpret their mother's lack of initial acknowledgement as a need for more information and so learned to elaborate. On the other hand, because fathers usually did not return to the conversation after a breakdown, the children learned to interpret their fathers' non-acknowledgements as a lack of interest and so learned to abandon talk.

While much research has been concerned with first language development, a few studies (e.g. Snow et al., 1991; Wu et al., 1994) provide equally compelling data on the relationship between communicative activities and the development of additional languages. In the study by Snow et al., for example, it was found that school-aged children's abilities to produce formal definitions in both English and French were tied to their involvement in activities in which the lexical, syntactic and discourse structures typical of such definitions were frequently and regularly used. They concluded that the development of linguistic skills in an additional language, if not first acquired in the first language, is strongly related to children's engagement in activities employing those skills in the target language rather than to their access to decontextualised, linguistic structures associated with the target language.

Similarly, Wu and colleagues (1994) looked at performance differences across tasks in which students used either English or French. They found that those learners who were restricted to learning French in the classroom showed a difference in written and oral performances across conditions, doing better on writing tasks, and doing most poorly on oral contextualised tasks. One reason for their different performances, the authors argued, was due to the learners' lack of opportunities to develop oral contextualising skills in their classroom activities. Thus, it was concluded that the kinds of communicative activities constituting the environments of language class-rooms shaped in fundamental ways the learners' abilities and skills to use the target language.

To recap, current research on language development reveals it to be a consequence of extended involvement in regularly occurring commun-icative activities in which children or novices and their more capable interlocutors 'have various pragmatic goals towards the world and towards one another' (Tomasello, 2001: 136). Contextual conditions playing a fundamental role in the process include the frequency with which par-ticular features appear in the linguistic environment, the clarity of their form–function relationships, the children's or novice participants' regular engagement in the activity, and its connection to their interests. In addition, language development depends on children's and other novices' ability to understand the purposeful, communicative intentions of their more experienced interlocutors in constructing their shared worlds in particular communicative circumstances. The linguistic resources used in the various courses of actions taken with them are linked to language development in that they structure both the form and content of what is learned.

3.6 Social activity and cognitive development

Alongside this research on the social constitution of language development are recent advances in developmental psycholinguistics examining the relation between language and cognition. A number of recent cross-linguistic studies, for example, have demonstrated differences in young children's spatial representations in populations from different language groups. These differences are not, as universal claims about cognition development would have it, aged-related. Rather, findings show that young children's descriptions of spatial arrangements are more similar to descrip-tions by adult speakers of their particular language group than they are to descriptions by children of the same age group but in different language groups.

Bowerman (1996) and Bowerman and Choi (2001) provide examples of these cross-group differences in their studies on spatial semantic representa-tion across various language groups. One example they provide concerns the differences in the way that spatial configurations are construed in English and Korean. According to the authors, English makes a distinction between putting a figure into contact with a supporting, external ground object [on] and putting a figure into some kind of container [in]. In contrast, Korean makes a spatial distinction that cuts across the *in–on* distinction, and for which no morpheme exists in English. The Korean verb *kkita* describes the fitting together of two objects with complementary, interlocking shapes. The verb is used to describe a figure interlocking with an external flat ground, such as fitting a finger into a ring ([on] is typically used in English to describe such a relationship, i.e. put the ring *on* the finger). *Kkita* is also used to describe an arrangement where the figure is placed tightly within the ground, such as slipping a video cassette into its container ([in] is typically used in English to describe such a relationship, i.e. put the cassette *in* the box). As a final example, *kkita* is used to describe a spatial configuration in which the figure is placed in and through the ground object, such as placing a button through a buttonhole (a relationship for which neither [in] nor [on] is used in English. Instead, the verb 'to button' is typically used, as in 'button the [article]').

In their examinations of spontaneous speech of English- and Korean-speaking children between the ages of 1 and 3, the authors found that, rather than relying on some universal set of basic spatial concepts, these children, from as early as the one-word stage of language development, categorised their spatial events according to their language-specific means for doing so. That is, each group's encoding of spatial configurations reflected the major semantic distinctions and grouping principles of their respective languages. These findings, they argue, demonstrate 'a pervasive interaction between nonlinguistic conceptual development and the semantic categories of the input language' (Bowerman and Choi, 2001: 477).

Findings from these and other studies (e.g. Bowerman and Levinson, 2001; Hickmann, 2001; Slobin, 1997), revealing the inextricable links between at least some cognitive patterns acquired by children and their native languages, have led to the claim that language-specific development plays an essential role in the construction of non-linguistic concepts such as space, time and object classification. It gives shape to cognitive organisations and perceptions by filtering 'incoming information, leading children to pay more or less attention to different aspects of reality, which therefore become more or less salient and available in everyday functioning' (Hickmann, 2001: 113). As Slobin (1996: 91) notes, 'the language or languages that we learn in childhood are not neutral coding systems of an objective reality. Rather, each one is a subjective orientation to the world of human experience.' In conceiving of language not as mere expression of cognitive development, but as shaper and change agent of cognition, this research provides ample evidence in support of Whorf's (1940/1956) notion of linguistic relativity, and Vygotsky's (1978, 1981) and others' (e.g. A.N. Leontiev, 1981; Wertsch, 1994) theoretical insights linking language use to the development of mind.

> **Quote 3.6** Michael Tomasello on the significance of linguistic symbols in perceptual development
>
> Linguistic symbols are especially important symbolic artifacts for developing children because they embody the ways that previous generations of human beings in a social group have found it useful to categorize and construe the world for purposes of interpersonal communication. For example, in different communicative situations one and the same object may be construed as a dog, an animal, a pet, or a pest; one and the same event may be construed as running, moving, fleeing, or surviving; one and the same place may be construed as the coast, the shore, the beach, or the sand – all depending on the communicative goals of the speaker. As the child masters the linguistic symbols of her culture she thereby acquires the ability to adopt multiple perspectives simultaneously on one and the same perceptual situation. As perspectivally based cognitive representations, then, linguistic symbols are based ... on the ways in which individuals choose to construe things out of a number of other ways they might have construed them, as embodied in the other available linguistic symbols that they might have chosen, but did not.
>
> Tomasello (1999: 8–9)

3.7   Language classrooms as fundamental sites of learning

Historically, language teaching has always been considered one of the field's more significant concerns. In fact, one of the earliest official uses of the term *applied linguistics* dates back to the late 1940s when the University of Michigan offered a course on the topic, with the central focus on the teaching of foreign languages. However, irrespective of how strong, historically, the scholarly interests in language pedagogy have been in the field of applied linguistics, they have been treated as distinct from scholarly interests in learning. In fact, some applied linguists working in the area of language learning have expressed scepticism as to whether research on language learning *should* have anything to say to language teachers. These feelings of uncertainty have persisted over the years with researchers and practitioners both being urged to be cautious in applying findings of research on the learning of language to language teaching practices (Ellis, 1997). Given the assumptions about language and learning embedded in the more traditional 'linguistics applied' approach to the study of language learning, these doubts about the relevance of learning to teaching are understandable.

Current insights and research findings on language learning, however, have broadened and in many ways transformed our understanding of its link to language teaching. We know, for example, that much of our language development is intimately tied to our extended participation and active apprenticeship in sociocultural events and activities considered significant to our everyday worlds. Because schools are important sociocultural contexts, their classrooms and, more specifically, their discursively formed instructional environments are considered consequential to individual learners' development. A fairly large body of work examining school-based learning from this sociocultural perspective (e.g. Barnes, 1992; Cazden, 1988; Gutierrez, 1994; Mehan, 1979; Nystrand et al., 1997; Smagorinsky and Fly, 1993) provides compelling evidence for claims linking learning to teaching. This research is reviewed in Chapter 5, but for our purposes here it is useful to point out that, among other findings, it has been demonstrated that recurring classroom activities, with their fairly conventionalised semiotic resources for sense making, set up structures of expectations within which their communicative values can be learned. Through their extended participation in these activities with other more experienced participants, such as their teachers, learners develop particular habits of participation. These habits are consequential in that they socialise students into particular understandings of the roles and relationships considered important to their lives as students. Likewise, they are socialised into particular formulations of what counts as the official curriculum and of themselves as students of that subject matter. Students draw upon these patterns and norms to participate in subsequent classroom activities and thus the patterns and norms are consequential in terms of shaping not only what students ultimately learn, but also, more broadly, their participation in future educational events and the roles and group memberships that they hold within these events.

One illustrative example of the links between students' participation in their classroom instructional activities and their development as language learners and users is Smagorinsky and Fly's (1993) investigation of large and small literature discussion groups in two high school English language arts classrooms. In a comparison of the norms and patterns of the discussions as realised by both large and small groups in each classroom, they found that the students' small group linguistic actions reflected the values and processes that were evident in their teacher's actions in the large group discussions. In one classroom, both teacher-directed large group discussions and student-directed small group discussions were characterised by brief unelaborated interactions that did not draw on external knowledge sources. In contrast, in the other classroom, both large and small group discussions were characterized by lengthy, detailed interactions that drew on a variety of external sources. Smagorinsky and Fly argued that the different ways in which literature discussions were accomplished in the two classrooms led to the creation of two distinct communities of learners with different interpretive frameworks and communicative means for engaging in discussions on literature. They concluded that differences in instructional discourse patterns across classrooms, in terms of the kinds of learning opportunities teachers make available to their students in their interactions with them, help to shape individual developmental outcomes in distinct and consequential ways.

Such findings on classroom discourse and learning help us to understand that, rather than being peripheral to learning, teaching is at its centre. That is, in locating learning in social activity, and defining it as a process of sociocultural transformation, it makes it impossible to consider the process and outcomes of learning apart from their specific sociocultural contexts. No aspect of learning can be considered context-free, i.e. 'uncontaminated', or isolatable from the specific context in which it occurs. Understanding individual language behaviour can only come about through examinations of its sociocultural origins and evolution, i.e. through investigations of its lived histories. In other words, as Wertsch (1994) suggests, the key to understanding the process of language learning lies in learners' language-based activity settings. Thus, the communicative activities of the classroom and their resources, the particular participants and their histories, and the very processes by which the participants conjointly use the resources to accomplish their lives as members of their classrooms or other learning contexts, become the fundamental units of analysis. Such a focus provides the grounds for the development of an integrated theory of language teaching and learning (Vygotsky, 1981; Wertsch and Bivens, 1992).

Research on language learning from this perspective has begun to broaden our understanding of the conditions by which language learners' involvement in the various constellations of their classroom communicative practices is shaped, and how, over time, such involvement affects the development of their social and psychological identities both as learners and users of language. A review of some current research on language classrooms is provided in Chapter 5.

Quote 3.7 According to Gordon Wells, a sociocultural theory of language learning should

. . . not only explain how language is learned and how cultural knowledge is learned through language. It should also show how this knowledge arises out of collaborative practical and intellectual activities and, in turn, mediates the actions and operations by means of which these activities are carried out, in the light of the conditions and exigencies that obtain in particular situations.

Wells (1994: 84)

Table 3.1	Traditional and sociocultural perspectives on language, culture and learning in the field of applied linguistics	

	'Linguistics applied' perspective	Sociocultural perspective
Language	Internally coherent structural systems, knowledge of which precedes use	Tools and resources for social action, structural and functional regularities of which result from use
Culture	Logical systems of representational knowledge	Social systems of communicatively realised practices
Learning	Internal activation of the language acquisition device for the assimilation of new knowledge structures into existing systems	Process of being socialised into the communicative and other social activities of sociocultural importance to the group(s) or community(ies) one aspires to be a member of
Individual	Self-reliant, autonomous, internally coherent and stable across contexts	Historically constructed, complex nexus of socially contingent identities
Purpose of research on language and culture learning	To uncover the universal properties of the innate language capacity and the role of cognitive processes in the assimilation of new language systems and cultural knowledge	To examine the developmental consequences of appropriation into particular communicative activities in terms of an individual's developing repertoire of means for taking action

A final point worth noting is that, while classrooms are indeed important sites of learning, they are not the only places where language learning occurs. In living our daily lives we come into extended contact with others, develop significant interpersonal relationships with them, and thereby exert influence on each other's language learning and use in consequential ways. Acknowledging this, recent investigations of language learning have begun to move outside the classroom, to such community-based institutions as recreational organisations, neighbourhood hangouts, daycare centres and social clubs as potentially significant sites of learning (see, e.g., Norton, 2000). Investigations of the specific conditions for and consequences of learning that exist at these different sites will contribute to a more complete understanding of the socioculturally mediated nature of language learning.

3.8 Summary

To recap, unlike the more traditional 'linguistics applied' approach, which views language learning as an innate process of linguistic system-building, a sociocultural perspective views it as the jointly constructed process of transforming socially formed knowledge and skills into individual abilities. It is, as Gee and Green (1998: 147) explain, a socioculturally constructed process of 'changing patterns of participation in specific social practices within communities of practice'. In this view, language development is considered to be both an evolutionary and a historical process (Williams, 1977). That is to say, while acknowledging that one needs to have a biological capability to learn language, a sociocultural perspective argues that what we actually learn, including a conceptual understanding of language itself, is shaped by our history of lived experiences in our communicative environments, including the relationships we develop with more expert language users, and the particular opportunities provided to and created by us to use the means associated with these contexts. On this view, language learning is also, and at the same time, culture learning.

Important to research on language learning, then, is not the articulation of a hierarchy of language systems; rather, it entails

- the identification and characterisation of the constellations of communicative activities, including the means for their accomplishment, that comprise different contexts of learning;
- specifications of how learners' appropriation into the resources of the activities both reflect and create particular kinds of 'learner' identities; and
- examination of the developmental consequences resulting from the varied paths down which the processes of appropriation lead.

Current understandings of learning also transform our understanding of language teaching. It is not merely an activity that may or may not be relevant to the process of language learning. Rather, it defines the very nature of both the processes and products of language learning, for it is in and through the processes of teaching – and more specifically the processes of appropriating learners into the communicative activities of their learning environments – that the conditions for and substance of learning are given shape. It is not the case, then, that language pedagogy is distinct from and peripheral to research on language learning. Rather, it forms its very core. Some of the more significant implications of current thinking on language teaching and learning are the central topics of discussion in Section II.

Further reading

Bruner, J. (1990) *Acts of meaning*. Cambridge, MA: Harvard University Press. This book is a compilation of lectures given by the author in 1989–99. The text opens with a critique of the information-processing model of the mind, a model that Bruner considers to be both antihistorical and anticultural. In the rest of the essays, the author presents an understanding of language and culture as socially linked, mutually constitutive, and fundamental to the shaping of self and mind.

Bybee, J. and Hopper, P. (eds) (2001) *Frequency and the emergence of linguistic structure*. Philadelphia: John Benjamins. This collection of essays presents research tying the emergence of language forms to their frequency and distribution of use in naturally occurring discursive contexts. They are revisions of papers that were first presented at an invitational symposium sponsored by Carnegie Mellon University in 1999. Together, they provide persuasive support for a view of language structure as a product of, rather than a condition for, communication.

Lantolf, J.P. (ed.) (2000) *Sociocultural theory and second language learning*. Oxford: Oxford University Press. This collection includes eleven chapters that address current theoretical and empirical research on second language learning from a sociocultural perspective. Topics covered include the roles of language play and the use of L1 in mediating L2 learning, identity development and second language learning, and interactional engagement in the zone of proximal development.

MacWhinney, B. (ed.) (1999) *The emergence of language*. Mahwah, NJ: Lawrence Erlbaum. The essays in this volume offer compelling evidence for an understanding of language development that moves away from the nature–nurture dichotomy. Labelled *emergentism*, the approach views the process of language development as fundamentally linked to, and emerging from, the interaction between innate predispositions and the social environment. Of the sixteen chapters comprising the volume, several chapters deal explicitly with language acquisition; one chapter, by Snow, explores specific features of social context that help to shape language development.

Nelson, K. (1996) *Language in cognitive development: The emergence of the mediated mind*. Cambridge, UK: Cambridge University Press. This book presents a sociocultural understanding of the relationship between language and cognitive development. Arguing for a view of language as mediational tool, the author presents evidence illustrating how individual aspects of cognition such as memory and conceptual knowledge are tied to social action in fundamental ways.

Newman, F. and Holzman, L. (1993) *Lev Vygotsky: Revolutionary scientist*. Routledge: London. The authors of this text analyse the insights of Lev Vygotsky into the study of learning, development, thinking, speaking and playing, and from these draw implications for education, psychotherapy and everyday life. They propose the notion of *revolutionary activity* as a normal characteristic of human life, and discuss how this notion transforms our understanding of development and change.

II Teaching language and culture

Chapter 4

The sociocultural worlds of learners

This chapter will...

- provide an overview of current research investigating learners' sociocultural worlds;
- describe some pedagogical innovations arising from this research.

4.1 Introduction

Language and culture teaching has always been considered an important component of applied linguistics. More traditional approaches to teaching, however, rarely took into account learners' linguistic and cultural worlds outside the classroom. Rather, it was assumed that learners entered the classroom as empty vessels to be filled with information about the world. The information itself was thought to consist of immutable, discrete elements that existed independently of individuals' worlds. The process of knowledge acquisition, as noted previously, was assumed to be an internally driven one in which the elements were pieced together, unit by unit, in the building of autonomous systems of rules.

Since learning was viewed as primarily a cognitive process, realised by internal mechanisms that all normally developing individuals possessed, learners' experiences in their sociocultural worlds were not considered significant to the process. When they *were* given consideration, they were usually treated as independent variables needing to be controlled in order to get a clear, unimpeded view of the internal process and outcomes of language learning.

The view of language as internally coherent systems and learning as an internally driven, universal process of assimilation resulted in a conceptualisation of learner *differences* as individual *deficiencies*. That is to say, differences in levels of academic achievement were often attributed to differences in individual learners' linguistic and cognitive capabilities. Those who did not succeed were considered deficient or lacking in requisite cognitive and linguistic skills. Where learners' home contexts were considered, lack of academic success was often attributed to the learner's upbringing in settings considered to be linguistically and culturally deprived.

In making apparent the inextricable links between learners' sociocultural worlds and learning, a sociocultural perspective embodies a fundamental change from the more traditional perspective. We now know that, rather than being peripheral to learning, the sociocultural worlds into which learners are appropriated play a fundamental role in shaping their language and cognitive abilities and, more generally, their cultural beliefs about the language and their identities as language users.

These understandings of the significance of learners' linguistic and cultural worlds, coupled with a growing awareness of the inadequacy of the deficiency view on learning for explaining the academic difficulties of learners who are not generally considered to be linguistically or culturally mainstream, have given direction to two strands of research in applied linguistics. While taking slightly different tacks, each strand combines interests in the linguistic and cultural worlds of learners with concerns with schooling. The purpose of this chapter is to overview the directions this research has taken, discuss the insights on the teaching of language and culture arising from the research findings, and present some current pedagogical practices and programmes that have been developed from these insights.

4.2 Language socialisation practices: Home and school connections

One direction of research concerned with learners' sociocultural worlds and schooling draws primarily from linguistic anthropology and, in particular, the research on language socialisation practices (e.g. Ochs, 1988; Schieffelin and Ochs, 1986). A primary aim of this research has been to compare the particular sociocultural practices into which learners are socialised *outside* their schools with the practices they encounter *inside* their schools. The studies by Shirley Brice Heath (1983) and Susan Phillips (1983) are arguably two of the more influential investigations in this area. Each provides comparative descriptive analyses of the language socialisation activities and practices, and larger sociocultural beliefs and values found in home communities of learners who are not considered to be standard English speakers with those found in their mainstream schooling institutions.

Heath's study was a longitudinal, comparative investigation of the socialisation practices of two rural communities – Trackton, a black community, and Roadville, a white community – and one urban, middle-class community comprising both black and white families. Her analysis revealed that the two rural communities differed from each other in fairly significant ways in terms of how the children were raised to use language and to see themselves as language users. For example, Heath discovered that the children in each community were socialised into different understandings of the activity of 'storytelling' and into using different linguistic resources for accomplishing the activity. The Trackton children were encouraged to exaggerate and to fantasise when telling their stories, whereas children from Roadville were expected to stick to the facts, providing details where necessary, but never straying from what the adults considered to be 'the truth'.

Not only did the socialisation practices of these two rural communities differ from each other, but they also differed from the instructional practices found in schools, which, Heath revealed, more closely mirrored the socialisation practices of the urban, middle-class community. These differences, she argued, resulted in different learning outcomes in school. Children from the rural communities whose practices differed from their schools' practices had more difficulty succeeding academically than did their urban counterparts, whose home practices more closely resembled the practices of school. This was so, Heath argued, because the contexts of schooling were a natural extension of the home contexts of the middle-class children. Consequently, the children were able to use what they had learned at home as a foundation for their learning in schools, whereas those from the rural communities could not. In her comparative study on the socialisation practices of the Warm Springs Indian home and school communities, Susan Phillips (1983) reported similar findings. Like Heath, she argued that the differences in language socialisation practices found in the Warm Spring Indian children's home and school contexts made it more difficult for the children to do as well as their Anglo counterparts in schools, whose home practices more closely reflected the school's practices.

This concern with understanding the links between learners' *language* practices in and out of school has been taken up by those interested in the comparative study of *literacy* practices. Like research on language practices, the studies here have aimed to understand more fully the social, cultural and historical links between the ways that learners are socialised into the activities of reading and writing in their home contexts and to use this knowledge to inform school-based instructional practices (Barton, 1991).

For example, Fishman's (1991) investigation of the literacy practices of one Amish community residing in the state of Pennsylvania in the United States revealed a fairly significant variation in their practices in and out of school. Similar findings revealing differences between home and school literacy practices were reported in the more recent studies by, to name but a few: McCarty and Watahomigie (1998), who investigated the literacy practices of American Indian and Alaskan native communities; Dien (1998), who investigated the literacy practices of Vietnamese American communities; and Martin-Jones and Bhatt (1998), who investigated the literacy practices of immigrant Gujarati-speaking groups living in Britain.

These studies on the language and literacy practices of different communities and groups have added greatly to our understandings of the links between learners' sociocultural worlds *outside* the classroom and their worlds *inside* the classroom. We know, for example, that home practices, particularly those of non-mainstream groups and communities, often differ from those found in schools. We also know that children whose worlds differ do not perform as well as those learners whose worlds are more similar. The reason for the differences in performances, however, is not because some home practices are inherently inferior. That is, it is not anything intrinsic to the language and literacy practices found in students' homes that impacts on students' abilities to do well in school. Rather, it is more a matter of compatibility. Children whose home activities reflect the dominant practices of schools are likely to have more opportunities for success since they only need to build on and extend what they have learned at home. On the other hand, children whose home practices differ from those of their school are likely to have more difficulty since they will need to add additional repertoires of learning practices to those they already know.

4.3 Language variation

In addition to studies of home and school socialisation practices, research on language variation has helped to shape pedagogical concerns with the teaching of language and culture. The focus of much of this research has been on describing the regular features of languages and dialects of particular groups and communities with the general purpose of informing discussions on linguistic diversity. By revealing the systematic regularities of language varieties, such studies aim to counter the view on language variation as a deficient or incomplete version of the standard variety. This has been considered especially significant for schooling contexts, since it is often the case that teachers, administrators and other institutional authorities who are unfamiliar with the linguistic varieties that non-mainstream students bring with them to school consider these students to be linguistically deprived (Baugh, 1999).

Early research on variation sought to illustrate the patterned phonological, syntactic and lexical features typical of different varieties of English found in the United States. Linguistic descriptions have been done, for example, of American varieties of English such as African American Vernacular English (Labov, 1972), Appalachian and Ozark Englishes (Wolfram and Christian, 1976; Christian et al., 1988), and Puerto Rican English (Wolfram, 1974). More recent studies have moved beyond descriptions of linguistic features to investigations of speech activities specific to particular groups such as African American English speakers (e.g. Baugh, 1983; Smitherman, 1994), Chicano speakers (Bixler-Márquez and Ornstein-Galicia, 1988) and urban and suburban Puerto Rican communities (Zentella, 1997; Urciuoli, 1996; Torres, 1997).

The substantial evidence on the regularities of language varieties documented in these and other studies reveals that instead of reflecting some deficient version of an idealised notion of language, these varieties, and more specifically their linguistic resources, are legitimate, meaningful tools by which members of linguistically diverse groups and communities participate in their sociocultural worlds. These findings, and those from studies on home and school language and literacy practices, have led to the development of three pedagogical innovations for teaching language and culture that use the richness of learners' sociocultural worlds *outside* the classroom to inform the worlds created *inside* the classroom. These approaches are described in the sections that follow.

4.4   Redesigning curriculum and instruction

Taking a broad-based approach to redesigning school programmes, two pedagogical innovations to the teaching of language and culture call attention to the importance of sociocultural compatibility between the students' home lives and their school lives for promoting academic success. Although their emphases are slightly different, both approaches are based on the following two premises. First, they recognise that classroom-based curricula and instruction have historically drawn on the activities, knowledge, skills, beliefs and values of certain mainstream sociocultural groups, which, as the research on home and school links has shown, do not usually include those of non-mainstream groups such as language minority students. Although the practices of these groups are different, however, it does not make them any less valuable as sources of learning.

A second premise recognises that effective learning begins with making learning culturally relevant and meaningful to learners. To do this depends not so much on changing the learners so that they become interested in the more mainstream ways of knowing. Rather, in recognising learners' experiences as important sources of knowledge, these approaches call for using the sociocultural worlds that students bring with them to school to create culturally relevant and meaningful curricula and instructional practices in the classroom.

4.4.1   Culturally responsive educational programmes

One early educational response to studies documenting differences between home and school practices was to develop instructional programmes specific to particular culture groups whose levels of academic achievement were below average and whose sociocultural activities, norms of participation and other patterns and beliefs, were found to differ fairly significantly from mainstream, school-based norms and patterns. One of the first such culture-specific programmes in the United States was the Kamehameha Early Education Program (KEEP).

KEEP was first developed in 1972 to improve the academic achievement of low-income, elementary school-aged Native Hawaiian children. Early studies (e.g. Gallimore et al., 1974; Au, 1980; Au and Mason, 1983) demonstrated incompatibility between the school and home environments of Native Hawaiian children. It was found, for example, that when at home, children often sought help from peers and siblings rather than from adults. It was also found that the children's home culture promoted joint turn-taking during conversation rather than the one-person-at-a-time pattern typically found in school contexts.

KEEP drew on this research to develop instructional practices and classroom management techniques that were more compatible with the Native Hawaiian children's home activities. Key features of the instructional programme included organising opportunities not around teacher-directed, large group activities, but rather around small, cooperative learning groups and peer-based learning centres in which 'the students have a fair degree of responsibility for their own learning, much like the Hawaiian children have in their own homes' (Villegas, 1991: 14). It also entailed incorporating the students' preferred means of interaction in the classroom. For example, they were allowed to engage in the joint construction of stories, taking turns as they wished, instead of depending on the teacher for allocation of turns. Villegas (1991: 14) notes:

> By design, the allocation of turns at speaking during the lessons resembles the rules for participation in the *talk story*, a recurrent speech event in Hawaiian culture. Specifically, students are allowed to build joint responses during story time, either among themselves or together with the teacher. This strategy of collective turn-taking parallels the joint narration of a story by two or more individuals, which is typical of the talk story.

Given KEEP's success in enhancing Hawaiian children's academic performance, other socioculturally congruous elementary school programmes in the United States have been developed. For example, Rough Rock Community Elementary School, located on the Navajo reservation in Arizona, was initially begun as a collaboration between the KEEP team and the Rough Rock elementary school team to investigate whether the classroom conditions that were successful in KEEP would be equally successful in a school for Navajo children (McCarty, 1989; Begay et al., 1995).

This collaboration led to the finding that while some factors were indeed equally successful in fostering learning, other practices worked better for the Navajo children, as they were more congruent with the Navajo home culture. For example, because of the traditional separation of children by gender in Navajo homes, children at Rough Rock were found to prefer to work alone on tasks or in same-sex groups rather than participating in mixed teams (Begay et al., 1995). Similar to KEEP, it was found that changing instructional practices so that they affirmed and built on the Navajo children's home socialisation practices was successful in raising their levels of academic achievement in school. Similar findings on the value of socioculturally congruent home and school practices are emerging in other culture-specific school programmes (e.g. Tharp et al., 1998).

4.4.2 Funds of knowledge

A similar innovation emerging from pedagogical concerns with connecting to learners' worlds outside the classroom is the *funds of knowledge* approach to curricular development and design. First developed by Luis Moll (1992), and expanded by others (e.g. González and Amanti, 1992; González et al., 1993, 1995), this approach combines Vygotsky's insights on learning with ethnographic methods for conducting research on learners' sociocultural worlds outside the classroom. The purpose of such research is to use the findings on learners' worlds to transform school curricula. The concept of *funds of knowledge* refers to the historically developed, significant sociocultural practices, skills, abilities, beliefs and bodies of knowledge that embody the households of learners in the immediate school community (Moll, 2000).

Similar to the culture-specific programmes mentioned above, this particular approach seeks to redesign curricula and instruction so that they are more culturally meaningful to students. It differs slightly in that it focuses on involving classroom teachers in redesigning instructional programmes. It rests on the premise that rather than being told what to do, teachers must actively be engaged in the transformation process itself, from conducting research on the sociocultural worlds of their students outside school to creating and implementing new curricula and instructional activities, if educational innovations are to have any chance of long-term success.

Example 4.1 *Funds of Knowledge* Teachers' Project

Purpose of the *Funds of Knowledge* Teachers' Project: To draw upon the knowledge and other resources found in local households to develop, transform and enrich classroom curriculum and instructional activities. This teacher-research project designed by González et al. comprised the following three activities:

1. *Community investigations.* This entailed ethnographic studies of the origin, use and distribution of funds of knowledge among households in a predominantly Mexican working-class community of Tucson, Arizona. Before engaging in the community study, teachers were trained in the use of ethnographic methods for collecting data, with a central focus on the ethnographic interview. It also entailed training teachers in methods for conducting thematic analyses of the data.

2. *After-school teacher study groups.* These groups, comprising teacher-researchers and university-based researchers, met on a regular basis to discuss research findings and to plan and design innovative curricula and instructional activities using the content and methods of home learning, gleaned from the household study of funds of knowledge, to inform the content and methods of school learning.

3. *Classroom investigations.* This component entailed teacher-researchers engaging in studies of existing methods of instruction in their own classrooms. They then used these findings to compare the ways the children learned at home and in the community with the opportunities provided at school. Based on these comparisons, the teachers made curricular and instructional changes, using the activities designed in the study groups.

Source: Based on González et al., 1993, 1995

The *funds of knowledge* approach begins with the engagement of teachers in the ethnographic study of the origin, use and distribution of the communicative activities and events, and ways of thinking about, believing in and valuing these activities that are significant to their students' home and community lives. Collecting the data usually involves extended visits to learners' communities and homes and interviews with important family and community members with the purpose of identifying and documenting existing knowledge, skills, behaviour and beliefs. Once the data have been collected and analysed, teachers compare existing curricula and instructional methods with content and methods of home learning, and use findings from their comparative analyses to devise new academic materials and instructional activities that build on what language minority learners know and can do outside school.

Most *funds of knowledge* projects have been conducted by teachers from public schools, primarily at the elementary level, in the United States

(González and Amanti, 1992; Moll et al., 1992). In the study by Moll and colleagues, for example, teachers visited their Mexican American students' homes to collect evidence of the *funds of knowledge* manifested in their homes. The teachers used their new understandings to create curriculum units on topics and activities considered to be significant to those households. In one case, it was found that when returning from their regular trips to Mexico, one family often brought back products to sell, such as candy. Building on this family's specific fund of knowledge, the teacher developed an integrated instructional unit based on various aspects of the nutritional content of candy. The class then made an inquiry-based comparison of US and Mexican candy and sugar-processing operations. Members of the family became participants and 'resident experts', visiting the class to share their knowledge and experience (González et al., 1993).

According to González et al. (1993: 1), participation in the project engendered 'pivotal and transformative shifts in teachers and in relations between households and schools and between parents and teachers'. For example, their research efforts helped teachers to redefine their understanding of the notion of culture by moving them away from a traditional perspective of culture as an accumulation of disembodied facts on foods, clothes, history and holidays or, as González et al. noted, 'as a static and uniform grab bag of tamales, *quinceañeras*, and *cinco de mayo* celebrations' (p. 10). Instead, the teachers came to understand culture as a vital, dynamic process, which 'emphasized the lived contexts and practices of the students and their families' (ibid.).

Quote 4.1 The transformative effect that engaging in a *funds of knowledge* project had on participating teachers

Each teacher, as she came to know the households personally and emotionally, came away changed in some way. Some were struck by the sheer survival of the household against seemingly overwhelming odds. Others were astonished at the sacrifices the households made in order to gain a better education for their children. They all found parents who were engineers, teachers, and small business owners in Mexico, who pulled up stakes and now work in jobs far below their capabilities in order to obtain a better life and education for their children. They found immigrant families with 15 people in a household, with all adult males and females working in order to pay for rent and everyday necessities. As Raquel Gonzáles notes, 'I came away from the household visits changed in the way that I viewed the children. I became aware of the whole child, who had a life outside the classroom, and that I had to be sensitive to that. I feel that I was somewhat sensitive before the visits, but it doesn't compare to my outlook following the visits.'

González et al. (1993: 11–12)

The approach also helped teachers to understand the value of their non-mainstream students' home lives. As pointed out earlier in the chapter, non-mainstream students' homes were traditionally viewed as places lacking in cultural knowledge and experiences and from which children needed to be rescued if they were to have any chance of academic success. The teachers' research experiences helped them to see things differently and, consequently, they came away with an understanding of their learners' homes as rich reservoirs of knowledge and experience. This recognition in turn helped the teachers to see their students as rich sources of linguistic and cultural knowledge and experiences, which ultimately resulted in increasing expectations of the learners' abilities (Civil et al., 1998).

4.4.3   Language awareness curriculum

A third response to concerns with the sociocultural worlds that learners bring with them to the classroom is the development of *language awareness* curricula. The scope of this response differs from the other two in that it is far more modest in its aims. Unlike the other two, which seek to transform entire programmes, this response seeks to add a curricular component to currently existing programmes. Its purpose is to raise individuals' awareness of the social nature of language, and thereby sensitise them to an understanding of language use as 'a uniquely social and human activity reflecting an array of choices to be made, not isolated or decontextualized rules to be *obeyed*' (Andrews, 1998: xxii; emphasis in the original). Such study helps learners to understand the communicative capabilities not only of their own varieties but of others as well. It also helps them to realise the social, historical and political conditions within which and by which language standards are defined and maintained.

As one example, Wolfram et al. (1999) developed an approach they call *Dialect Education* designed specifically for adolescent and young adult learners. Its purpose is to help students to understand how languages are structured and how they are used. One way they do this is by promoting the involvement of learners in their own studies of language variation in their communities. Example 4.2 outlines the general steps for engaging in dialect study as proposed by Wolfram, Adger and Christian.

In addition to conducting their own studies on community language use, students undertaking dialect education are provided with lessons that serve to raise their awareness of different linguistic features. Example 4.3 contains a sample lesson plan from Wolfram, Adger and Christian's dialect education curriculum.

Example 4.2 Steps for engaging in dialect study

1. Identify a possible dialect feature for study.
2. Collect data.
   (a) Listen to casual talk in the speech community to determine that the structure is widely used.
   (b) Write down actual examples from casual talk.
   (c) Identify corresponding form(s) in other dialects.
3. Analyse data.
   (a) Develop hypotheses about the linguistic context in which the form occurs. Hunt for patterns in the data, considering:
      (i)   Linguistic forms preceding and following the features.
      (ii) Various forms the feature can assume.
      (iii) Etcetera.
   (b) Check the hypotheses against more data.
   (c) Accept hypotheses, reject or refine.
   (d) Repeat the two previous steps, looking for both differences and similarities with other dialects and testing stereotyped explanations.
   (e) Stop when no new information appears.

Source: Wolfram et al. (1999: 43)

Example 4.3 Sample lesson from a curriculum on dialect and language variation

A Southern vowel pronunciation
In some Southern dialects of English, words like *pin* and *pen* are pronounced the same. Usually, both words are pronounced as *pin*. This pattern of pronunciation is also found in other words. List A has words where the *i* and *e* are pronounced the SAME in these dialects.

List A: *i* and *e* pronounced the same
1. *tin* and *ten*
2. *kin* and *Ken*
3. *Lin* and *Len*
4. *windy* and *Wendy*
5. *sinned* and *send*

Although *i* and *e* in List A are pronounced the SAME, there are other words where *i* and *e* are pronounced differently. List B has word pairs where the vowels are pronounced DIFFERENTLY.

List B: *i* and *e* pronounced differently
1. *lit* and *let*
2. *pick* and *peck*
3. *pig* and *peg*
4. *rip* and *rep*
5. *litter* and *letter*

Is there a pattern that can explain why the words in List A are pronounced the SAME and why the words in List B are pronounced DIFFERENTLY? To answer this question, you have to look at the sounds that are next to the vowels. Look at the sounds that come after the vowel. What sound is found next to the vowel in all of the examples given in List A?

Source: Wolfram et al. (1999: 194)

In addition to lessons, books and courses designed specifically for students in first and second language programmes, several books and courses on language awareness have been developed for teacher preparation programmes (e.g. Andrews, 1998; McCarthy, 1991; Mittens, 1991). These curricula for teachers are based on the premise that raising teachers' awareness of issues and concerns with language variation will enhance their understandings of and appreciation for their learners' linguistic and cultural worlds (Adger et al., 1999; Fillmore and Snow, 2000).

4.5 Summary

As we have seen in this chapter, research on learners' linguistic and cultural worlds has helped to make visible their vitality and richness as sources of significant experiences, knowledge, skills and beliefs. It has also made visible the significant role they play in shaping learners' developmental paths. These understandings, in turn, have helped to transform pedagogical concerns with the teaching of language and culture. The different worlds that non-mainstream learners bring with them to the classroom are no longer viewed as sources of linguistic and cultural deprivation, or explained away as individual deficiencies. Rather, they are viewed as linguistically and culturally significant resources on which to build. Consequently, rather than trying to change learners so that they fit more squarely into traditional schooling practices, current pedagogical practices seek to change schools so that they more adequately reflect and build on the linguistic and cultural diversity of learners' worlds.

The efforts described in this chapter have enjoyed success in transforming educational programmes and enhancing the academic performances of linguistically and culturally diverse learners. However, to continue doing so, future research and education concerns must face two challenges. The first has to do with the conceptualisation of learners' worlds. As we discussed in Chapter 2, current understandings of the complexities of cultures are making visible the need to move away from treating learners' worlds as consensual and homogeneous, participation in which is shared equally among members of a particular group or community (Cazden, 1993; Williams, 1992). Additional research efforts are needed to help us to understand more fully the social, historical and political conditions of learners' lived experiences. The study by Schecter and Bayley (1997) is just one example of a useful direction that such research can take. In this study, Schecter and Bayley look at the kinds of identities that four families – who historically have been treated as members of one cultural group, Mexican Americans – construct for themselves in their home and community activities. They find more differences across families than similarities in terms of, for example, when and with whom they use English and Spanish, and, more generally, their beliefs about their different uses. At the very least, studies like this will help us to understand more fully the dynamic, locally situated nature of language and cultural practices.

A related challenge concerns the issue of representation. Educational programmes like KEEP and the *funds of knowledge* that we examined here are based on the assumption that communities in which schools are nested consist of one homogeneous culture group. Such a view, however, does not reflect current demographics showing that many communities actually comprise many groups, with many languages and many cultures. These groups, in turn, comprise individuals who have multiple identities and multiple group memberships and so take different stances towards their positioning in their groups. Certainly, changing schools to better reflect their communities becomes more complicated as the number and diversity of groups increase. The heterogeneous nature of communities gives rise to a number of social, economic and political issues that will need to be addressed by applied linguists and educators concerned with connecting learners' sociocultural worlds to educational programmes.

Further reading

Burns, A. and Coffin, C. (eds) (2001) *Analysing English in a global context: A reader*. London: Routledge. This collection of essays presents an international perspective on the varieties of English as found in specific institutional, geographic, and cultural contexts world wide. Topics include the internationalization of English, the significance of language variation and current discussions on the question of standard versus non-standard varieties.

Celce-Murcia, M. and Olshtain, E. (2000) *Discourse and context in language teaching.* Cambridge: Cambridge University Press. This is a handbook designed specifically for language teachers. Its purpose is to raise teachers' awareness of the many elements of discourse analysis and pragmatics and to demonstrate how they can apply this understanding to the teaching of spoken and written language in their classrooms.

Delpit, L. (1995) *Other people's children: Cultural conflict in the classroom.* New York: The New Press. In this text, the author demonstrates how many of the academic problems experienced by non-mainstream learners are a result of lack of congruence between the learners' home and school worlds and the miscommunication that arises between the learners and their mainstream teachers due to the lack of fit. Drawing from her own diverse experiences in teaching, Delpit presents a compelling argument for the value of incorporating learners' home worlds into the classroom.

Gay, G. (2000) *Culturally responsive teaching: Theory, research and practice.* New York: Teachers College Press. Drawing on insights from research on culturally responsive pedagogy, Gay makes a case for transforming school curricula and instructional practices so that they are responsive to the diverse knowledge, skills and abilities that learners bring with them to the classrooms. Included is a discussion of some of what the author considers to be essential components of culturally responsive pedagogy such as teacher attitudes and expectations, culturally informed classroom discourse, and cultural congruity in teaching and learning strategies.

Hollins, E. and Oliver, E. (eds) (1999) *Pathways to success in school: Culturally responsive teaching.* Mahwah, NJ: Lawrence Erlbaum. The aim of this text is to help teachers to identify ways in which they might transform their instructional practices to reach students from diverse backgrounds more effectively. The essays in the collection cover such issues as how to select and develop culturally responsive curricula and instructional approaches that build on students' backgrounds, including their linguistic, cognitive and social knowledge, skills, abilities and beliefs.

Chapter 5

Language and culture of the classroom

This chapter will . . .

- provide an overview of current research concerned with the communicative environments of schools and classrooms;
- describe some pedagogical innovations that focus on creating particular kinds of communities in the classroom.

5.1 Introduction

In addition to making visible the significance of learners' worlds outside the classroom, a sociocultural perspective on language, culture and learning has drawn attention to the significance of classrooms as bona fide sociocultural communities and thus to the importance of the languages and cultures *of* classrooms. In their classrooms, teachers and students together create communities based on shared goals, shared resources and shared patterns and norms for participating as legitimate members of the communities. In their interactions with each other, teachers and students assume particular identities and roles, and together they develop understandings of what constitutes not only the substance of what is to be learned, but also the very process of learning itself. These understandings, in turn, give fundamental shape to learners' development as language learners and users.

The role that teachers of these classrooms play is regarded as especially consequential. Given the jointly constructed nature of development, it is assumed that the differences in learning opportunities that teachers make available to their students in their classroom practices, and differences in these practices across classrooms lead to the development of different communities of language learners, and within those communities, differently developed individual learners.

This idea of the classroom as fundamental to development is relatively new in applied linguistics. The more traditional view has considered the activity of teaching to be conceptually separate from the process of learning. That is, while teaching could make language learning easier or more fun, it has not been considered intrinsically linked to learners' development. Rather, as we discussed in earlier chapters, the process of learning has traditionally been considered an internal, inherently individual process that relies on the use of different cognitive mechanisms for taking in new information, assessing it, and assimilating it with already known information.

The role that teaching has been assumed to play in the process is to help students to utilise what are fundamentally immutable cognitive processes. Accordingly, research on teaching has been concerned primarily with discovering ways that teachers can help learners to make more effective use of cognitive processes such as noticing, attending to, and analysing new information about language and culture so that they can assimilate and eventually internalise this new knowledge (e.g. Gass, 1997, 1998; Long, 1997; Long and Crookes, 1993; Long and Robinson, 1998). Beyond their generic role as neutral sites where findings from the research could be implemented, classrooms themselves have been given little attention in studies on language and culture learning.

An understanding of classrooms as sociocultural communities important in their own right as sites of development has informed several current strands of research in applied linguistics. This chapter details the directions that research concerned with communities in classrooms has taken. For the most part, the review will be limited to two kinds of classrooms: language classrooms, be they first, second or foreign, and mainstream classrooms comprising linguistically and culturally diverse learners. A sociocultural understanding of classrooms also forms the foundation of at least two approaches concerned with the teaching of language and culture. Details on these approaches are also provided in this chapter.

5.2 Schools and classrooms as communicative environments

One strand of current research concerned with the language and culture *of* classrooms looks at the communicative environments of schools and classrooms. Drawing on Hymes's ethnography of communication approach to describe features typical of particular classroom environments, these studies seek to answer questions such as: What do classroom communities look like? What are the typical communicative events and activities? What are the conventional norms and patterns of participation? Who are the participants, and what roles do they play?

Early studies, like those of Saville-Troike and Kleifgen (1986) and Saville-Troike (1987), used Hymes's framework to investigate the various social activities and their conventional patterns and norms of participation found in elementary classrooms in the United States that include linguistically and culturally diverse students. Foster (1989) used Hymes's framework to examine the communicative events of a classroom in an urban community college taught by an African American teacher to African American students to uncover the social conventions particular to a community of learners who were considered non-standard English users. As a final example, Duff (1995) used the ethnography of communication approach to examine the different patterns of language use found in content-based English immersion classrooms in Hungary.

Additional studies on classrooms, and on language classrooms in particular, have used more general ethnographic methods. Data come from varied sources and include videotapes of classroom activities, interviews with teachers and students, and institutional archives and written documents that are typical of the learning communities. Some of these studies take a language socialisation perspective – which ties learner development to their contexts of learning – and examine the content and patterns of language use in school contexts. Their aim is to uncover the particular cultural assumptions embodied in the classroom routines and activities so that we may understand more fully the sociocultural worlds into which learners are being socialised along with the participants' own understandings of their worlds and their positions within them. Other studies have been concerned with linking learners' classroom lives to the larger social, political, economic and historical conditions that give them shape. Still others have been concerned with uncovering the cultural and ideological assumptions embodied in the particular identities that teachers and students adopt, or are appropriated into, within their learning communities.

Taking the classroom as his unit of analysis, and using ethnographic methods to collect and analyse his data, Canagarajah (1993) investigated students' attitudes towards learning English as they were reflected in their involvement in a university-level English classroom in Sri Lanka. He noticed that while they were resistant to the Americanised cultural discourses found in their textbooks, the learners were strongly motivated to learn English for socioeconomic advancement in their communities. He concluded that full understanding of what happens inside a classroom must also be based on an understanding of the sociopolitical forces with which students must contend outside the school.

Using similar methods, Harklau (1994) compared the communicative activities found in two instructional contexts – English as a second language (ESL) and mainstream classrooms – for adolescent learners of English as a second language in the United States. She found that while each context served *some* of the needs of language minorities, neither served *all* of their needs. Sharing a concern with learning environments, Willett (1995) and Toohey (1998) examined the socialisation practices found in elementary classrooms that included ESL learners. Their findings reveal how the children's involvement in their different routines with the teachers led their teachers to have different perceptions of language abilities and prospects as good language learners. These perceptions, in turn, led to further differentiation in the kinds of learning opportunities the teachers made available to the learners, which influenced the children's subsequent language and academic development.

Other ethnographic studies have focused on individuals, following them through their schooling contexts. McKay and Wong (1996), for example, examined the participation of four Mandarin-speaking adolescents in the regularly occurring academic and social events and activities of a mainstream English-medium school. Their findings reveal the varied ways the individuals negotiated their identities as English language learners and users, and the consequences of their attempts relative to the development of their academic skills in English.

Along similar lines, Duff and Uchida (1997) explored the multiple and varied social identities of four teachers of English in Japan that emerged from the teachers' participation in their schooling contexts. Duff and Uchida were interested specifically in the teachers' identities as 'instructors and purveyors of (American) English language and culture(s)' (p. 453). They found that although the teachers did not perceive themselves as sources of American culture, 'implicit cultural transmission was very evident' (p. 467), particularly in the way they structured their instructional environments. One teacher, for example, emphasised sociopolitical issues and popular American culture in his daily lessons. Another encouraged autonomous learning by relying on communicative language methods. The ways these teachers constructed their social identities as (tacit) sources of culture, the authors argue, were linked to their personal circumstances, professional histories and perceptions of their roles as teachers in their teaching contexts.

Quote 5.1   Duff and Uchida describe the import of their findings examining EFL teacher identities

Sociocultural identities and ideologies are not static, deterministic constructs that EFL teachers and students bring to the classroom and then take away unchanged at the end of the lesson or course . . . Nor are they simply dictated by membership in a larger social, cultural or linguistic group . . . Rather, in educational practice as in other facets of social life, identities and beliefs are co-constructed, negotiated, and transformed on an ongoing basis by means of language.

Duff and Uchida (1997: 452)

Findings from these and other ethnographic studies have added much to our understanding of the nature of classrooms as legitimate sociocultural communities. We understand more fully the complexities of sociocultural contexts of learning. In particular, we understand more fully the kinds of activities and events typical of different types of classrooms, the varied roles that teachers and students play in their communities, and the subtle yet significant influences that teachers and students' understandings of their roles have on the learning environments they create. Likewise, we have gained an understanding of how the social, economic, historical and political conditions of larger social communities give shape to the types of learning communities that evolve in these classrooms, and, more particularly, the identities that teachers and learners assume or are ascribed, and how both teachers and students position themselves in relation to these various identities and the communicative means by which they are constructed.

5.3   The role of classroom discourse

A related strand of research concerned with the language and culture of the classroom has looked more closely at how the worlds of classrooms are constructed *through* language. General interest here is in uncovering links between students' participation in particular patterns of interaction and their subsequent communicative and academic development.

5.3.1   The IRE

Early research focused on uncovering patterns of discourse considered to be typical of classrooms. One of the earliest descriptions is provided in Sinclair and Coulthard's (1975) study. Drawing on Halliday's functional theory of language, Sinclair and Coulthard were interested in describing the form–function relationship of typical classroom utterances, and the larger patterned sequences of activity into which the utterances fell. They described what they found to be the basic unit of classroom discourse, a three-part sequential exchange (IRE) consisting of the teacher's initiation (I), the learner's response (R), and the teacher's evaluation of the response (E). Other, more recent, research on classroom discourse by, for example, Barnes (1992), Cazden (1988), Gutierrez (1994), Mehan (1979) and Nystrand et al. (1997), to name but a few, has revealed the ubiquity of the IRE pattern in western schooling, from kindergarten to the university and across content areas.

Commonly referred to as recitation script, the IRE pattern of interaction involves the teacher, in the role of expert, eliciting information from individual students in order to ascertain whether the students know the material. The teacher does this by asking a known-answer question to which one student is expected to provide a brief but 'correct' response. The teacher then provides an evaluation of the student's response with such phrases as 'Good', 'That's right' or 'No, that's not right'. After completing a sequence with one student, the teacher typically moves into another round by asking either a follow-up question of the same student or the same or related question of another student.

In addition to describing the patterns of discourse characteristic of classrooms, more recent research has sought to draw connections between the patterns of language use and language development. Using data from her own and other classrooms, Cazden (1988), for example, revealed how the use of the IRE pattern more often facilitated teacher control of the interaction rather than student learning of the content of the lesson. Similarly, in his study of classroom discourse, Barnes (1992) found that the frequent use of the IRE sequence did not allow for complex ways of communicating between the teacher and students.

Gutierrez (1994) came to the same conclusion in her study of 'journal sharing' in language arts classrooms. Her analysis revealed that in classrooms in which the activity was based on a strict use of the IRE, the teacher did most of the talking by commenting or elaborating on the journal entries of individual students. Student participation, on the other hand, was limited to providing brief responses to the teacher's questions. Gutierrez concluded that prolonged participation in this script gave students few opportunities to develop the skills they needed to construct extended oral and written texts. An example of the typical pattern of interaction found in Gutierrez's study is given in Example 5.1.

Example 5.1 Recitation script

1 ((Teacher calls on Louisa; Louisa reads her journal))
2 T: Very nice Louisa … great … okay … she told us how he got burned and the [title
3 L: [Oh yeah … and it took place at the house
4 T: At the house … great … Yolanda
5 ((T calls on Yolanda: Yolanda reads her journal))

Source: Gutierrez (1994: 348). Use of [indicates simultaneous talk.

Other recent studies have also confirmed the ubiquity of the IRE pattern of interaction in second and foreign language classrooms, revealing that its extended use creates similarly limited conditions for language learning. Hall (1995), for example, revealed its pervasiveness in a high school Spanish-as-a-foreign-language classroom. She argued that persistent use of the IRE pattern limited students' involvement to listing and labelling in the target language, and gave them no opportunity to participate in more communicatively complex language events.

Lin (1999a, 1999b, 2000) reported similar findings in her investigations of junior form English language classrooms in Hong Kong. In her analysis of the discourse of these classrooms, Lin found that, with one exception, the recitation script was the common pattern, and this was linked to limited student participation. Moreover, she found that it most often occurred in classrooms consisting primarily of students from socio-economically disadvantaged backgrounds. Lin argued that by keeping to a strict IRE pattern of interaction, the teachers in her study ran the risk of pushing their students 'further away from any possibility of developing an interest in English as a language and culture that they can appropriate for their own communicative and sociocultural purposes' (2000: 75).

While many of the earlier studies on classroom interaction have argued that prolonged participation in the recitation script provides limited learning opportunities, few have actually documented in detail links between long-term participation and academic achievement. The Nystrand et al. (1997) study is a notable exception. In their investigation of 112 eighth and ninth grade language arts and English classrooms, the researchers found that the overwhelming majority of teachers in these classrooms used the recitation script almost exclusively and that its use was negatively correlated with learning. Students whose learning was accomplished almost exclusively through the recitation script were less able to recall and understand the topical content than students who were involved in more topically-related, self-initiated discussions. Moreover, like Lin, Nystrand et al. found that the use of the IRE was more prevalent in lower-track classes, leading, they argued, to the construction of significant inequalities in student opportunities to develop intellectually and communicatively complex knowledge and skills.

5.3.2   The IRF

In an attempt to understand more fully the links between particular patterns of classroom discourse and learning, Wells (1993, 1996) conducted an extensive analysis of the interactions of classrooms where extended student participation was common. He was surprised by his initial analysis of transcriptions of the interactions, which revealed what appeared to be a sizeable number of IRE sequences. Closer inspection, however, uncovered a subtle but significant difference from the more typical IRE pattern. More specifically, it was found that the teachers in the classrooms often initiated questions to students, but instead of closing down the sequence with a narrow evaluation of their responses in the third part of the three-part sequence, they more often followed up by asking students to elaborate or clarify, and in other ways treated students' responses as valuable contributions to the ongoing discussion.

Wells (1993) concluded that it was not the use of the full teacher-directed IRE pattern that constrained students' learning opportunities; rather, it was the teacher's evaluation (E) of the student response in the third part of the sequence that was limiting. Where the teacher followed up (F) on students' responses by asking them to expand their thinking, justify or clarify their opinions, or make connections to their own experiences, student participation was increased and their opportunities for learning were enhanced. Based on these findings, Wells argued for a consideration of the IRF pattern as potentially beneficial to learner development.

These differences between the IRE and IRF patterns of interaction were confirmed in the Nystrand et al. (1997) study of language arts classrooms, noted above, and in the comprehensive six-year study by Nassaji and Wells (2000) involving nine elementary and middle school classrooms. In contrast to their finding in the lower-tracked classroom, Nystrand and his colleagues found that, in higher-tracked classrooms, the teacher's third-part contribution served to open up the discussion rather than close it down. In addition to ratifying students' responses, the teacher incorporated them into the discourse of the class by elaborating on them or asking follow-up questions. These teacher actions, the researchers argued, affirmed student participation in the process of knowledge building, challenged them to extend their thinking and engagement with the subject matter, and provided opportunities for the learners to take ownership of the ideas. These strategies, in turn, helped to create an inclusive classroom culture that valued participation and learning, and ultimately enhanced students' academic performances in the language arts classroom. Along similar lines, Nassaji and Wells found that the choice of move in the third-part sequence of interaction determined to a large extent the direction of subsequent talk. Just as suspected, teacher contributions that evaluated rather than encouraged tended to suppress student participation. Conversely, teacher follow-ups that invited students to expound upon or qualify their initial responses opened the door to further discussion, and provided more opportunities for learning.

The potential value of the IRF for supporting and promoting student interaction has also been confirmed in studies of foreign language classrooms. For example, in her study of a high school Spanish-as-a-foreign language classroom, Hall (1998) found that when the teacher asked students to elaborate and expand each other's contributions, more participation occurred. When the teacher limited her responses to a short evaluation of the students' responses, participation was constrained and learning opportunities were limited. Likewise, in his examination of the interaction of nine English language classrooms in Brazil, Consolo (2000) found that in classrooms characterised by ample student participation, teachers more often followed up on student responses in ways that validated student contributions and helped to create topical connections among them. As a final example, Duff's (2000) study of a high school English immersion classroom in Hungary revealed that in interactions that promoted student participation, the teacher often followed up student responses by repeating or paraphrasing their contributions, and offering them back to the class for further discussion. Such follow-ups, Duff argued, served as an important means of encouraging learners' attempts to express their own thoughts and opinions on the topics, to validate the concepts and ideas initially raised by students, and to draw their attention to key concepts and linguistic forms.

Studies of the classroom interaction in two university second language classrooms (Boyd and Maloof, 2000; Boxer and Cortés-Conde, 2000) also found that teachers who were effective in stimulating student involvement followed up on student contributions in such a way as to affirm their contributions and make them available to the full class for their consideration. Similar findings on the facilitative aspects of the IRF have also come from studies of mainstream classrooms with linguistically diverse learners (e.g. Damhuis, 2000; Hajer, 2000; Verplaetse, 2000). Taken together, finding from these studies show that regardless of the medium or content matter of the classroom, teacher follow-ups that expanded student responses, invited elaboration from others, and in other ways treated the students' contributions as valuable and legitimate fostered active student participation in communicatively and intellectually rich interactions.

In summary, studies on the discourse of a range of classrooms have revealed the ubiquity of one pattern, the IRE. Moreover, they have revealed that pervasive use of the pattern creates fairly deprived learning environments with limited opportunity for participation calling for socially, communicatively or cognitively complex actions. Additional research has shown that with subtle changes to this pattern, specifically in terms of teacher follow-ups to student responses, significantly different learning conditions can be created. In their responses to student-posed questions and comments, and their own reflections and musing on the topics, teachers not only help to create communicatively and cognitively rich interactional environments, but they also provide models of appropriate academic and social discourse for the students.

5.4   Redesigning curriculum and instruction

This view of classrooms as significant sociocultural communities in their own right, coupled with an understanding of the intrinsic relationship between teaching and learning, has led to the design of two pedagogical approaches concerned with creating effectual learning conditions in the classroom. One approach is broad-based in that it focuses on reconceptualising classrooms as communities of learners. The second is more restricted in that it focuses on incorporating cooperative learning practices into the traditional classroom. While they are slightly different in scope, they share a view of the importance of using language and other cultural resources to create supportive and effective learning environments.

5.4.1   Communities of learners in the classroom

A recent response to concerns with classroom environments has been to reconceptualise classrooms as communities of learners (Wells, 1999, 2000). According to this approach, if what we do in the classroom is intimately tied to learners' development, then what we need to do is create effectual classroom communities of learners. In such communities, learning and teaching are considered to be inseparable parts of a socially situated, collaborative and mutually beneficial process in which learners, through their participation in their classroom activities, assume new understandings, take on new skills, and ultimately develop new sociocultural identities. Because language is considered to be a primary tool for socialising learners into these communities, classroom interaction is seen as fundamental to the process. In their interactions with each other, teachers and students work together to address issues, concerns and problems that are of particular concern to their community. The role of the teachers is to provide ample opportunities for learners to appropriate the particular communicative and cultural knowledge and skills that have been deemed important to participation in their larger social communities.

Communities of practice

The concept of a community of learners draws in part from the anthropological work on *communities of practice* (e.g. Chaiklin and Lave, 1993; Lave and Wenger, 1991; Rogoff, 1984; Scribner, 1997a, 1997b; Wenger, 1998). Drawing from Vygotsky's theoretical insights on the fundamentally social nature of learning, this work locates learning within the *communities of practice* to which we belong or aspire to belong. Communities of practice are social activity units consisting of individuals who share a common identity and come together for shared purposes organised, for example, around professional or community goals. As newcomers or novices to these communities, we appropriate the particular behaviours, beliefs and ways of orienting to the world and to each other as bona fide members of these groups via our participation with more experienced members.

Concept 5.1   **Legitimate peripheral participation**

Legitimate peripheral participation captures the socially situated, relational nature of learning, in which learners are viewed as novice members who are given increased access to opportunities for developing expertise in those activities in which they aspire to develop competence. As they move from limited – *peripheral* – participation to full participation, they appropriate the knowledge, skills, abilities and attitudes towards their role in the activity evidenced by those who are considered to be expert.

Much of the scholarship on communities of practice has its roots in early ethnographic studies of community-based apprenticeship programmes in different cultural communities. These studies focused on the social processes by which inexperienced individuals were apprenticed into particular professional trades. Using findings from these studies, Lave and Wenger (1991) proposed an apprenticeship model of the learning process in communities of practice, which they call *legitimate peripheral participation*. According to Lave and Wenger, newcomers to a community of practice begin on its periphery. Their interest in wanting to become full participating members and their acceptance by the more experienced members as potential, full participating members give them legitimacy for being there. As they become more active and engage with more experienced members in working towards a common set of goals, the newcomers or novices move from the periphery of the community to its centre, eventually assuming roles as experts.

This apprenticeship model of learning has been used as a lens with which to conceptualise what happens in classrooms. It is argued that in these sites teachers and students come together as mentors and apprentices in *communities of learners*, with the shared goal of moving the learners from limited, novice participation to full, expert participation (Rogoff et al., 1996). This occurs as the learners gradually increase their involvement, and gain access to a wide range of activities and roles in their classroom experiences. In the process, teachers and students serve as resources for each other, each taking 'varying roles according to their understanding of the activity at hand and differing (and shifting) responsibilities in the system' (Rogoff et al., 1996: 397). In a community of learners, learning is then considered to be a mutually constituted transformation of skills and knowledge and, at a more fundamental level, a mutually constituted experience of identity transformation.

Key features of a community of learners

A *community of learners* is based on the following principles:

- *Language is a primary tool for learning.* Language is not only the primary means of communication; it is also the principal tool for thinking. As noted by Halliday, 'language is the essential condition of knowing, the process by which experience *becomes* knowledge' (1993: 94; emphasis in the original). Learners are given opportunities to use language in a range of challenging communicative activities such as interpreting, offering opinions, predicting, reasoning and evaluating.

- *Through joint activity learners are socialised into their community's practices.* Through interaction among members of a community of learners individuals are able to achieve the social and communicative goals of the larger community.

- *Learning requires taking on successively more complex roles and identities.* In the context of language learning, or any kind of learning, learners acquire the communicative skills and knowledge needed to participate in a wide variety of communicative activities in the process of assuming successively complex roles and participation opportunities in these activities.

- *Learners share responsibility for learning.* Authority and control over the processes and content of what is to be learned do not rest with the teacher. Instead, they are shared with learners, thus enabling the learners to enhance their investment in the activities of the community.

- *The teacher plays an essential role.* Teachers' actions as coach, mentor, instructor and supporter in the activities they undertake with learners serve to assist learners in appropriating the knowledge, skills and meanings learners need to gain entry into the sociocultural activities considered important to full participation in their larger social worlds (Rogoff et al., 1996). Teacher actions also function to help learners to stand back from and become fully aware of the knowledge and skills they are developing so that they may act responsibly and creatively in achieving their goals (Wells, 1999).

- *The affective is integrated with cognitive.* In addition to building meaningful and challenging academic learning environments, teachers and learners work to develop strong interpersonal connections, and feelings of solidarity and affiliation among the members of their classroom communities.

- *Knowledge and skill building are intrinsically tied to a community's instructional activities.* Classroom activities are structured around specific patterns of social interaction where members, in collaboration with each other, have opportunities to observe, reflect on, and practice the means and modes by which socially accepted and valued communicative events and activities are accomplished.

Classrooms as communities of inquiry

A recent move within the larger conceptual framework of *communities of learners* has been to conceptualise classrooms as *communities of inquiry*. In such communities of learners, inquiry is not viewed as a particular instructional method, undertaken occasionally for particular kinds of projects. It is, instead, as Wells (1999) points out, the fundamental principle around which curriculum and instruction are organised. In communities of inquiry, classroom activities are organised around the open-ended, exploratory study of questions or topics that are generated from real experiences of the group members and thus are of genuine interest to the group. Wells (2000) notes that topics and questions are also suitably open-ended to allow alternative possibilities for consideration, and to enable students to collaborate with each other in constructing their understandings and perspectives.

Concept 5.2   **Principles embodied in a concept of classrooms as communities of inquiry**

- The classroom is a collaborative community in which participants come together not as a collection of individuals, but as a community that works towards shared goals, the achievement of which depends upon collaboration.

- Purposeful activities involve whole persons whose transformation occurs as a function of their participation in activities that have real meaning and purpose; learning is not simply the acquisition of isolated skills or items of information, but involves the whole person and contributes to the formation of individual identity.

- Activities are situated in place and time, and are unique in that they involve the coming together of particular individuals in a particular setting with particular artifacts, all of which have their own histories that, in turn, affect the way in which the activities actually unfold.

- Curriculum is a means not an end. The specified knowledge and skills that make up the prescribed curriculum should be seen as items in the cultural tool-kit which are to be used as means in carrying out activities of personal and social significance.

- Outcomes of activity cannot be completely known or prescribed in advance. While there may be prior agreement about the intended goal, the route taken depends upon emergent properties of the situation – the problems encountered and the human and material resources available for their resolution.

- Activities must allow for diversity and originality. Without novelty, there would be no development; both individuals and societies would be trapped in continual recyclings of current activities, with all their limitations.

- Communities of inquiry are shaped by institutional and societal values and expectations as well as by material conditions including availability of resources.

Source: Paraphrased from Wells (2000: 60–1)

5.4.2   Cooperative learning practices

A second pedagogical approach concerned with the language and culture of the classroom is *cooperative learning*. *Cooperative learning* refers to various methods and activities for organising classroom instruction. Unlike an approach based on a *community of learners* concept, which involves a full transformation of education programmes, this approach is better viewed as a particular instructional strategy for fostering cooperation among learners to accomplish shared goals in supportive learning environments.

Originally based on Allport's (1954) contact theory of intergroup relations, cooperative learning was first developed as a means of helping students from different social and cultural backgrounds to develop interpersonal relationships in schools. According to Allport's theory, the kinds of contact that occur between individuals from different social groups shape the kinds of social relationship they develop. The more the purpose of the contact is cooperative, built on common goals and officially supported by the larger institution that is bringing the individuals together, the more likely that the individuals will view each other positively and work towards building mutually beneficial relationships.

Early research on cooperative learning methods in classrooms (e.g. Weigel et al., 1975; Sharan, 1980, 1984) revealed the value of such methods for enhancing relationship building between socially and culturally diverse learners. More recent research (e.g. Calderon et al., 1998; Slavin, 1988, 1995) has revealed its effectiveness for enhancing academic performance, fostering self-esteem and increasing motivation for learning in addition to promoting the development of prosocial interpersonal relationships among learners from different linguistic, cultural, ethnic and socioeconomic backgrounds.

Components of cooperative learning practices

The primary aim of cooperative learning practices is to develop learning opportunities that are based on cooperation and mutual respect. According to Johnson and colleagues (Johnson and Johnson, 1991, 1997; Johnson et al., 1993) their essential components include the following:

- *Small, heterogeneous teams.* Groups are usually composed of four or five members and represent different social identities in terms of ability level, gender, social class, and linguistic and cultural backgrounds. The value of heterogeneous grouping is based on the premise that each individual brings different abilities and perspectives to a task, and that these differences constitute a valuable resource for learning (Cohen, 1994; Lotan, 1997).

- *Positive interdependence.* Positive interdependence involves designing instructional tasks so that each group member's efforts are required for group success and each group member has a unique contribution to make to the joint effort. There are three ways to structure positive interdependence: *interdependent goals*, where students share a group goal of producing a project, or learning the assigned material; *interdependent reward*, where each group member receives the same reward when the group achieves its goals; and *interdependent resources*, where each group member has only a portion of the resources but it must be combined with the other members' resources to complete the task and enable the group to achieve its goals.

- *Individual and group accountability.* Learners are held accountable at two levels in their cooperative tasks. As members of the group, they are, together, accountable for achieving the task's goals. As individuals, each is accountable for contributing his or her share of the work.

- *Facilitative interaction.* Cooperation among students is promoted by encouraging students to share resources and to support each other's efforts. Such supportive behaviours include explaining to each other how to solve problems, providing direct instruction, tutoring, modelling and assisting.

- *Interpersonal and small group skills.* In addition to needing skills to assist each other in completing task work, learners need social skills if the group is to work together productively. These include skills for conflict management, consensual decision making and trust-building. It is assumed here that, like task-based skills, social skills are essential to learning and need to be taught to learners.

It is worth reiterating that many of the premises on which cooperative learning practices are based are similar to those underlying the concept of *community of learners*. Where they vary is in terms of scope. Literature on cooperative learning methods (e.g. Aronson and Patnoe, 1997; Johnson and Johnson, 1991, 1997) often discuss them as particular types of group-based activities, among other kinds that can be incorporated into classrooms without making major changes to the curriculum.

Example 5.1 Two methods of cooperative learning

A. Student Team Learning (STL)

Originally developed by Robert Slavin (1980, 1989/1990, 1995) at Johns Hopkins University, *Student Team Learning* emphasises individual accountability, team goals and team success. Two forms of SLT adaptable to most ages and levels are:

1. *STAD: Student teams-achievement divisions.* This is a means for organising students into small groups for learning. Students are assigned to
   teams of four, mixed by ability, ethnicity and gender. The teacher presents
   a lesson and the teams work together to ensure that all members have
   mastered the lesson. Students are tested individually on the lesson.
   Teams are awarded points based on how well each member meets
   or exceeds his or her own past performances. Teams that meet certain
   criteria earn rewards.

2. *Teams–Games–Tournaments (TCT).* Similar to STAD but instead of
   quizzes and tests students play academic games with members of other
   teams to contribute points to the team score. Cross-team players are
   at the same ability levels (low achievers compete with low achievers,
   and so on) to ensure that each has an equal opportunity for success.
   Team-mates can help each other to prepare for the games.

B. Jigsaw

Originally designed by Elliot Aronson and his colleagues (Aronson and Yates,
1983; Aronson and Thibodeau, 1992; Aronson and Patnoe, 1997), this
technique emphasises group cooperation and individual accountability.
Students are assigned to small groups of five or six members to work on
segmented academic material. Each team member reads an assigned
section, and members from different teams who have studied the same
sections then meet in 'expert groups' to work on their sections. Together,
they gather information and rehearse their presentations. Once they feel
prepared, students return to their own teams and take turns teaching their
team-mates about their section. Students are tested on what they learned
about the topic. This technique is based on the premise that giving each
student of the group an essential role in the activity encourages active
engagement with the task, facilitates interaction among all students in the
class, and leads them to value each other as contributors to the achievement
of their common goal.

5.5 Summary

As we have discussed in this chapter, a recent concern of research on
teaching and learning in applied linguistics has been with investigating the
worlds of classrooms as authentic communities, with particular communicative activities and events that socialise learners into culturally specific
ways of knowing, thinking and valuing their communities, themselves, and
each other as participants in those communities. In addition to making
visible the worlds within classrooms, some studies have made visible the
influences that the larger social, historical and political forces outside the

classrooms exert on what takes place within them, including the kinds of identities participants assume and the activities and resources that are made available to them for appropriation.

Other studies have looked more closely within classroom communities to uncover the particular means by which individuals become socialised into their worlds *through* language. Among other matters, findings have shown the consequential role that teachers play in structuring and managing the particular kinds of worlds into which learners are socialised. In the learning environments that they design, teachers make relevant to the learners what they are to learn and how they are to learn it. They also make relevant their own assumptions about the value of what they are learning, and of the routes learners take in the process.

Pedagogical approaches that take a sociocultural view of classrooms and learning have sought to create particular kinds of learning communities in the classroom. These are characterised by an atmosphere of cooperation, shared trust, and mutual respect, built on shared goals, and realized through jointly constructed activities. Language is viewed as especially significant in these communities since the way in which language is used in the classroom creates both the shape and content of the language that learners learn. That is, language is not just a means by which information is conveyed. It is also, and more significantly, the quintessential sociocognitive tool by which learners move through, respond to, and make sense of their worlds.

While two approaches described in this chapter vary in scope, both have had some success in transforming classrooms. Cooperative learning methods, for example, have been shown to be effective in various kinds of classrooms, and in particular, in classrooms with linguistically and culturally diverse learners (e.g. Holt, 1993; Gumperz et al., 1999). Given the relative newness of the concept of communities of learners, it is impossible to consider its effects on transforming classroom environments and, more particularly, learners' development. It is, however, at least, beginning to inform discussions on the implications that such a concept has for designing language classrooms. I used the concept and its underlying principles, for example, in the design of an instructional framework for teaching foreign languages to adolescent and young adult learners (Hall, 2002). Likewise, the concept has been used by Kwan (2002) in her proposal for transforming English language programmes for adolescents and young adults in Hong Kong.

Where do we go from here? Given the intrinsic link between teaching and learning, and the importance of classrooms as sites of development, we still know very little of the various shapes that learning communities take in different sociocultural contexts. Given our current limited knowledge, a goal of future research on the sociocultural worlds of classroom communities should be to understand these worlds more fully. What are needed are additional investigations identifying the specific social, historical and political contexts within which classroom communities are nested, and the communicative events and activities through which learning communities are formed in classrooms. Also needed are investigations that examine the varied paths that are created by teacher and learner involvement in their classroom communities and through their constitutive role relationships, the different ways that individual learners position themselves relative to the activities and the processes by which they are being socialised into them, and the varied consequences – in terms of identity and ideological development in addition to communicative development – that arise from these actions. Once we have a deeper understanding of what we are doing in our classroom communities and the myriad conditions that influence what we do, we can make informed decisions about how we might design communities of learners that will shape learners' development in ways that are considered to be appropriate to their specific social, cultural, communicative and other needs.

Further reading

Hymes, D. (1996) *Ethnography, linguistics, narrative inequality: Toward an understanding of voice.* London: Taylor & Francis. This collection of essays, written by Hymes over the last three decades, addresses the contributions of ethnography and linguistics to education, and the contribution of research in education to anthropology and linguistics. The first of three sections presents a historical overview of the role of ethnography in education. The second section discusses the significance of language in social life with a particular emphasis on how such understanding can help overcome inequality. The third section examines the special role of narratives in both ethnography and linguistics.

Lensmire, T. (1996) *When children write: Critical re-visions of the writing workshop.* New York: Teachers College Press. Lensmire examines the social and ideological underpinnings of classroom communities through an investigation of a writing workshop comprising a group of elementary school children. He shows in compelling ways the directions that children's participation in their writing community took when the teacher did not take into account the larger social contexts in which they were writing. He concludes with suggestions for creating just and caring classroom communities of writers.

Toohey, K. (2000) *Learning English at school: Identity, social relations and classroom practice.* Clevedon: Multilingual Matters. This book presents a three-year ethnography of a group of children learning English in a Canadian school, following them from the beginning of kindergarten to the end of Grade 2. Toohey uses sociocultural understandings of language and learning to frame her examination. She focuses in particular on how the children's participation in their classroom practices led to differential resource distribution and identity development, and how these, in turn, affected their opportunities for learning English.

Edwards, A.D. and Westgate, D.P. (1994) *Investigating classroom talk*. London: The Falmer Press. The authors of this text draw on a wide range of classroom studies to demonstrate the value of analysing teacher–student interaction and its role in learning. They focus in particular on methods for collecting and analysing data taken from classrooms, and on the possibilities and limitations of interpreting talk as evidence for learning.

Mercer, N. (1995) *The guided construction of knowledge: Talk amongst teachers and learners*. Clevedon: Multilingual Matters. Taking a sociocultural perspective on language and learning, and using examples of interactions from classrooms and other contexts, the author demonstrates how learning is accomplished through talk. The author also provides descriptions of language techniques commonly used by teachers for developing shared understandings, and more generally, for creating effective classroom communities of learners.

Putnam, J.W. (1998) *Cooperative learning and strategies for inclusion* (2nd edn). Baltimore: Paul H. Brooks Publishing Co. This guide discusses how to use cooperative learning strategies effectively in kindergarten to high school classrooms. It includes overviews of current research on multiple intelligences theory, cultural and ethic diversity, conflict resolution, and the educational benefits of cooperative learning.

Chapter 6

Language and culture as curricular content

This chapter will . . .

- examine how language and culture are treated as curricular content in classrooms based on a sociocultural perspective;
- describe some pedagogical approaches to teaching language and culture.

6.1 Introduction

Several popular practices for teaching language and culture in applied linguistics have evolved from traditional perspectives on language and learning. These include the Natural Approach (Krashen and Terrell, 1983), developed in the early 1980s as an extension of Chomsky's linguistic theory of language, and the more recent cognitive approaches including input enhancement (e.g. Van Patten, 1990; Van Patten and Cadierno, 1993), focus-on-form instruction (e.g. Doughty and Williams, 1998), consciousness-raising tasks (Ellis, 1994; Fotos, 1994), and TBLT [task-based language teaching] (e.g. Long and Crookes, 1993; Long and Robinson, 1998).

While these approaches differ in terms of, for example, the role that interaction is thought to play and the degree and kind of instructional intervention they call for, they are similar in that they all give primacy to linguistic structures as forming the curricular content of language classrooms. Moreover, they agree that even though the process of acquiring linguistic structures is influenced primarily by the learners' internal grammar, they do see a role for instruction. Specifically, they agree that instruction should create opportunities in the classroom that facilitate learners' ability to make use of general cognitive processing capacities to speed up the rate at which learners gain control of the linguistic forms in an other-wise naturally occurring, internally driven process (Long and Crookes, 1993; Willis, 1996).

Given the significantly different understandings of language and culture embodied in a sociocultural perspective, what is configured as curricular content in these classrooms is significantly different. The purpose of this chapter is to present an overview of how language and culture as content are dealt with from a sociocultural perspective, to discuss concerns with defining norms and standards for learning raised by this perspective, and to consider pedagogical approaches that incorporate current understandings of language, culture and learning into their curricular and instructional designs.

6.2   Defining knowledge of language and culture

6.2.1   Communicative competence

An early attempt in applied linguistics to define the content of language classrooms from a sociocultural perspective for the purposes of curriculum design is Canale and Swain's framework of *communicative competence* that was proposed in 1980. The concept of communicative competence was first made popular by Dell Hymes (1964, 1971, 1972b) in the mid-1960s as an alternative to the concept of linguistic competence, as first proposed by Chomsky (1965, 1966). According to Chomsky's theory of language, individuals are born with a universal grammar, a mental blueprint for processing and generating language. Presumed to be a fixed property of mind, the capacity for language was defined as sets of principles and conditions from which the grammatical rules for language systems are derived. Chomsky proposed the concept of linguistic competence to capture those sets of principles, conditions and rules for generating the structural components of a language, which any 'speaker of a language knows implicitly' (1966: 9).

For Hymes, Chomsky's definition of language knowledge could not account for the knowledge and skills that individuals must have to understand and produce utterances appropriate to the particular cultural contexts in which they occur. Drawing on rich ethnographic data on language use from a variety of social groups, Hymes called for a significantly different understanding of competence. He defined it in terms of both the knowledge and ability that individuals need to understand and use linguistic resources in ways that are structurally well formed, socially and contextually appropriate, and culturally feasible in communicative contexts constitutive of the different groups and communities of which the individuals are members. It is important to note that, for Hymes, the notion of ability was defined in terms of accessibility rather than considered to be an innate trait.

He labelled this *communicative competence* and defined it in terms of four dimensions. The first, *systemic potential*, is knowledge of and ability to use the generative base of language. This dimension most directly contrasts with Chomsky's concept of linguistic competence in that Hymes considered the abstract system that Chomsky called competence as only *systemic potential*, a resource that is *potentially* but not *necessarily* available to individual language users (Cazden, 1996). The second dimension of communicative competence is *appropriateness*, defined as knowledge of language behaviour and its contextual features and the ability to use language appropriately. The third is *occurrence*, which Hymes defined as knowledge of whether and to what extent action is taken with language, and the ability to use language to take such action. The last dimension is *feasibility*, which includes knowledge of whether and to what extent something is possible, and the ability to be practical or feasible.

> **Quote 6.1** Dell Hymes on the link between knowledge and ability in his concept of communicative competence
>
> Knowledge also is to be understood as subtending all four parameters of communication just noted. There is knowledge of each. Ability for use also may relate to all four parameters. Certainly, it may be the case that individuals differ with regard to ability to use knowledge of each: to interpret, differentiate, etc. The specification of ability for use as part of competence allows for the role of non-cognitive factors, such as motivations, as partly determining competence.
>
> Hymes (1972b: 282–3)

Canale and Swain (1980) were among the first in applied linguistics to attempt to use Hymes's notion of communicative competence to design a framework for second and foreign language curriculum design and evaluation. Their initial model of communicative competence contained three components: *grammatical*, which included knowledge of lexical items and rules of morphology, syntax, semantics and phonology; *sociolinguistic*, which included knowledge of the rules of language use; and *strategic*, which included knowledge of strategies to compensate for breakdowns in communication. Acknowledging that their initial model was more concerned with oral language use, Canale (1982) added a fourth component, *discourse competence*, which dealt with the knowledge needed to participate in literacy activities.

In order to determine which components to teach, Canale and Swain argued that each should be addressed in terms of its probability of occurrence as based on authentic texts. That is, choices for what to include in a curriculum for language classrooms should be based on an analysis of the linguistic, sociolinguistic, discourse and strategic components comprising those communicative activities in which learners of additional languages were interested in becoming competent.

Since its appearance in applied linguistics, others have attempted to use the concept of communicative competence, and its underlying theory of language, to construct frameworks for the design of language curricula and tests (e.g. Bachman, 1990; Bachman and Palmer, 1996). One of the more comprehensive frameworks to date is that by Celce-Murcia et al. (1995). Their model, depicted in Figure 6.1, consists of five interrelated areas of competence: discourse, linguistic, actional or rhetorical, sociocultural, and strategic.

The authors define *discourse competence* as the core of communicative competence. It includes not only knowledge of and the ability to use linguistic resources to create cohesion and coherence in both oral and written texts. It includes also knowledge of and ability to use conversational conventions for taking turns, holding on to the conversational floor,

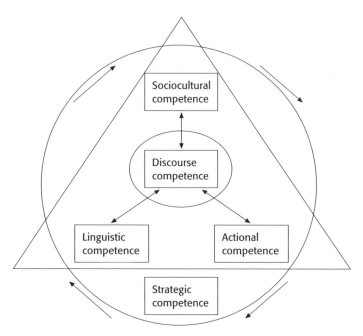

Figure 6.1   Model of communicative competence (Celce-Murcia et al., 1995: 10)

interrupting and providing 'listener feedback' cues such as 'umm' and 'uh huh'.

Giving shape to, and being shaped by, discourse competence are three additional components. The first of these is *linguistic competence*, which consists of the basic elements of the linguistic system that are used to interpret and construct grammatically accurate utterances and texts. This also includes knowledge of and ability to use syntax, involving sentence patterns, word order, coordination, subordination and embedding in addition to morphology, phonology, vocabulary and orthography.

Also linked to discourse competence is *actional* or *rhetorical competence*. Celce-Murcia et al. define this component as the knowledge of and ability to match 'actional intent with linguistic form based on the knowledge of an inventory of verbal schemata that carry illocutionary force' (p. 17). Entailed here, therefore, is knowing how to use language to do something, to perform certain functions, such as making a promise, giving orders, complaining and so on. It also involves knowing how to combine individual acts into larger, meaningful sets of actions to create an appropriate communicative activity such as making a purchase, setting up an appointment, recounting a story and so on. When discussing written texts, Celce-Murcia et al. prefer the parallel term *rhetorical competence*. This aspect includes knowledge of the speech acts and speech act sets conventionally associated with particular written genres.

A third component linked to discourse competence is *sociocultural competence*. This comprises the non-linguistic, contextual knowledge that communicators rely on to understand and contribute to a given communicative activity. This aspect of competence is broader than actional or rhetorical competence in that it includes knowledge of, and ability to use, the rules, norms and expectations governing the larger social context of the activity. Weaving through all components is *strategic competence*, the final component of Celce-Murcia et al.'s model. This competence includes the knowledge, skills and ability to resolve communicative difficulties and enhance communicative effectiveness.

The notion of communicative competence helps us to see that language use involves not just knowledge of and ability to use language forms, it also involves knowledge and ability to use language in ways that are, to use Hymes's terms, socially appropriate, feasible and contextually called for. The many attempts over the years to conceptualise the various socially constituted dimensions of our linguistic resources with this concept in mind have helped in the design of curricula and syllabi for language classrooms by providing blueprints for identifying the substance of the communicative plans that more experienced participants use to guide their participation in activities and events deemed to be important to learners. As such, they provide some basis for making decisions about the curricular content of language classrooms.

> **Quote 6.2** Henry Widdowson on the significance of the concept of communicative competence for language teaching
>
> Hymes originally proposed the concept of communicative competence in opposition to the concept of grammatical competence. If one follows through the implications of his proposal...I think we arrive at a recognition of the need to shift grammar from its preeminence and to allow for the rightful claims of lexis. Linguistics may be about grammar rather than language. But the study and teaching of language is about a lot more than that, and grammar needs to be put in its place. 'There are rules of use...', etc. But rules, of use, or of anything else, are useless unless they can be effectively acted upon, unless the scope and conditions of their employment are understood.
>
> Widdowson (1989: 136)

6.2.2   Intercultural communicative competence

Alongside attempts to create an adequate framework for conceptualising the knowledge, skills and abilities that are tied to our communicative actions is the recent work concerned with building a curricular framework based on the notion of *intercultural communicative competence* (ICC). Made popular by Byram (1997) and his colleagues (Byram and Zarate, 1997; Byram and Fleming, 1998) this concept was developed as an expansion of communicative competence in response to what Byram argued was the need to consider the competence that learners of additional languages develop as qualitatively different from the competence that members develop as native speakers of social groups and communities. Learners of other languages, he argued, should be treated not as aspiring native speakers but as developing intercultural communicators.

   To capture some of the knowledge and skills that users of more than one language develop, Byram (1997) proposed the concept of intercultural communicative competence, and defined it as the knowledge, skills and abilities to participate in activities where the target language is the primary communicative code and in situations where it is the common code for those with different preferred languages. Specific components of ICC include the following, grouped into four dimensions:

- *Savoirs*: Included here is general knowledge of relevant sociocultural groups and their significant communicative activities and events.
- *Savoir-apprendre*: This includes the ability to use this knowledge to communicate with others in conventional or expected ways at the levels of both the individual and group, and the ability to sort through, reflect on and use one's understanding of the differences and similarities across

individuals and across groups to form open, flexible communicative plans and perspectives.

- *Savoir-faire*: This includes skills of identification, interpretation, analysis and synthesis of patterns and perspectives and of potential sources of miscommunication and incompatibilities. It also includes skills needed to negotiate agreement on places of conflict and acceptance of differences and incompatibilities.

- *Savoir-être*: This refers to general attitudinal dispositions, including a curiosity with and openness to difference, a readiness to suspend disbelief and judgement with respect to others' meanings, beliefs and behaviours, and a willingness to understand and be sensitive to the perspectives of others.

According to Byram, the model of ICC is intended to encourage the development of both culture-specific knowledge and skills, and culture-general knowledge and skills for learning about, becoming involved in, and successfully negotiating intercultural communicative interactions. Like its companion concept, communicative competence, the concept of intercultural communicative competence affords course designers some basis for making decisions about what to include in a curriculum. It has gained some currency in the field of applied linguistics, as it was recently adopted by the European Council on Modern Languages Section (Council of Europe, 1994) as a goal of foreign language learning, and is currently being used in research on the teaching of foreign languages in Europe. Sercu (2000), for example, uses ICC as a conceptual base for an investigation of whether and to what extent foreign language textbooks contribute to promoting adolescent pupils' acquisition of intercultural communicative competence.

6.2.3   Learning outcomes: Where are we going?

It is generally agreed that the goal of language learning from a sociocultural perspective is for learners to add alternative knowledge, skills and abilities for understanding and participating in a wide range of intellectual and practical activities to their already established repertoires of sense-making knowledge and abilities. This is to enable learners to broaden their communicative experiences, their worldviews, and their understandings of the active, creative roles they as individuals play in constructing these worlds (Firth and Wagner, 1997; Kramsch, 1993, 1998; Valdes, 1998).

While the concepts of communicative competence and intercultural communicative competence have provided the field with useful frameworks with which to consider the various dimensions of knowledge, skills and abilities embodied in communicative activities, they are incomplete in that they leave open the question of *whose* knowledge, skills and abilities learners are expected to learn. That is, a view of learning as socialisation into particular sociocultural worlds with sanctioned tools and signs for mediating participation in various communicative activities and events constitutive of these worlds implies a commitment, howsoever tacit, to some outcome and some end point (Wertsch, 1998). While the two concepts discussed above afford us a framework for understanding what *could* be involved, they do not address the issue of whose communicative worlds, and, more specifically, whose sociocultural tools and whose ways of using the tools learners are to be socialised into.

It has been suggested that learners' individual goals for learning languages must be balanced with educational goals embodied in the learners' sociocultural worlds (e.g., Hall, 2002; Nunan, 1995; Widdowson, 1998a). While on one level this suggestion seems practical, we are still left with having to decide on not only the specific worlds we wish to draw on for curricular content but also the norms by which learning outcomes are to be assessed. If, for example, one of the goals of learning another language is to be able to use it in contexts considered significant by users of the target language – given the variety of groups that speak the languages we typically teach in language classrooms, the cultural, linguistic and other differences that exist across these groups, and across social identities within language groups – we are still left with the question of *whose contexts*. For learners of English for example, are the contexts of groups from the United States? From Australia? From England? From India? Likewise, for learners of Spanish, are the contexts we bring to the classroom those of groups from Spain? From Mexico? From the Dominican Republic? Do these contexts consist primarily of adults? Adolescents? Are they typical of affluent communities? Of middle-class communities? In what social institutions are communicative activities to be based? The family? The school? The workplace? These are just a few of the many questions raised by concerns with curriculum design.

Even if we cannot articulate the kinds of communicative contexts we would like to make part of the curricular content in our language classrooms, the textbooks and materials we use in our classrooms often do (Ramirez and Hall, 1990; Cook, 1999). A close inspection of them may reveal that what we are making available to learners in terms of communicative options, is at best incomplete. Perhaps, as Widdowson (1998b) suggests, rather than attempt to bring unfamiliar worlds to the classroom, we should strive to create communities with their own cultural realities within them. Whatever curricular decisions we make, as current research on learning shows (National Research Council, 1999), they need to be made. For having a clear understanding of what learners are to learn – in the case of language classrooms, this entails understanding fully the communicative worlds and their various dimensions into which learners are to be socialised, no matter whose worlds they are – and being able to articulate the directions their learning is supposed to be taking, provides learners with a clear sense of where they are going and thus can help them to share in the responsibility for getting there.

> **Quote 6.3** Henry Widdowson on curricular considerations for language classrooms
>
> Learners cannot be rehearsed in patterns of appropriate cultural behavior, and of course they will not be prepared in every particular to cope with all the niceties of communication, but the crucial requirement is that they should have a basic capacity which enables them to learn how to cope when occasion arises. The extent to which they subsequently fine-tune their behavior to conform to particular norms for appropriate use will depend on a number of circumstantial and attitudinal factors which simply cannot be anticipated and accounted for in the classroom context. What the classroom context can do is to create a community with its own cultural reality, with its own conventions of what is feasible and appropriate; conventions which are contrived, but which carry conviction. Such a context is bound to set limits on what language learners are explicitly taught, and these cannot of their nature contain 'real world communication'. But the crucial point is that this is not language to be learned as such, but language to be learned from. It is the business of pedagogy to decide on what can be feasibly and effectively taught within these limits so as to activate a learning investment for future use.
>
> Widdowson (1998b: 331)

6.3 Pedagogical approaches for redesigning language classrooms

Concerns with the need to define curricular content and learning outcomes notwithstanding, several approaches to teaching language and culture from a sociocultural perspective have emerged in the field of applied linguistics. In general, these approaches aim to develop in learners an extensive cultural repertoire that includes the development of communicative competence in a variety of communicative contexts. They also aim to develop in learners a conscious awareness of their knowledge and skills so that they may act responsibly and creatively in achieving their own individually created personal goals as well as larger mutually constructed social goals. Moreover, their general instructional concern is expanded not just to include the knowledge and ability to use language that is contextually relevant, socially appropriate, systemically possible and feasible, it is also to develop learners' abilities to analyse, critique and identify ways to transform their lives both in and out of the classroom.

In this section, two pedagogical approaches concerned with these issues, and currently found in various kinds of language classrooms, are discussed. While their general goals are similar, they differ slightly in terms of the kinds of instructional environments they seek to create in their classrooms. The first, *participatory pedagogy*, takes more of a learner-centred approach in that it uses the worlds of the learners as the primary basis for designing curriculum and instructional activities. The second general approach, the *multiliteracies project*, combines a learner-centred focus with what has been termed a knowledge-centred focus (National Research Council, 1999) in that it seeks to design a learning environment that not only helps learners to understand and live within their own worlds, but is also concerned with helping students to acquire the knowledge, skills and abilities they need to expand their communicative horizons, and move into other worlds.

6.3.1 Participatory pedagogy

Participatory pedagogy is a general approach to language education that draws on the work of Brazilian educator Paulo Freire (1972, 1973). Freire developed an alternative model of education as a response to what he perceived to be shortcomings in the more traditional model. The more traditional model, he argued, is based on an understanding of learning as a process of transmitting or depositing neutral, value-free and universally applicable information into the empty heads of learners. For their part, learners are thought to be little more than passive and uncritical receptors of the deposited information. Their only role is to store the information for use at a later date. In such a view of pedagogy, Freire argued, social, cultural, political and historical concerns are kept invisible, the status quo is maintained, and learners continue to think they are powerless, unable to make a difference in their worlds.

In response to these shortcomings, Freire (1972, 1973) developed an approach in which the overall aim is to help learners to develop their own voices in response to their local conditions and circumstances, and in so doing, transform their lives in socially meaningful ways. Building on these insights, and keeping within a sociocultural perspective on learning, current formulations of participatory language pedagogy consider learning to be a socially situated, collaborative process of transformation whereby teachers and students, together, build a common base of knowledge, frameworks of understanding, and a shared system of meanings, values and beliefs for purposes of mutual growth (Auerbach, 2000; Wallerstein, 1983; S. Wong, 2000).

While participatory pedagogy draws on similar concepts and ideas as other sociocultural approaches presented in earlier chapters, two features distinguish it from other methods (Auerbach, 2000). First, as noted earlier, participatory pedagogy does not locate curricular issues and concerns in differences between learners' home and school cultures – nor does it begin with a predetermined, content-based curriculum – but rather it locates the focus of learning in a nexus of political, social, and economic conditions defining the communities within which learners live. This concern with learners' lives both in and out of the classroom is translated into a curriculum that is organised around experiences, needs and concerns that learners themselves have identified as central to their lives.

Sometimes referred to as critical pedagogy (cf. Pennycook, 2001), participatory pedagogy aims to create environments that assist learners in appropriating the knowledge and skills needed for full participation in their larger social worlds in ways that fully account for, and ultimately help to transform, their particular circumstances. Classroom activities are structured in such a way as to provide learners with opportunities to explore concerns and issues that are of utmost important to them, to raise their awareness of the social, cultural and political inequities manifested in their experiences, and to work to transform them by articulating their own directions for living. In addition to helping learners to identify their concerns and transform them into curricular content, the role of the teacher is to ensure a safe environment in which learners feel comfortable and validated as they raise questions and consider alternatives.

A second distinguishing feature of participatory pedagogy is its focus on informed action as a central aim of learning. In other words, language learning is not considered to be about just developing a deeper understanding of one's lived experiences. It is also about knowing how to take action to make a difference to one's world. Thus, rather than being imposed on them, the specific communicative skills and knowledge that become part of the curriculum emerge from learners' needs and concerns as they are expressed in their classroom discussions. Learned both as tools and resources for analysing their contexts as well as for taking action, the communicative resources that learners take hold of afford them the means to engage in a 'language of critique' and a 'language of possibility' (Stanley, 1992). In this way, language learning becomes not an end in itself but a means for learners to participate fully in their lives inside and outside school.

Problem-posing approach

One kind of participatory pedagogy commonly found in many adult immigrant community-based language programmes is the *problem-posing approach* (Auerbach and Wallerstein, 1987; Wallerstein, 1983). This approach begins with learners' experiences, and in particular the problems or complex concerns or issues they face in their communities outside the classroom. Its aim is to help to make visible the social, political and cultural underpinnings of their experiences, to raise learners' awareness of these links, and to help them to acquire the specific communicative skills and knowledge necessary for taking action in ways that they feel will be beneficial.

A problem-posing approach begins by bringing the lived experiences of students to the classroom as the focal thematic content. This is typically done using such media as pictures, comics, short stories, songs and dramas to generate discussion centred on the problem depicted in the materials. Wallerstein (1983) points out that in order to represent these experiences adequately and meaningfully in the classroom, it is essential that teachers be intimately connected with the lives of their students outside the classroom and have some shared understandings of these experiences and the realities the students face. It may also mean bringing the classroom to the learners and locating it in a safe site in their community, rather than expecting learners to come to the classroom (Auerbach, 2000).

Quote 6.3 Ira Shor on the role of the teacher in a problem-posing approach

The responsibility of the problem-posing teacher is to diversify subject matter and to use students' thought and speech as the base for developing critical understanding of personal experience, unequal conditions in society, and existing knowledge. In this democratic pedagogy, the teacher is not filling empty minds with official or unofficial knowledge but is posing knowledge in any form as a problem for mutual inquiry.

Shor (1992: 33)

To help to generate discussion, the teacher typically asks a series of open-ended questions about the situation depicted in the materials. The aim of the questions is to encourage students to define the real-life problem, share their experiences and elaborate on what they see. The objective is not to generate a particular solution but to explore the complexities of the issue, and to identify actions that respond constructively to the issue at hand. The particular language skills and resources that form the content of class lessons evolve from these conversations and identified actions, and thus provide learners with personally meaningful purposes for their development. As Auerbach (2000) notes, in integrating learning of communicative skills and knowledge with the particular social activities of reflection and analysis, they become appropriated by learners as new tools for implementing real change in their lived experiences.

Concept 6.1   **Basic components of a problem-posing approach**

This approach consists of the following three components:

1. *Listening*: Through listening to and observing students in and out of class, the teacher defines and codifies student concerns for use in structured language learning and dialogue.

2. *Dialogue*: Using the codified concerns as springboards, the teacher and students engage in dialogue about the concerns or issues, and ways to view and respond to them.

3. *Action*: The discussions move students to use what they have learned to take action outside the classroom.

Source: Wallerstein (1983)

Concept 6.2   **Instructional procedures typical of a problem-posing approach**

1. Present a problem in the form of a story, narrative, role-play, drawings, pictures, or dialogue.

2. Ask informational questions (e.g. What do you see? What is happening?).

3. Ask question to reveal the problem encountered by the characters (e.g. Is there a problem? What is it? Why do you think there is a problem?).

4. Apply the issues and concerns depicted in the situation to the students' lives (e.g. Have you ever had an experience like this? What happened? Why did it happen? What did you do about it?).

5. Compare students' experiences to the situation depicted in the problem-posing scenario (e.g. How do your experiences compare to what is happening here?).

6. Ask students for ideas that they would propose to change or improve their current situation (e.g. How could you address the problem differently? What additional information would be helpful? What steps would you take now that differ from those you have taken? Why?).

Source: Wallerstein (1983)

Advocates (e.g. Auerbach, 1991, 2000, 2001; Auerbach and Wallerstein, 1987; Wallerstein, 1983) acknowledge that student resistance to this approach is possible. Learners may prefer a more seemingly neutral approach, one that stays away from rather than embraces what some might consider controversial matters. The advocates remind teachers that the aim of participatory pedagogy is not to lay out a particular agenda or point of view for learners to follow. Rather, it is to provide them with opportunities to engage with critical issues, and to voice their concerns. Thus, if learners are resistant, teachers need to make official space for their resistances. Auerbach (2000) notes that once students have named their resistances, they can become objects of collaborative reflection and dialogue. In other words, the resistances themselves can become the basis for curricular development by affording learners the chance to talk about their needs and learning strategies and, more generally, to analyse social and pedagogical issues that are of great importance to them.

Classroom-based social research

A more recent form of participatory pedagogy developed for community-based adult immigrant language programmes is what Bonnie Norton (Pierce, 1995; Norton, 2000) calls *classroom-based social research* (CBSR). Similar to the problem-posing approach, the aim of CBSR is to help 'language learners claim the right to speak outside the classroom' (Pierce, 1995: 27). It does so by engaging learners in explorations of their lives in their local communities. Using primarily ethnographic methods such as interviews, observation charts and logbooks and with the active guidance and support of their teachers, learners examine the opportunities they are given or seek to have to interact with target language speakers in different contexts and in the varied role relationships they assume as members of their communities. After systematic documentation of such opportunities, learners, with help from their teachers and other learners, describe, critically reflect on, and share their thoughts about their involvement in these opportunities. Together, learners 'may begin to see one another as part of a social network in which their symbolic resources can be produced, validated, and exchanged' (Pierce, 1995: 28). Moreover, teachers can use the learners' experiences as a basis for developing classroom activities and materials that will ultimately help students to strengthen their voices in their communities.

While Pierce's approach is geared to adult immigrant language learners, Heath and Mangiola (1991) have used a similar participatory approach with linguistically diverse school-aged children. Using basic ethnographic skills of observation, interviewing and reporting, students record their language habits or language games with the target language and then use the data for discussions on language and language use. The focus is not so much on helping learners to participate in their lives outside school as it is on providing opportunities within the classroom that develop learners' understanding of and ability to use language in school and thereby succeed as students. Like other forms of participatory pedagogy, it uses the learners' own experiences as the curricular base, and thereby empowers them to invest in their own learning.

6.3.2   The multiliteracies project

A second general approach to language pedagogy that embodies a socio-cultural perspective is the *multiliteracies project* (New London Group, 1996, 2000). The project was developed by a group of international scholars in response to what they had identified as two important challenges to education. The first is the increasing cultural and linguistic diversity of communities around the world, which, they argue, has changed the nature of schooling. Students are now required to learn 'to negotiate regional, ethnic, or class-based dialects; cultural discourses; the code switching often to be found within a text among different languages, dialects, or registers; different visual and iconic meanings; and variation in the gestural relationships among people, language, and material objects' (New London Group, 2000: 14). The second challenge is the proliferation of means for communicating within and across these communities. Not only have additional communication technologies been created, but communicating through them is 'increasingly multimodal – in which written-linguistic modes of meaning are part and parcel of visual, audio, and spatial patterns of meaning' (Cope and Kalantzis, 2000: 5).

According to the group of scholars, pedagogies based on one formal, standard notion of language and literacy are inadequate for meeting these challenges. What is required is a pedagogy that opens doors to new communicative practices and resources, that expands students' options for participating in their worlds, and enables them to use their resources to bring their cultural worlds into existence, maintain them, and transform them for their own purposes. Such a pedagogy, the New London Group argues, will need to 'recruit, rather than attempt to ignore and erase, the different subjectivities, interests, intentions, commitments and purposes that students bring to learning. Curriculum now needs to mesh with different subjectivities, and with their attendant languages, discourses, and registers, and use these as a resource for learning' (The New London Group, 2000: 18).

For this, they propose *a pedagogy of multiliteracies*, consisting of four interrelated spheres of learning opportunities: *situated practice*, *overt instruction*, *critical framing* and *transformed practice* (see Figure 6.2).

Figure 6.2   Spheres of learning opportunities in a pedagogy of multiliteracies as proposed by the New London Group (1996, 2000)

Situated practice

The purpose of *situated practice* learning opportunities is to socialise learners into those communicative activities in which they are expected to become competent. As discussed in Chapter 3, and again in Chapter 5, learners' communicative development is linked to the opportunities they have to actually participate in their communicative activities with others who are more expert. This contrasts with a more traditional approach to teaching, in which it is thought that learners should participate in communicative activities only after they have mastered a range of skills. The assumption embodied in situated practice is that mastery of skills and knowledge needed for competent performance is partially dependent on learner involvement in the very activities in which they wish to become competent from the beginning of instruction. If learners are expected to become competent participants in certain academic tasks like engaging in discussions on literary texts, or presenting oral research reports, for example, *situated practice* learning experiences immerse learners in such activities from the beginning of instruction.

According to the New London Group, such opportunities afford students the chance to develop a familiarity, or a 'feel' for these activities, the means for accomplishing them, and their roles as participants. As expert-mentor, the teacher's tasks are to model the linguistic actions needed for participation in the activities, to guide the learners in recognising these actions and understanding their meanings, and to assist them in using the activities' tools to take appropriate action themselves. The teacher is also responsible for creating an environment where learners feel safe to take on different roles and explore alternative linguistic actions for accomplishing the goals of the activities.

Overt instruction

The purpose of *overt instruction* is to provide opportunities for learners to focus on, practice and eventually take control of the various linguistic and other relevant conventions needed for competent engagement in their communicative activities. For example, writing a story involves not only knowing how to use certain grammatical conventions, it also includes knowing the conventions of spelling, punctuation and vocabulary, and knowing how to organise the telling of events and ideas so that the story is coherent. Likewise, requesting help from someone involves knowing how to formulate structurally feasible and socially acceptable utterances as well as knowing the conventional ways to get another's attention, to take turns, to take action in ways considered appropriate to the particular roles of the participants, and to identify and resolve misdirected talk.

Overt instructional activities help learners to become conscious of and eventually take control of these various conventions. An additional purpose is to help students to develop a meta-language for describing the contextual connections between communicative functions and forms. Being able to extract and consider conventional aspects of communication as they relate to their particular contexts of use is considered to be as important to language learners' communicative development as is their learning to use the forms and functions in ways that are appropriate and feasible (New London Group, 1996).

Critical framing

The third sphere of learning opportunities is *critical framing*. The purpose of these opportunities is to help learners to stand apart from their activities and identify the diverse and multiple perspectives embodied in them, with the aim of understanding their historical, social, cultural, political and ideological contexts. Such analyses can help learners to discern the conventional ways linguistic resources are used, how the uses are subject to wider sociohistorical and political forces that constrain both the meanings of the resources and their access to them, and how individuals attempt to use the resources towards their own social or political ends.

The New London Group argues that such reflective explorations will facilitate learners' development of a broader perspective of the ways in which locally situated meanings both converge and diverge from the learners' own worldviews. They will also learn to recognise that meanings and rules for the use of communicative resources are arbitrary, and tied to their contexts of use in complex, and sometimes contradictory, ways. This awareness, in turn, will enable learners to make informed choices about their participation.

Concept 6.3   **Multiliteracies pedagogy**

Designs of meaning

The starting point for *multiliteracies* is an understanding of how texts are historically and socially located and produced, how they are 'designed' artifacts. As proposed by the New London Group there are three aspects of the meaning-as-design:

- *the designed*: the available meaning-making resources; patterns and conventions of meaning;

- *the designing*: the process of shaping emergent meaning, which involves representation, recontextualisation;

- *the redesigned*: the outcome of designing, something through which the meaning-maker has remade – a new meaning-making resource.

Four dimensions of learning opportunities

Situated practice (doing)
Being immersed in designs of meaning that make 'intuitive' sense, common sense, or at least something more than half sense. In a learning situation this might be either:

- designs in the students' lives, the students' own experiences, or
- throwing students in at the deep end with designs that will make perhaps only half sense at first, but provide lots of contextual clues.

Assessment: What works, e.g. a problem solved, albeit intuitively, with an expert's help, by looking up answers, with scaffolded assistance.

Overt instruction (reflecting)
Developing a language that describes how we make meaning and the designs in those meanings.

- Describe the patterns in available designs of meaning: the resources we can find and use to make meaning.
- Talk about how we do designing.
- Talk about how meaning becomes redesigned; how much does new text express voice, experience, etc.?

Assessment: Students have a way to describe the processes and patterns of design in a meaningful way.

Critical framing (reflecting)
How a design fits in with local meanings and more global meanings.

- What is the purpose of the design? What's it doing: to whom? for whom? by whom? why? to what effect?
- What's the local social context (structure, function, connections, systems, relationships, effects)?
- What's the global social context (culture, history, society, politics, values)?

Assessment: The students show that they know what the design is for, what it does and why it does it.

Transformed practice (doing)
Applying the design in a different context, making a new design.

- Transfer: taking a meaning out of context and making it work.
- Adding something of myself/ourselves.
- Intertextuality (the connections, influences, recreation of other texts, cross-references of history, culture and experience) and hybridity.
- Meaning-making, designing, that changes the designer.

Assessment: Good reproduction (if that's the game); or the extent and value of creativity in the transformation; aptness of the transformation or transfer to another context (does it work)?

Source: Paraphrased from Cope and Kalantzis (2001)

As noted by the New London Group (1996: 87), 'through critical framing learners can gain the necessary personal and theoretical distance from what they have learned, constructively critique it, [and] account for its cultural location'. In so doing, they gradually see that the use of language is not neutral. Instead, they find that its use at particular moments of time by particular users represent particular perspectives – perspectives that give voice to some while silencing others. Such understanding influences the ways that learners live their everyday lives.

Transformed practice

The knowledge and skills developed in *critical framing* learning opportunities form the base for the fourth sphere of opportunities, *transformed practice*. Its purpose is to provide learners with opportunities to take the lead in their own learning, to use what they know to chart alternative courses of action for realising both their personal and social goals. As noted by the New London Group (2000: 35), in transformed practice 'teachers need to develop ways in which the students can demonstrate how they can design and carry out, in a reflective manner, new practices embedded in their own goals and values'.

In transformed practice, then, students use their new understandings, knowledge, and skills to try out different voices in familiar contexts, to invent new means and, where possible, create new contexts and new goals for self-expression and connecting with others.

Conclusion

The New London Group points out that these four spheres of learning opportunities are not to be viewed as hierarchical stages of learning. Rather, they are complexly interrelated, 'elements of each [which] may occur simultaneously, while at different times one or the other will predominate, and all of them are repeatedly revisited at different levels' (ibid.: 85). Together, the conditions for learning fostered in each of the spheres promote learners' development of a complex range of understandings and perspectives, knowledge and skills, and values and motivations needed for full personal, social and cultural participation in their classroom communities as well as in their larger, social communities. In addition to learning how to use language in a wide range of practical and intellectual activities and to critically examine their use and that of others, learners develop the ability to see from multiple perspectives, to be flexible in their thinking, to direct their own learning, to solve problems creatively, and, ultimately, to develop new ways of becoming involved in their worlds.

6.4 Summary

In classrooms concerned with teaching language and culture from a socio-cultural perspective, the general instructional aim is not to teach language and culture per se, as subject matter removed from any specific contexts of activity. Rather it is to help learners to understand the means by which their activities are constructed, and the myriad ways in which language use is tied to culture. It is also to help them to understand the roles and identities they are appropriated into by their use of particular resources, the social, cultural and other forces that give shape to these constructions, and how to negotiate with others to position themselves in relation to these roles and identities, and larger social forces in ways that are mutually beneficial. While not ignoring the importance of language forms, in these classrooms they are treated as 'tool[s] or resource[s] to be used in the com-prehension and creation of oral and written discourse rather than some-thing to be learned as an end in itself' (Celce-Murcia, 1991: 466).

While there is general agreement with these goals among practitioners operating within a sociocultural perspective, there is still the question of how we define where we are going in terms of development. While the concepts of communicative competence and intercultural communicative competence have been helpful in conceptualising the kinds of knowledge, skills and abilities learners use to take action in their worlds, language teachers continue to operate in and make decisions about communicative worlds that are ill-defined. Even as we acknowledge the importance of expanding learners' worlds, and the usefulness of ethnographies of com-munication for illuminating the conventions and norms for their realisa-tion, not forgetting the roles they play in the lives of those for whom they are important, we still know little about the communicative activities of the many linguistically and culturally diverse groups that comprise our worlds. However, because the activities we make available to our students in our language classrooms fundamentally shape their development, the choices we make about the kinds of communicative activities to include in the curriculum are of great significance. Consequently, even having some knowledge about these worlds leaves us with the value-laden decision of whose worlds we are to orient to in our classrooms.

Finally, assuming that we are able to make such decisions, we still know little about the pedagogical effectiveness of the practices described in this chapter for expanding learners' communicative horizons. That is, we still cannot answer how effective, if at all, it is to engage learners in the differ-ent instructional activities advocated by these approaches. Arguing that they should be effective, as the approaches discussed in this chapter do, is certainly not the same as documenting not only that they are effective, but how they manage to be effective. For this, we need longitudinal studies that tease apart the links that appear to exist between students' involvement in specific instructional activities and their appropriation of particular communicative resources. We might find that the specific curricular choices we make about the kinds of communicative practices to include in the classroom and the instructional practices we use to socialise students into them are consequential to learners' communicative development in ways we may not have imagined.

Further reading

Byram, M. and Risager, K. (1999) *Language teachers, politics and cultures*. Clevedon: Multilingual Matters. This text explores the social and political dimensions of foreign language teaching using comparative data from research conducted in Denmark and England. Using discussions with teachers as a base, the authors demonstrate the links between curricular and instructional decisions made by the teachers and current social and political changes.

Byram, M., Nichols, A. and Stevens, D. (eds) (2001) *Developing intercultural competence in practice*. Clevedon: Multilingual Matters. The aim of this collection of essays is to provide examples of good practice in the teaching of intercultural competence in foreign language classrooms. Chapter topics range from discussions of large-scale projects to stories and examples of classroom activities.

Lustig, M. and Koester, J. (1999) *Intercultural competence: Interpersonal communication across cultures* (3rd edn). New York: Longman. This book presents theories and practical considerations underlying the concepts of intercultural competence and intercultural communicative competence, drawing out their links to the notion of communication. Topics discussed also include verbal and non-verbal communicative codes, cultural identity and intercultural relationships.

Morgan, B. (1998) *The ESL classroom: Teaching, critical practice, and community*. Toronto, Canada: University of Toronto Press. The author of this text draws on his own teaching experience in Canada and China to reconsider the goals of English language teaching and to propose an approach that accounts for the social, political and cultural conditions of learners. He suggests using curricular content that is meaningful to learners and includes sample lesson plans and examples of student work.

Smoke, T. (ed.) (1998) *Adult ESL: Politics, pedagogy, and participation in classroom and community programs*. Mahwah, NJ: Lawrence Erlbaum. The essays in this collection deal with a range of issues regarding adult ESL and literacy training in North America. The topics range from accounts of struggles to obtain funding for adult programmes to stories with examples and suggestions for implementing a curriculum based on critical pedagogy.

Scollon, R. and Scollon, S.W. (2001) *Intercultural communication: A discourse approach* (2nd edn). Oxford: Blackwell. This text is an introduction to the concepts and concerns of intercultural communication and provides an overview of methods for conducting research on intercultural communication. The authors present their own comparative research, based on Gumperz's framework of interactional sociolinguistics, comparing, for example, the discourse of westerners and Asians, of men and women, and intergenerational discourse.

III Researching language and culture

Chapter 7

The research enterprise

This chapter will . . .

- discuss methodological foundations of research on language, culture and learning from a sociocultural perspective;
- discuss some issues and concerns important to the doing of 'good' research.

7.1 Introduction

Traditional conceptualisations of research in applied linguists have often considered those who do research on language and learning to be a distinct, elite group of professionals who differ from those who teach. The task of researchers is to produce new knowledge, while the task of practitioners is to make use of this new knowledge to improve their teaching. A sociocultural perspective of research makes no such distinction. Instead, in defining research as a systematic quest for new understandings and new ways of attending to the world, such activity is viewed as a natural component of all applied linguists' activity. The distinction deemed relevant is that which distinguishes expert researchers from less proficient researchers. Rather than being based on one's professional position, the distinction is predicated on an individual's degree of expertise in a range of knowledge, skills and abilities needed to engaged in a complex and demanding task.

The purpose of this chapter is to lay out some of the general issues and concerns embodied in the enterprise of research with which anyone interested in doing research on language and culture from a sociocultural perspective should at least be familiar. The discussion is not meant to turn novice researchers into experts; for this, one needs extensive training and experience. Rather, it aims to highlight some of the basic issues involved in doing 'good' research that are worthy of consideration.

7.2   Methodological foundations of research on language and culture from a sociocultural perspective

One important aspect of research expertise involves being aware of and able to articulate the theoretical premises embodied in different approaches to research. The ways in which we perceive the world and our relationship to it, however tacit this understanding may be, frame our understanding of the nature of research, the purposes for which we engage in it, the kinds of research questions we ask, and the methods we choose to seek answers to those questions. Before undertaking a discussion on possibilities for research on language and culture, it is useful to review some of the more fundamental presuppositions embodied in a sociocultural perspective.

A first premise has to do with the nature of knowledge. As we have discussed in earlier chapters, a more traditional 'linguistics applied' perspective configures knowledge as a rational, universal entity with unchanging properties that exists separate from and independent of the knower. Language knowledge specifically is perceived as abstract, symbolic representations that, although located in the head of individuals, can be extracted from individual mind, and subjected to inquiry independently of the varied ways in which they are used.

In contrast, a sociocultural perspective defines knowledge not as some rational system existing apart from its users, but as a socially constituted cultural construct. This construct exists not within universal mind but within our communities, and is given shape by the communicative activities in which we engage as members of our communities, their tools and the ways we use the tools to mediate our actions in our activities with others. It is from our mediated actions that knowledge takes shape, including its forms and functions, and from which referential understandings of the world are drawn. From this view, then, language forms cannot be understood apart from their contexts of use. Rather, they are bound together, existing as two mutually constitutive components of systems of action.

A second premise has to do with how we gain knowledge. In the more traditional view, gaining knowledge is seen as a universal, natural process of assimilating new knowledge structures into already existing structures.

Since the structures themselves have their own shapes, embedded within and yet external to the individual, the individual does not, in fact cannot, play any fundamental role in giving shape to the new knowledge. Rather, the new knowledge stands apart from the knower, and the shape it takes is imposed on it by the coherent, logical and universal systems already in the mind.

In contrast, a sociocultural perspective does not separate individual social actors from the process of 'coming to know'. Rather, they are intimately connected in what is considered to be a fundamentally social activity. As we discussed in earlier chapters, individuals gain knowledge from their involvement with more experienced others in their sociocultural worlds. These more experienced members guide – in both explicit and tacit ways – less experienced individuals in taking notice of particular aspects of their worlds as they (re)create them in their jointly enacted experiences. By their actions they give shape to both the form and substance of the knowledge that less experienced individuals eventually accept as their own. Also structuring both the processes and outcomes of knowing are individuals' past experiences. That is to say, because individuals are culturally structured social beings, continually (re)created in their sociocultural practices enacted within specific sociohistorical contexts, the knowledge they create in any locally situated context of activity is also shaped by the histories individuals bring with them to these contexts.

A third premise has to do with the nature of inquiry. A traditional view makes a distinction between two kinds of research: basic or theoretical, and applied or practical. The purpose of basic research is to expand our theoretical understandings of the universal principles by which the world operates so that we may better predict and control what happens in it. In assuming language and culture knowledge to consist of internally coherent systems by which their existence – apart from any context – is governed, the role of such inquiry is to understand the structural specifications, the formal properties, of the knowledge systems as fully as possible so that we can predict how individuals, universally inscribed, make use of them. In such inquiry, sites of language use become sources of data only in that they allow for the collection of samples from which forms can be extracted and isolated, and hypotheses about the formal properties of systems can be made. Other sources of data are researchers' own intuitions. Since language systems are thought to be internal to all native speakers, it is assumed that, as native speakers of the language, the use of their own insights as sources of data is a plausible means for researchers to hypothesise about the formal properties of the systems and construct models of them.

Another concern of basic research from this traditional perspective, at least as it has related to applied linguistics, lies in uncovering the internally driven linguistic and cognitive principles and processes involved in assimilating, storing and accessing knowledge of other language systems for the purpose of constructing a more adequate theory to explain these phenomena. Here, research begins with the formulation of propositions or hypotheses about the kinds of natural, lawful relationships thought to obtain between sets of variables. Studies are designed to test assumptions about the relationships, and the findings are used to revise the theory with which the researcher began. Investigations concerned with language learning in applied linguistics that have taken this approach have sought answers to such questions as: What are the linguistic and cognitive mechanisms that move a learner from one state of knowledge to another? How do individual differences in terms of innate cognitive and linguistics abilities affect this movement? How does the manipulation of external forces influence the efficacy of the internal process? The answers to such questions lead researchers towards the construction of a universal theory of language development.

In contrast to basic research, the purpose of applied or practical research from a traditional perspective is to use our understandings of the nature of language and culture systems – and human development arising from basic, theoretical investigations – to address real-world concerns. As originally conceived, this was the realm of applied linguistics. A primary goal was to relate theory to practice, that is, to apply findings about the nature of language and culture to the solving of problems concerned with, for example, the teaching of languages, language policy decision making, the assessment of language abilities and disabilities, and workplace communication (Davies, 1999; Widdowson, 2000). In this view, the linguist – or in the case of research on language learning, the psycholinguist – is the scientist whose task is to build theories about language and about learning, while the applied linguist is the practitioner whose task is to take to the road in search of real-world problems that can be remedied – or at least better understood – by applying these theories on language and language learning.

A sociocultural perspective on the nature of inquiry differs fairly significantly from the more traditional view. Here, the worlds we live in form the very heart of research activity. That is to say, a sociocultural perspective makes no distinction between basic and applied research as used in the traditional paradigm. The goal of research is not to reveal some underlying truth or sets of universal principles and properties of human nature. Rather, it is to understand the communicative worlds in which and by which we live our lives – that is, to understand how we make our way in the world, not how the world is made inside us (Reed, 1996).

To reach such understanding entails the examination of our particular language games or lived experiences, the meanings residing in them, the social, cultural and political forces that give rise to these meanings, and the consequences that participation in these games have for individual language use and development. Such examinations will reveal intricacies of our communicative worlds and make clear how our worlds, our social identities and the roles we play, are connected to, and partially constructed by, our communicative actions and those of others, and by the larger socio-historical forces embodied in them. So doing will make visible the 'taken-for-granted' nature of our everyday lives and thereby 'render the character of our own and other people's practices publicly discussable and teachable' (Shotter, 1997: 304). Such understanding can also lead to the development of a theory of practice (de Certeau, 1984; Lave and Wenger, 1991). The goal of such a theory is to help to explain, on a broader scale, the communicative actions by which individuals within groups, and groups within communities, (re)create and respond to both their sociohistorical and locally situated interactive conditions, and the consequences – linguistic, social, cognitive and otherwise – of their doing so.

Quote 7.1 **John Shotter on the goal of research on communication from a sociocultural perspective**

We must study how, by interweaving our talk with our other actions and activities, we can first develop and sustain between us different, particular *ways* of relating ourselves to each other. That is, that we should first study how we construct what Wittgenstein calls our different shared *forms of life* with their associated *language games* . . . And then, once we have a grasp of the general character of our (normative) relations both with each other and to our surroundings – a grasp of their logical grammar – we should turn to a study of how, as distinct individuals, we can 'reach out' *from within* these forms of life, so to speak, to make the myriad different kinds of contact with our surroundings *through* the various ways of making sense of such contacts our forms of life provide.

Shotter (1996: 299–300; emphasis in the original)

In terms of learning, the goal of research is to lead us to an understanding of the conditions by which learners' involvement in the various constellations of their language socialisation practices – in and out of the classrooms – is shaped, and how their evolving participation affects their development as language users and language learners. This entails identification and characterisation of the communicative practices, the social institutions in which they are embedded, and the resources by which such practices are constituted in communities of language learners, be they in more formal learning settings like schools, or in other less formal settings like community clubs, civic organisations or the workplace. Also called for is the specification of the ways in which the participants in these activities use the resources of their learning practices to reflect and create particular settings, their individual identities and role relationships within these settings, and their collective identities across them. The third strand of research involves the examination of the consequences that result from individuals' long-term participation both within practices across time and across communities of learners.

Identifying the complex webs of communicative activity through which communities of language learners are formed, their sociohist-orical conditions and the varied trajectories of language use giving rise to different formations of individual identities and social relations, and following the developmental paths down which individual participation in the activities lead, can help us to understand more fully the intrinsic link between the kinds of communicative environments into which learners are socialised and their developmental consequences. More generally, they can help us to construct a theory of learning – a psychological theory of communicative action (A.A. Leontiev, 1981) – that explains the fundamental relationship between social activity and learning in ways that more mainstream theories of language learning do not, and indeed, cannot. Such an understanding in turn will provide us with a principled basis for creating and sustaining communities of learners that help to shape learners' language development in ways that are considered to be appropriate to their social, academic and other needs.

Quote 7.2 Jean Lave and Etienne Wenger on a theory of social practice

Briefly, a theory of social practice emphasizes the relational interdependency of agent and world, activity, meaning, cognition, learning, and knowing. It emphasizes the inherently socially negotiated character of meaning and the interested, concerned character of the thought and action of persons-in-activity. This view also claims that learning, thinking, and knowing are relations among people in activity in, with, and arising from the socially and culturally structured world. This world is socially constituted; objective forms and systems of activity, on the one hand, and agents' subjective and intersubjective understandings of them, on the other, mutually constitute both the world and its experienced forms.

Lave and Wenger (1991: 50–1)

7.2.1   Choice of methods: quantitative versus qualitative

In addition to making one's assumptions clear, doing good research involves choosing appropriate methods for collecting and analysing data, since the methods we choose to use will shape the kinds of data we gather and ultimately what we find. Data generally take two forms: quantitative and qualitative. The basic distinction between the two is that quantitative data are usually expressed in terms of numbers or amounts while qualitative data are not. Instead, qualitative data can take many forms, including verbal and non-verbal means of social action, pictorial and other kinds of visual representations, and so on. Although this division is a common one, a closer look reveals that they are not distinct categories. Rather, they are intimately connected in that quantitative data are based upon qualitative judgements, and all qualitative data can be described and manipulated numerically.

The purpose of research on language and culture is to discern, examine, and interpret meaningful communicative patterns and plans, and to explain them in terms of larger ideological themes and topics that emerge from the patterns. To generate well-grounded, warranted claims about the patterns and themes detected through analysis of the data, we must rely on counting – a basic means for determining quantity. The more often an action takes place, or a form appears, or a concept or idea is generated, the more basis we have for determining whether there is a pattern or theme. Once we have determined the existence of a pattern or a theme, we generally rely on the number of times it occurs to determine its significance. The more often something happens, the more warranted is our claim of conventionality. Similarly, the more a theme appears in particular oral or written texts, the stronger our claim can be of its significance to the person or persons to whom the texts belong.

The more we build our analysis on the basis of frequency, the less concern there is that the examples we have chosen to illustrate a claim are selective, representing our own hunches, rather than illustrative of the whole body of data from which the examples are drawn. Our use of such quantitative methods allows us to see patterns of language use that we might not have seen if we relied on our intuitions, and thus can 'act as a check on the insights derived from qualitative analysis' (Layder, 1993: 127).

On the other side, no matter which particular means of quantifying data we choose to use, the meaningfulness of the quantified data can only be determined through qualitative judgements based on the perceptions of those from whose lives the data are drawn. That is to say, detecting patterns of communicative behaviour can tell us how ubiquitous something is in the full body of empirical evidence. However, what it cannot tell us is the meaning such patterns have for those whose patterns they are. It can, as Widdowson (2000: 7) has pointed out, 'only analyze the textual traces of the processes whereby meaning is achieved; it cannot account for the complex interplay of linguistic and contextual factors whereby discourse is enacted'. Without some form of qualitative evaluation of the data, the numbers remain meaningless.

In some corners in applied linguistics, a great divide exists between those who use quantitative data and those who use qualitative data. Because traditional approaches to language learning have often used quantitative methods for collecting and analysing data, it is sometimes assumed that all quantitative methods carry with them the same assumptions underlying the methodology for which they are used. That is, quantitative methods have become associated with deductive, hypothesis testing research whose goal is to uncover universal, context-independent accounts of meaning-based systems. Similarly, all qualitative methods have become associated with ethnographic, inductive research whose goal is to understand particular cultural worlds (Schutz et al., in press). Such a divide, however, as pointed out by Potter (1996) and others (Bryman, 1984), is founded on a misunderstanding in that it fails to distinguish between the methodology (general epistemological assumptions underlying the general purposes and goals for undertaking a research project) and methods (the various tools and strategies that can be used to gather and analyse data in the attempt to reach the articulated goals).

Quote 7.3 Shirley Brice Heath on the value of enhancing qualitative data with electronic means for gathering quantitative data

[E]lectronic supports for quantitative analysis, often simple frequency counts of word usage, have the potential to enhance greatly certain behavioral or attitudinal issues. For example, if a frequency count of negatives turns out to be much higher for one teacher as compared with another, linguists are alerted to consider a host of contextual factors ranging from the type of lesson to the possibility of different ideological positions the two teachers may hold with regard to students' ability to handle the subject matter...The constant interplay of rich descriptive materials from field notes and such simple quantitative steps as frequency counts or ratios helps researchers guard against rushing to select the 'perfect' example from their qualitative data to illustrate a point.

Heath (2000: 54–5)

From a sociocultural perspective, both quantitative and qualitative data can help us to gain an understanding of the worlds in which we live, and thus should be viewed as complementary rather than competing forms of data (Layder, 1993). The question, then, becomes not *whether* qualitative and quantitative methods can be combined but *how* can they be combined to enhance our understanding of the data? The choices we make in terms of the kinds of data we collect and the methods we use to analyse them depend on the research questions we ask. Our task as researchers is to choose the most appropriate tools for the study. In the end, what will make our research 'good' is using the methods we have chosen systematically and rigorously so that the claims we make represent our data accurately and fairly even if the answers to our questions are not what we thought or hoped they would be.

Quote 7.4 Susan Berkowitz on judging the validity and quality of qualitative research

... there is broad consensus concerning the qualitative analyst's need to be self-aware, honest, and reflective about the analytic process. Analysis is not just the end product, it is also the repertoire of processes used to arrive at that particular place. In qualitative analysis, it is not necessary or even desirable that anyone else who did a similar study should find exactly the same thing or interpret his or her findings in precisely the same way. However, once the notion of analysis as a set of uniform, impersonal, universally applicable procedures is set aside, qualitative analysts are obliged to describe and discuss how they did their work in ways that are, at the very least, accessible to other researchers. Open and honest presentation of analytic processes provides an important check on an individual analyst's tendencies to get carried away, allowing others to judge for themselves whether the analysis and interpretation are credible in light of the data.

Berkowitz (1997)

7.2.2   Transcription issues

Since data for studies of language and culture from a sociocultural perspective are taken from naturally occurring events, collection methods, as noted earlier, often involve video- and audiotapings of these events. For the purposes of analysis, these taped events must be transcribed, or represented in another form, which most often is writing. While on the surface the process of re-presenting the activity graphically may seem unproblematic and fairly straightforward, it is, as Elinor Ochs (1979) and others (e.g. Duranti, 1997; Edwards and Westgate, 1994) have pointed out, a theoretical task in itself.

It is theoretical in that it entails our making choices about what to include and what to ignore. That is to say, in the process of transcribing, we select certain actions from a much larger repertoire to re-present in another form. In turn, the specific aspects we select shape what we determine to be relevant in the analysis. For example, in noting only verbal cues in our encoding of a communicative activity, we give primacy to verbal cues as significant tools in the realisation of the event before we have even begun the analysis. The decision to leave out non-verbal and paralinguistic actions makes it impossible to consider communicative acts realised non-verbally, such as a pointed finger to direct attention, raised eyebrows to indicate surprise, eye gaze to signal a change of turns and so on. Consequently, we are constrained in reaching a full understanding of the event as experienced by those whose event it is. The point is not that all possible actions be included, since no transcript can fully recapture the totality of experience. Rather, our task as researchers is to be clear about the criteria we use in choosing what to transcribe, and to construct a transcript that represents the particular aspects of the activity in ways that are consistent with our research goals (Duranti, 1997).

Transcription systems have been developed to represent a wide variety of communicative actions, including paralinguistic and non-verbal actions in addition to linguistically instantiated actions. For example, because a major concern of conversation analysis – a field of research interested in talk-in-interaction – is with the sequential rendering of social order between participants, transcription symbols have been designed specifically to reveal the sequence of actions. One typical symbol used for this purpose is the left bracket ([) to indicate overlapping turns, as illustrated in Example 7.1. Where the bracket occurs in the transcript indicates the point at which the participants are speaking at the same time. Example 7.2 contains a list of additional transcription conventions. Psathas (1995) points out that one system of symbols is not necessarily better than another. What is important is that we choose the one that makes salient those particular aspects of the event that we are interested in, and are consistent in our use of symbols to render the findings 'readable' by others doing similar kinds of research.

Example 7.1 Use of left bracket to indicate overlapping turns

Tom: I used to smoke [a lot
Bob: [he thinks he's real tough

Source: Taken from Psathas (1995: 71)

Edward and Westgate (1994) note that whatever we choose to transcribe, it is important when reporting our findings to state our criteria for selecting sections of transcribed data to illustrate an analysis. Where the issue is not even recognised, the question arises as to whether the selected samples of transcribed data are convenient rather than representative examples of the whole body of data. As such, we run the risk of using data to support our own version of reality, whether or not it adequately reflects the reality of those whose communicative experiences they are.

Example 7.2 Some commonly used transcription symbols in research on language use

.	(period) Falling intonation
?	(question mark) Rising intonation
,	(comma) Continuing intonation
-	(hyphen) Marks an abrupt cut-off
::	(colon(s)) Prolonging of sound
<u>never</u>	(underlining) Stressed syllable or word
WORD	(all caps) Loud speech
°word°	(degree symbols) Quiet speech
>word<	(more than and less than) Quicker speech
<word>	(less than and more than) Slowed speech
hh	(series of h's) Aspiration or laughter
.hh	(h's preceded by dot) Inhalation
[ ]	(brackets) Simultaneous or overlapping speech
=	(equals sign) Contiguous utterances
(2.4)	(number in parentheses) Length of a silence
(.)	(period in parentheses) Micro-pause, 2/10 second or less
( )	(empty parentheses) Non-transcribable segment of talk
(word)	(word or phrase in parentheses) Transcriptionist doubt
((gazing))	(double parentheses) Description of non-speech activity

(From the journal *Research on Language and Social Interaction*)

7.3   Research ethics

A final, important issue in the development of research expertise concerns *ethics*. All good research requires that researchers conduct themselves responsibly and ethically. Ethical approaches to research begin with a well-designed research project that includes the clear and adequate articulation of the theoretical presuppositions framing the study. It also entails the setting out of a clear rationale for undertaking the study, a clear statement of the questions with which the researcher is concerned, identification of the kinds of data needed to answer them, and clear articulation of the sources of data and the methods to be used for gathering and analysing the data.

In addition to a well-planned study, ethical research requires behaving responsibly towards participants. Responsible behaviour involves securing informed permission to participate from all participants from whom or about whom data will be collected. Informed permission means that prospective participants must be fully acquainted with the procedures and risks involved in the research before giving their written consent to participate. Moreover, ethical behaviour towards participants requires that all participation in the research project be voluntary and not in any way coerced. This means, for example, that individual learner involvement in a study of language learning should never be tied to course requirements; nor should the involvement of classroom teachers be required as part of their official positions as teachers.

Finally, ethical behaviour towards participants requires guaranteeing prospective participants that their participation will remain confidential. This means ensuring the participants that any identifying information will not be made available to anyone who is not directly involved in the study. Thus, for example, when sharing the findings with a wider audience, only pseudonyms should be used, unless the researcher has been given participants' permission to use their real names. Depending on the nature of the research, the researcher or the participants may wish to keep all identities anonymous. In this case participant identities are unknown even to the researcher. This might be warranted in a study in which individuals are asked for personal opinions. If they do not have to identify themselves on the form they may be more willing to share their opinions. Additional components of responsible behaviour towards participants include allowing for adequate time to arrange data collection procedures with participants rather than doing it at the last minute, keeping to the schedule that has been agreed by the participants; and formally thanking participants for their involvement at the end of the project (Wallace, 1998).

Most professional groups have a code of ethics that sets out standards of ethical and professional behaviour for their members. The British Association of Applied Linguistics, for example, produced a set of guidelines in 1994 that are intended to help applied linguists to maintain high standards and respond to new opportunities, 'acting in the spirit of good equal opportunities practice and showing due respect to all participants, to the values of truth, fairness and open democracy, and to the integrity of applied linguistics as a body of knowledge and a mode of inquiry'.*

More recently, the International Association of Applied Linguistics/ Association Internationale de Linguistique Appliquée adapted these suggestions into a code of good practice for applied linguists world wide.

In addition, most professional institutions and organisations have official review boards whose task is to ensure that research projects involving human participants proposed by their members meet standards of ethical behaviour. These boards determine, for example, whether and how well

---

* Readers should refer to http://www.baal.org.uk/goodprac.htm.

the rights of the research participants are protected, how well risks to the participants are minimised and whether the anticipated benefits outweigh any potential risk. They also determine the adequacy and appropriateness of the plans for obtaining informed consent, and of the qualifications of the researcher to conduct research involving human participants. In addition to becoming familiar with the standards of good practice endorsed by the professional associations in which they hold membership, those conducting research in applied linguistics, or hoping to, should be familiar with and willing to abide by their home institutions' procedures and regulations for engaging in research activity.

Quote 7.5   Introduction to the document *Recommendations on Good Practice in Applied Linguistics* endorsed by the British Association of Applied Linguistics

In the course of their work, which includes teaching, research, administration and consultancy, applied linguists often face a variety of conflicting interests and competing obligations. This document aims to assist applied linguists in their awareness and response to these dilemmas and the choices they entail. To do so, it points to a range of principles and values. Some, such as the commitment to equal opportunities and to fair employment practices, are general in their scope. Others are more specific to academic work and to applied linguistics. Ethical priorities are the central concern throughout this text, but it leans more to discussion in terms of 'could' than prescription in terms of 'must'.

Source: http://www.baal.org.uk/goodprac.htm

7.4 Summary

As discussed in this chapter, good research is dependent not on one's professional role – that is, whether one is, say, a university professor or classroom teacher. Rather, it depends on one's degree of research expertise. Among other knowledge, skills and abilities, this expertise involves understanding and being able to articulate one's assumptions about the nature of knowledge, of knowing, and of both the nature and purpose of inquiry. It is also a matter of asking relevant questions, choosing the most appropriate tools for answering the questions, and adhering to ethical standards of professional behaviour throughout.

Such expertise does not just happen once we decide to gather data. Rather, it is a life-long process, involving extensive, active experiences in communities of researchers. Part of the process of becoming bona fide members of these communities involves regularly engaging in professional conferences, reading and contributing to professional journals and books, and connecting with others via professional electronic discussion lists and bulletin boards. It also entails a collective willingness to look past our current understandings, to encourage exploration in unfamiliar territories, and to be open to unexpected experiences and discoveries in these quests.

In the chapters that follow, I present an overview of some of the more common approaches to the study of language, culture and learning from a sociocultural perspective along with a set of basic guidelines for undertaking research. Also included are suggestions for research projects that individuals at any level of experience in various contexts can undertake, and a collection of additional resources that readers may find useful in their teaching and research endeavours.

Further reading

Booth, W.C., Colomb, G. and Williams, J.M. (1995) *Craft of research*. Chicago: University of Chicago. This instructional text provides a detailed, practical overview of how to plan, carry out, and report on research for any field and at any level. Aimed especially at novice researchers, the book discusses how to choose a topic, and plan for, organise and implement a research study. It also details how to write a convincing report of findings.

Cameron, D., Frazer, E., Harvey, P. Rampton, B. and Richardson, K. (1992) *Researching language: Issues of power and method*. London: Routledge. This text addresses issues of the different kinds of power relationships that develop between researchers and their participants, with the authors providing examples from their own research experiences to illustrate their points. Also provided are suggestions for those who engage in research for developing a mutually beneficial research process.

Creswell, J. (2001) *Educational research: Planning, conducting, and evaluating quantitative and qualitative research*. Upper Saddle River, NJ: Merrill. This offers an integrated overview of both quantitative and qualitative approaches to educational research. It includes descriptions of eight research designs: experimental, correlational, survey, grounded theory, ethnography, narrative, mixed method, and action research.

Edwards, J.A. and Lampert, M.D. (eds) (1993) *Talking data: Transcription and coding in discourse research*. Hillsdale, NJ: Lawrence Erlbaum. This collection of essays examines the details of transcribing and coding data that are primarily oral. The chapters are divided into three sections – transcription, coding and resources – and topics include systems of discourse transcription, the analysis of prosody and conversational exchanges, and the coding of child language data.

Vogt, W.P. (1999) *Dictionary of statistics and methodology: A nontechnical guide for the social sciences* (2nd edn). Newbury Park, CA: Sage. This book provides about 2,000 definitions of statistical and methodological terms that are used in the social and behavioural sciences. The definitions are written clearly, and many include examples. All are designed to help readers to understand their use in research reports and articles.

Chapter 8

Approaches to research on language, culture and learning

This chapter will . . .

- describe six general approaches used to research language, culture and learning from a sociocultural perspective.

8.1 Introduction

While there is a variety of research approaches from which one can choose when planning research, six are commonly used to engage in research on language, culture and learning from a sociocultural perspective. They are: the ethnography of communication, interactional sociolinguistics, conversational analysis, discourse analysis, critical discourse analysis, and the microgenetic approach. Although the six approaches have their roots in different fields, they share the following features. First, they approach the study of language and culture as one dialogic, mutually constituted unit. Thus, all studies of language are also considered to be studies of culture. Second, they consider social activity to be their unit of analysis. While the size of the unit may vary from one-word actions to larger cultural, institutional and historical activities, the general concern is with uncovering the sociocultural worlds that are constituted in the actions we take and, conversely, uncovering the actions by which our worlds are constituted. This means that the approaches are empirically based, relying on data taken from naturally occurring contexts of action. Finally, while the data are generally qualitative in nature, these approaches recognise the value of using a mix of quantitative and qualitative methods for collecting and analysing data.

The purpose of this chapter is to provide a short overview of each of these six approaches. The overviews are not meant to be comprehensive, but are meant to serve as primers, particularly for novice researchers. For more detailed explanations, readers are encouraged to explore each approach more fully on their own. To help, I have included a list of readings for each that cites studies using the approach, and essays about the approach itself. Rather than including the lists at the end of the chapter, as I have done for previous chapters, I have included them after each section describing the particular approach. The lists are not meant to be inclusive, only illustrative. A search of any database of academic journals and books will surely lead readers to many more examples.

8.2   Ethnography of communication

As discussed in Chapter 1, Dell Hymes developed an approach to the study of language and culture called the *ethnography of communication*. The focus of this approach is on capturing patterns of language use as used by members of particular sociocultural groups in particular contexts to reflect and create their social worlds. Its central unit of analysis is the communicative event. As noted by Hymes (1962: 13),

> The starting point is the ethnographic analysis of the communicative habits of a community in their totality, determining what count as communicative events, and as their components, and conceiving no communicative behavior as independent of the set framed by some setting or implicit question. The communicative event is thus central.

Quote 8.1   Dell Hymes on the focus of an ethnography of communication

It [Ethnography of communication] is a mode of enquiry that carries with it a substantial content. Whatever one's focus of inquiry, as a matter of course, one takes into account the local form of general properties of social life – patterns of role and status, rights and duties, differential command of resources, transmitted values, environmental constraints. It locates the local situation in space, time, and kind, and discovers its particular forms and center of gravity, as it were, for the maintenance of social order and the satisfaction of expressive impulse.

Hymes (1980: 100)

As a way to describe systematically the links between the use of language forms and context in a communicative event, Hymes proposed the *SPEAKING* model. This framework was constructed as a guide to researchers to enable systematic descriptions of communicative events across communities and groups. That is, the framework is meant to help the researcher to connect linguistic forms to particular cultural practices and, on a broader scale, to uncover the particular ideologies about the participants' worlds embodied in their practices (Hymes, 1998). Each letter of the SPEAKING model represents one of the components of a communicative event to be described; all are interrelated in that each is defined by and helps to define the other. Likewise, the framework itself is contingent on the particular analysis of an event: i.e. as it is used to enhance our understanding of the event, the event itself helps to transform our understanding of the framework. The individual components of the SPEAKING model are:

- **S**ituation, including the physical and temporal setting and scene and its particular cultural definition;
- **P**articipants, including their identities in terms of age, gender, ethnicity, social status and other relevant features, and their roles, relationships and responsibilities as participants in the event;
- expected **E**nds or outcomes of the event and both group and individual participant goals;
- the particular speech **A**cts constituting the event, including their form, content and sequential arrangements;
- the **K**ey or tone underlying the event, for example, whether it is humorous, serious, or playful;
- the **I**nstrumentalities used to realise the event, including the code, e.g. which language or which language variety, and channel, e.g. whether it is accomplished via vocal versus non-vocal (e.g. oral vs written), and verbal versus non-verbal (e.g. prosodic features vs body movements) means;
- the **N**orms of interaction and interpretation of language behaviour including turn-taking patterns;
- the **G**enre with which the event is most closely associated, for example, storytelling, gossiping, joking, lecturing, interviewing and so on.

A primary source of data for doing ethnographies of communication is actual accomplishments of the events themselves. These are typically collected via audio and video recordings. During the period of time that the researcher is collecting data, the researcher plays the role of participant-observer. This involves acting as a member of the group whose communicative events are being studied in order to arrive at an in-group member's common-sense understanding of the activities and their significance. Other important sources of data include field notes of the researcher's own experiences and his or her observations of the experiences of the events' participants, interviews with participants, and related public documents and written records.

Analysis of communicative events is inductive and typically involves four stages. In the first, features important for the accomplishment of the event are noted. In the second, their patterned uses are described and, in the third stage, the conventional meanings of the patterns are interpreted in light of how they are typically used by the participants to take action. The SPEAKING framework, noted above, serves as a key for describing the events' significant features and patterns of behaviour and their systematic relationships. In the last stage of analysis, the participants' actions, and on a more general level the events themselves, are explained in light of the larger social, historical and political contexts they help to (re)create.

In addition to studies of everyday communicative events and practices, the ethnography of communication approach is the basis for research on language socialisation practices. As discussed earlier in the text, the particular concerns of research on language socialisation practices are with documenting the patterns of language use, and norms for participation specific to communicative events by which individuals are socialised into their particular groups and communities. Such research has added much to our understanding of the developmental paths that are created within culturally specific ways of using, teaching and learning language. Following this section are brief lists of studies that take an ethnography of communication approach to the study of language and culture in addition to readings about the approach itself.

One last point worth noting concerns the means by which communicative data are collected. Recent developments in electronic tools for capturing and representing social action such as digital video and audio recorders are transforming research on communicative activity. Such tools, for example, allow for the direct linking of transcriptions to digitised audio and video, and thus facilitate the instant retrieval of annotations and immediate access to data from annotations. In addition, in supporting the construction of repositories of digitised communication data, the tools allow for sharing and analysis of data across the Internet, and thus can facilitate cross-institution, geographically distributed, networked collaboration on collection and analysis of communicative data from a wide range of contexts and sites that have not traditionally been part of mainstream research. These cross-case and cross-corpora comparisons can help in the building of an international database of normative samples of social action for further research and use.

Finally, the tools can increase the potential to facilitate change through social research. Visually representing the trajectories of particular communicative actions through representative video clips, for example, can reveal the incredible complexity and dynamics of social action in a way that pages of description and written transcription cannot. For those viewing the video, it can reproduce the powerful processes of understanding and insight usually reserved for the researcher. In changing the way we use computers and other electronic tools in our research, the digital revolution that is now taking place will surely alter not only how we understand our communicative worlds but also how we represent them.

Further reading on the ethnography of communication approach

Bauman, R. and Sherzer, J. (eds) (1989) *Explorations in the ethnography of speaking* (2nd edn). Cambridge: Cambridge University Press. This classic collection of studies in the ethnography of speaking contains essays on the communicative practices of a wide range of groups and communities including traditional societies in North, Middle, and South America, Africa, and Oceania, as well as English- and French-speaking communities in Europe and North America and African American groups in North America. This edition includes an introduction by the editors that chronicles the development of the ethnography of speaking approach and provides directions for future research.

Duranti, A. (1988) Ethnography of speaking: Toward a linguistics of the praxis. In F. Newmeyer (ed.), *Linguistics: the Cambridge Survey, Vol. 4* (pp. 210–28). Cambridge: Cambridge University Press. This chapter provides a useful overview of the principles guiding an ethnography of speaking approach to the study of language use.

Philipsen, G. (1992) *Speaking culturally: Explorations in social communication.* Albany: SUNY Press. Ethnographies of communication of two cultural groups are presented in this text. The ethnography of the Teamsterville culture is drawn from the author's investigations into the ways of speaking found in an urban, working-class neighbourhood in Chicago; the second ethnography of communication is on the Nacirema culture, which focuses on ways of speaking as enacted by middle-class Americans, primarily on the West Coast.

Watson-Gegeo, K. (1997) Classroom ethnography. In N. Hornberger and D. Olson (eds), *Encyclopedia of language and education, Volume 8: Research methods in language and education* (pp. 135–44). The Netherlands: Kluwer Academic Publishers. This chapter reviews four ethnographic methods used in classroom research including ethnography of communication. In addition to summarising major contributions made by these methods, the chapter includes recommendations for future research on classrooms.

Further reading on language socialisation practices

Blum-Kulka, S. (1997) *Dinner talk: Cultural patterns of sociability and socialization in family discourse.* Mahwah, NJ: Lawrence Erlbaum. Using empirical data collected from over 100 episodes of family dinner conversations, the author examines the role that these interactions play in socialising children into their families' groups and cultures.

Schieffelin, B. and Gilmore, P. (eds) (1986) *The acquisition of literacy: Ethnographic perspectives.* Norwood, NJ: Ablex. This text contains a collection of reports of studies of home and school literacy socialisation practices of a diverse group of children from a variety of cultural contexts.

Moore, L.C. (1999) Language socialization research and French language education in Africa: A Cameroonian case study. *Canadian Modern Language Review*, 56 (2): 329–350. This study is on the multilingual socialisation practices of a community located in the Mandara Mountains, Cameroon, revealing the incongruities between home and schooling practices. The author concludes with suggestions for improving French language pedagogical practices.

Vasquez, O., Pease-Alvarez, L. and Shannon, S. (1994) *Pushing boundaries: Language and culture in a Mexicano community*. Cambridge: Cambridge University Press. This text presents findings from an ethnographic study of the language socialisation practices of a Mexicano community in California, illustrating how the children of this community learn to make use of their bilingual resources in myriad ways. The authors discuss ways in which educators can use these resources in classrooms to enhance the children's chances of academic success.

8.3   Interactional sociolinguistics

As discussed in Chapter 2, interactional sociolinguistics (IS) is an approach to the study of language and culture developed by John Gumperz enabling researchers to look more closely at actual movement in communicative activity. Where an ethnography of communication approach allows researchers to get an idea of the patterns of language use constitutive of a particular communicative event, and the presuppositions held by members of a particular group about the patterns and the event, this approach allows researchers to examine more closely how particular linguistic cues used by participants affect their interpretations of what is happening as a communicative event unfolds.

The focus is on those cues by which 'speakers signal and listeners interpret what the activity is, how semantic content is to be understood and how each sentence relates to what precedes or follows' (Gumperz, 1982a: 131). Of particular concern are interactions where participants with different cultural presuppositions about seemingly familiar events attempt to interact with each other. Such understanding, Gumperz argues, goes beyond what can be gained from doing only ethnographies of communication since they can only tell us what is shared among a group of participants. They cannot interpret communicative and other outcomes arising from cultural differences in language use. The main purpose of IS is therefore to 'show how diversity affects interpretation' (Gumperz, 1999: 459).

This is not to say that IS does not see the value of ethnographies. Quite the contrary, in fact, since the IS approach is predicated on findings arising from ethnographies of communication. That is to say, if researchers are to be able to account for these intercultural differences, they must know the conventional meanings that the cues hold for speakers, that is, how they are typically used to create 'culturally realistic scenes' (Gumperz, 1982a: 160). What IS proposes to do is extend our understanding of the cultural embeddedness of our linguistic actions by demonstrating the consequences that arise from interaction between individuals with different communicative practices for sense making.

Concept 8.1   **Conducting an interactional sociolinguistics study**

An interactional sociolinguistics study involves a two-stage recursive set of procedures.

Stage 1 involves conducting ethnographic research in order to:

(a) become familiar with the local socioculturally constituted environment of the events of interest;

(b) uncover and record recurrent types of communicative events relevant to the research problem at hand;

(c) discover, through participant-observations and interviews with key participants, their expectations and presuppositions for engaging in the activity.

Stage 2 involves analysing recorded events for:

(a) communicative moments of apparent misunderstanding between participants;

(b) prosodic and other cues used by participants to signal their presuppositions and their misunderstandings of each other's intentions at these moments.

Methodologically, IS studies differ slightly from ethnographies of communication in that they involve participants in the data analysis by asking them to view recordings of the event and point out whatever moments in the recordings they wish to respond to. This includes those times when they felt misunderstood or where they felt they might have misunderstood the other during the time the interaction was actually taking place. These moments are then examined to uncover how differences in the use and interpretation of linguistic cues between culturally different participants may have led to unintended consequences in their communicative encounters. The following list of further readings on interactional sociolinguistics includes recent studies utilizing this approach.

Further reading on interactional sociolinguistics

Auer, P. (ed.) (1998) *Code-switching in conversation: Language, interaction and identity.* London: Routledge. The studies reported in this volume combine methods of analysis from interactional sociolinguistic and conversation analysis approaches to examine the functions of code-switching in a wide variety of international contexts. In addition to reports of empirical data on the bilingual use of English and Cantonese, French and Italian, Danish and Turkish, and Hebrew and English, contributions include theoretical discussions on the nature of code-switching and bilingual conversation.

Auer, P. and DiLuzio, A. (eds) (1992) *The contextualization of language.* Amsterdam: John Benjamins. Contributions to this volume explore the theoretical and empirical aspects of interactional sociolinguistics, and in particular the notion of contextualisation and contextualisation cues, in the analysis of non-verbal communication and prosody.

Couper-Kuhlen, E. & Selting, M. (eds) (1996) *Prosody in conversation: Interactional studies.* Cambridge: Cambridge University Press. The essays in this volume take an interactional sociolinguistics approach to the study of prosody, primarily intonation and rhythm, and the role it plays in everyday conversation. The studies are based on empirical data from English, German and Italian conversations.

Hamilton, H. (1994) *Conversations with an Alzheimer's patient: An interactional sociolinguistic study.* Cambridge, UK: Cambridge University Press. This book takes an interactional sociolinguistic approach in the longitudinal study of communicative breakdowns that occur in conversations between the author and an elderly female with Alzheimer's disease. In her analysis, the author demonstrates how the patient's communicative abilities and disabilities are related, how they change, and how they are influenced by her own interactional behaviour.

Sarangi, S. and Roberts, C. (eds) (1999) *Talk, work and institutional order: Discourse in medical, mediation, and management settings.* Berlin: Mouton de Gruyter. Contributions in this volume take an interdisciplinary approach to the examination of talk and its role in creating workplace practices and relationships. Analyses draw primarily from three approaches: ethnography of communication, conversation analysis, and interactional sociolinguistics. Specific contexts include medical practices, health care delivery, management and social care.

8.4 Conversation analysis

Conversation analysis (CA) is an approach to the study of talk-in-interaction that developed as a field of study in the 1960s around the same time that Dell Hymes and John Gumperz were developing their approaches. It began in sociology as a reaction to the traditional view of language as a mere reflection of internal dispositions. Like the approaches developed by Hymes and Gumperz, and in contrast to the more traditional view, CA was predicated on a sociocultural perspective of language as social action, and asserted that individual social actors continually produce social order in the contexts of social action. That is, in their interactions with each other, and through the use of various devices or means, individuals continually produce order and, at the same time, display their understanding of what is taking place with their co-interactants. Thus, then, as now, the primary analytic concern of CA is with the socially constituted means by which such order is produced in interaction (Goodwin and Heritage, 1990).

As with the other approaches, conversation analysis is based on naturally occurring communicative activities. Data are collected via audio and video recordings of interactions, which are then transcribed and analysed for particular resources that participants use to recognise, produce and in other ways coordinate their locally situated actions with each other. The analytic focus of conversation analysis is finely grained as extralinguistic factors such as body position, eye gaze, and paralinguistic features like rhythm, intonation, and speed are taken into account as possibly meaningful resources in addition to linguistic features for bringing order to the interaction. Thus, transcriptions of recorded events are generally quite detailed in terms of what is represented graphically.

Similar to the other analytic approaches discussed in this chapter, the analysis of talk-in-interaction begins with the identification of the phenomenon of interest and the collection of particular instances of the phenomenon. The process of deciding on a unit of analysis is inductive in that the phenomenon of interest is identified via repeated viewings and transcriptions of the recordings. The samples in the collection are then analysed to construct a normative case, the meaning of which is interpreted in light of its use in interaction.

For those who do 'straight-ahead' (Heap, 1997: 223) conversation analysis, the focus is on explicating the various kinds of resources used to produce interactional order in general, and not on the contextually situated uses of the resources by particular individuals or groups. Meaningfulness of utterances is determined in reference to their functions in moving the interaction along and, consequently, there is little interest in collecting data from sources outside the interaction such as participant perspectives (Sanders, 1999). Outside CA proper, however, interest has been extended to the examination of interaction in institutional settings. Incorporating more ethnographically grounded data into their analyses, these studies take a particular interest in examining how participants interactionally enact their organisational roles and, more generally, in demonstrating links between particular resources participants in the interaction use and the larger contexts indexed by the use of the resources.

Such an ethnographically grounded approach to the study of talk-in-interaction is also sometimes referred to as micro-ethnography (Garcez, 1997; Watson-Gegeo, 1997). In comparison to ethnographies of communication, which entail complete descriptions of the various components of communicative events, a micro-ethnographic approach examines social interactions more closely, focusing on the particular means by which they are jointly constructed. Such studies 'may offer a detailed analysis of only one type of event or even a single instance of an event, perhaps contrasted with a second type of instance found in another context' (Watson-Gegeo, 1997: 138). It is worth noting that because of the overlap in interests in interaction, IS studies are also sometimes referred to as micro-ethnographies (Boxer, 2002).

Both the analytic techniques and findings arising from the multiple and varied studies of interaction have been valuable to those interested in researching language and culture from a sociocultural perspective. These studies make visible the multitude of means including, for example, patterns for turn initiations, turn projections, and self- and other-repair strategies in addition to the more traditional syntactic and semantic means we have at our disposal for sense-making in our communicative activities (Goodwin and Duranti, 1992; Jacoby and Ochs, 1995). Although the studies are generally descriptive in nature, they provide a base for taking a more explanatory approach in terms of being able to link the locally situated actions of individuals to the larger institutional and ideological structures embodied in them.

Further reading on conversation analysis

Drew, P. and Heritage, J. (eds) (1992) *Talk at work: Interaction in institutional settings.* New York: Cambridge University Press. The studies in this collection apply conversation analysis to the study of professional interaction. The studies cover a wide range of institutional settings, including doctor–patient consultations, legal hearings, and job interviews.

Firth, A. (ed.) (1995) *Discourse of negotiation: Studies of language in the workplace.* Oxford, UK: Pergamon. This collection of essays reports on studies of negotiation discourse that take a micro-ethnographic/conversation analytic approach. The studies examine negotiations in a variety of workplace settings, including the US Federal Trade Commission, management–union meetings, travel agencies, international trading houses in Denmark, Belgium and Australia, and consumer helplines.

Svennevig, J. (2000) *Getting acquainted in conversation: A study of initial interactions.* Amsterdam: John Benjamins. The study presented in this book is a detailed conversation analytic examination of the interactional accomplishment of the event 'getting acquainted' and the particular interactional means by which individuals establish and maintain interpersonal relationships in it.

McHoul and M. Rapley (eds) (2001) *How to analyse talk in institutional settings: A casebook of methods.* London: Continuum International. The contributions to this volume examine interaction in a variety of contexts from three different approaches, including applied conversation analysis. Studies include data from settings such as airline cockpits and medical interviews.

Ten Have, P. (1999) *Doing conversation analysis: A practical guide.* London: Sage. The author presents a comprehensive guide on doing conversation analysis. Included are chapters on methods for collecting data, transcribing recordings, and writing up and publishing results. Most chapters include examples of actual recordings of talk in ordinary settings, and all end with practical exercises and further readings.

8.5 Discourse analysis

A fourth approach to the study of language and culture, one that informs both ethnographies of communication and IS studies, is discourse analysis. Its focus is on uncovering the meanings of linguistic resources as used in naturally occurring oral and written texts. The resources of interest can range from single words like 'umm', 'well', and 'ok', which serve to mark particular junctures in the text and relate them to one another, to more complex units like speech acts and their sequential arrangements.

A discourse analysis of language use usually involves three steps. First, particular features for study are identified in the instances of the collected texts. The patterned uses of the feature or features are then identified and described and their meanings interpreted on the basis of how they are used by those whose texts they are. Currently, computerised innovations such as corpus-based linguistics are being employed for detecting patterns of language use across large collections of natural texts. They are useful in that they can provide quantitative descriptions of language patterns in terms of, for example, frequency distributions of single items and the collocation of a number of items. At the same time, since the analyses are based on forms rather than meanings, they limit the kinds of interpretations that can be made about the identified features (Widdowson, 2000).

Recently, in keeping with a sociocultural perspective on language and culture, calls have been made for a discourse analysis that is more explanatory, that is, that seeks to explain individuals' uses of their linguistic resources in terms of larger social, political and historical structures (Candlin, 1987). In tying the analysis of language use to its larger social, historical and political contexts, the goal of explanatory discourse analysis is, in almost all respects, similar to that of the ethnography of communication as developed by Hymes. That is, like ethnography, explanatory discourse analysis seeks to explain how language as used by particular groups and communities both reflects and creates the social actions by which they live their everyday lives. On another level, it seeks to explain how these actions serve to (re)construct particular visions of the world together with particular formations of individual identities and role relationships (Candlin, 1987). Consequently, in addition to samples of naturally occurring texts for analysis, other sources of data such as participant-observations and participant perspectives are drawn on in the analysis.

While the type of texts that are analysed by discourse analysts is quite varied, there has been a recent turn, at least in studies by applied linguists, to narratives as a particularly powerful form of discourse. According to Wortham (2001), telling a story about one's life affords individuals the chance to foreground what they consider significant. In turn, their representations of themselves provide narrators with examples of how the self

> **Quote 8.2**   Chris Candlin on an explanatory approach to discourse analysis
>
> An explanatory approach to discourse analysis seeks to demystify the hidden presuppositions and world-views against which meanings are co-constructed by participants. This approach does so by subjecting the use of particular terms, the choice of phonological and lexico-syntactic realizations, the conversational strategies and routines, the speech act values and the understandings by the participants of the norms of interaction and interpretation in encounters, to analysis and critique. In so doing, this approach seeks to illustrate the degree to which our use of language and our meaning-making, as well as our perceptions of role relationships, are determined by the properties of the social situation, its unstated values and interests, its economy; and from this the degree to which such use confirms the status quo and determines the values of the conversational 'goods' which are being exchanged ... It is this attempt to see discoursal features and pragmatic markers characteristic of particular types of encounters ... as being socially and culturally produced, reflective and reproductive of social relationships between participants, and, importantly, between groups, which marks off an explanatory approach to discourse analysis from one which is merely descriptive or even interpretive.
>
> Candlin (1987: 25–6)

wants to be. As Wortham (2001: 6) notes, 'when an autobiographical representation becomes compelling enough the narrator acts in accordance with the characteristics foregrounded in the narrative'. Given these interests, current concern with the analysis of narrative is on the linguistics cues that narrators use in the stories that they tell about themselves to construct themselves as particular kinds of individuals, with particular identities as characters within the story and, at the same time, as individuals who take particular stances in relation to the audience as their stories unfold. The following section contains a list of some recent discourse analyses along with some readings on the approach; this is followed by a list of some readings specific to narrative analysis.

Further reading on discourse analysis

Cameron, D. (2001) *Working with spoken discourse.* Thousand Oaks, CA: Sage. The author of this text provides a comprehensive account of the broad field of discourse analysis. Several current approaches are discussed along with practical strategies for applying the approaches in the analysis of naturally occurring data.

Gee, J.P. (1999) *An introduction to discourse analysis: Theory and method.* London: Routledge. This text presents the theoretical underpinnings of a view of language as social action and a discussion of discourse analysis as a method of research that embodies this view. Included is a discussion of tools of enquiry and strategies for using them in the study of language use.

Lemke, J. (1995) *Textual politics: Discourse and social dynamics.* London: Taylor & Francis. This text takes an explanatory approach to discourse analysis. It begins by examining the role of language in processes of social and cultural change, and the relationship between discourse and the notions of power and ideology. Included as part of the discussion is a review of the work of Mikhail Bakhtin, Michel Foucault and Michael Halliday. The text concludes with a discussion of potential sites of social change.

Schiffrin, D., Tannen, D. and Hamilton, H. (eds) (2001) *The handbook of discourse analysis.* Malden, MA: Blackwell. This collection of essays presents the theoretical foundation of a perspective of discourse as social action and examines some of the more significant methodological issues embodied in discourse analysis. Also included is a wide range of empirical studies of discourse as social and linguistic practice.

Titscher, S., Meyer, M., Wodak, R. and Vetter, E. (2000) *Methods of text and discourse analysis.* Thousand Oaks, CA: Sage. This text provides a comprehensive view of ten approaches to text and discourse analysis. In addition to a detailed description of a particular approach, each chapter provides examples of pertinent studies, a chart with key terms and an annotated list of additional sources of information.

Further reading on narrative analysis

Atkinson, R. (1998) *The life story interview.* Thousand Oaks, CA: Sage. The focus of this text is on how to use life story interviews in research. Included in the discussion is an overview of the role of narrative in research, and the presentation of a set of guidelines for collecting, transcribing and analysing the interview stories.

Bruner, J.S. (1997) *The culture of education.* Cambridge, MA: Harvard University Press. This collection of essays by the author presents a sociocultural view of narrative as a means for both representing and creating world views. Bruner uses this concept to examine ways that educational practices, and their accompanying narratives socialise children into particular understandings of themselves and their worlds. Included in the discussion is an examination of the work of scholars such as Lev Vygotsky and Pierre Bourdieu.

Lanehart, S.L. (2002) *Sista, speak! Black women kinfolk talk about language and literacy.* Austin: University of Texas Press. This book examines attitudes about language use through an analysis of narratives as told by women in the author's family. Using data from interviews and written statements by each woman, Lanehart demonstrates how differences in age, educational opportunities, and social circumstances lead to different attitudes towards using language as one goes about living one's everyday life.

Riessman, C.K. (1993) *Narrative analysis.* Thousand Oaks, CA: Sage. This text introduces the use of narratives in research. In addition to a discussion of the concept of narrative, the text examines the advantages of using narratives as a primary source of data in research, and overviews techniques and strategies for both collecting and analysing them.

Wortham, S. (1994) *Acting out participant examples in the classroom.* Amsterdam: John Benjamins. This book reports on a study of a particular pattern of classroom interaction that the author refers to as 'enactment of examples'. In this pattern teachers and students both narrate stories and enact relationships that are embedded in larger social issues. The text contains detailed examples of this pattern in addition to an overview of the methods used to collect and analyse the classroom data.

8.6   Critical discourse analysis

An approach to the study of text features that has its roots in discourse analysis is critical discourse analysis (CDA). Similar to an explanatory approach to discourse analysis, the purpose of this approach is to move beyond the textual interpretation of the patterned uses of language to explanation of their ideological underpinnings. What is arguably unique to CDA studies is their concern with how discourse structures are used to enact, confirm, legitimate, reproduce or challenge the dominant ideologies on social problems such as racism, inequality and discrimination.

In bringing together linguistic theory and social theory, CDA seeks to make visible 'how discourse is shaped by relations of power and ideologies, and the constructive effects that discourse has upon social identities, social relations and systems of knowledge and belief, none of which is normally apparent to discourse participants' (Fairclough, 1992: 12). Moreover, those who engage in CDA do so with the explicit aim of compelling broad social changes by the force of their findings. That is, the intention behind CDA is, as Mey (1985: 374) suggests, 'to define, and describe such language as can assist at least some people in preventing some social injustice in every-day life, and in changing some societal structures to the better'.

A very recent variation of CDA is what Ruth Wodak and her colleagues (Wodak et al., 1999) have termed discourse-historical methodology. Its purpose is to situate texts in their historical contexts and explore the ways in which they change through time. The more general aim of this method is similar to that of CDA in that it seeks to 'unmask ideologically perme-ated and often obscured structures of power, political control, and domi-nance, as well as strategies of discriminatory inclusion and exclusion in language use' (ibid.: 8). The following section contains a list of recent studies taking a critical approach to discourse analysis along with some readings on the approach itself.

Further reading on critical discourse analysis

Chouliaraki, L. and Fairclough, N. (2000) *Rethinking critical discourse analysis.* Edinburgh: Edinburgh University Press. This text presents a comprehensive over-view of the theoretical assumptions about language and social life embedded in a critical discourse analytic approach to the study of language use. The authors ground their discussion in contemporary social theory and clarify the relationship of this particular approach to other types of social analysis.

Collins, C. (1999) *Language, ideology and social consciousness: Developing a sociohistorical approach.* Aldershot, UK: Ashgate. The author presents an approach to a critical analysis of language use grounded in a sociohistorical perspective of language as found in the work of L.S. Vygotsky and V.N. Voloshinov. In the early chapters, the author outlines his theoretical framework, which he then applies in later chapters to critical analyses of language use from three particular contexts. Also included is a critique of the critical discourse approach to research.

Levett, A., Kottler, A., Burman, E. and Parker, I. (eds) (1997) *Culture, power and difference: Discourse analysis in South Africa.* New York: St Martin's Press. This volume contains essays that examine the sociopolitics of language use in South Africa in its transition to democracy. Studies provide critical perspectives on a wide range of social and political issues as they are discursively realized in a variety of social contexts. Methodological issues with conducting critical discourse analysis are also addressed.

Parker, I. (ed.) (1999) *Critical textwork: An introduction to varieties of discourse and analysis.* London: Taylor & Francis. This collection of essays is an introduction to critical discourse analysis. The different studies examine the use of symbolic resources in reflecting and creating social context. In addition to critical analyses of standard oral and written texts such as conversations and newspaper articles, there are studies of advertising, comics and sign language systems.

Wodak, R. and Meyer, M. (eds) (2002) *Methods of critical discourse analysis.* Thousand Oaks, CA: Sage. This book provides a comprehensive introduction to critical discourse analysis. It includes chapters that lay out the theoretical underpinnings of the approach, describe methods of data collection and analysis, and introduce some of the leading figures in this field of research.

8.7 Microgenetic approach

The last approach to be discussed differs from the others in that the concern is specifically with the study of language *learning*. In keeping with a sociocultural perspective, the goal of such research is to understand human action (Cole, 1996; Tomasello, 1999; Vygotsky, 1978, 1981; Wertsch, 1994, 1998). However, unlike traditional methods, which seek to study language behaviour in its final form, and apart from its contexts of learning, the concern here is with studying communicative action in the very processes of change, since, as Vygotsky and others have asserted, the only way to understand human action in its final form is by analysing its development.

Quote 8.3 Vygotsky on the significance of the historical method for studying development

To encompass in research the process of a given thing's development in all its phases and changes – from birth to death – fundamentally means to discover its nature, its essence, for 'it is only in movement that a body shows what it is'. Thus, the historical study of behavior is not an auxiliary aspect of theoretical study, but rather forms its very base.

Vygotsky (1978: 64–5)

Vygotsky posited four dimensions of historical, or developmental, study of human action: *phylogenesis*, which considers the development of human action in the evolution of the human species; *sociocultural history*, which considers its development over time in a particular culture; *ontogenesis*, which considers its development over the life of an individual; and *microgenesis*, which considers the development of human action over the duration of particular interactions in specific social settings. This last dimension is what studies of learning are centrally about.

Microgenetic studies (Siegler and Crowley, 1991; Wertsch and Stone, 1978) are small-scale, longitudinal studies in which learners' behaviours are observed to identify changes, and the specific contextual conditions of these changes. Specific methods involve a high density of observations of action over a specified period of time. Data sources include repeated video- and audio-recordings of the naturally occurring communicative event in which change is anticipated and, in some cases, other ethnographic data such as participant perceptions of their involvement. The goal is to link specific processes of learning with both quantitative and qualitative aspects of change. Crucial to this method is not so much the length of time over which change is observed, but the density of observations relative to the rate of change.

Another significant feature of this method is its use of both qualitative and quantitative measures for understanding change. To analyse change, the events are transcribed and coded in terms of the specific actions being investigated. Qualitative analyses of the longitudinal data can uncover the changing shapes of the linguistic actions as they happen. Quantitative measures such as frequency counts, sign tests, and other non-parametric measures, can also be employed to detect whether any changes in the observed actions are significant from one point to another, and how the changes relate to specific aspects of the event.

Most current studies using microgenetic methods are found in the field of psychology. Their primary concern has been with the development of conceptual knowledge and cognitive strategies (Siegler and Crowley, 1991; National Research Council, 1999). Only recently have such methods been used to study the learning of language. Because of the relative newness of this approach to the study of language learning in applied linguistics, it would be useful to describe in detail one recent study of foreign language learning utilising microgenetic methods.

Kim and Hall (2002) report on an investigation of the connection between the participation of a small group of native-speaking Korean children in an interactive book-reading programme and their development of particular linguistic and conversational resources in English. Twice a week for four months four children engaged in book-reading sessions with one of the researchers. Each of the sessions lasted 30 minutes.

During the first 20 minutes of the session, the children engaged in an 'interactive reading' session with the researcher using a book depicting a school-based story. Each session involved having the researcher read the story aloud to the children while actively involving them in the reading. He engaged the children by asking them questions and encouraging contributions from the children. He also expanded upon their comments and, in other ways, drew their attention to the story and the illustrations. During the last 10 minutes of each session, the children were encouraged to role-play the scenes depicted in the book read to them during the first 20 minutes.

To detect changes over time in the children's language use in the role-plays, the researchers used microgenetic methods. They first collected video-recordings of the role-play sessions in which the children created and participated in the pretend situations over the four-month period. The data were then transcribed and coded for several linguistic features including: vocabulary (including the number of words and number of school-specific vocabulary words), utterances (the number of utterances); talk management actions (including number of initiations, number of elaborations, number of conclusions and number of formulaic expressions), and meaning management actions (including number of self-corrections and number of other corrections). Quantitative changes in the children's use of the four features over the four months were measured using the sign test, a non-parametric statistic; and to determine whether the changes were related to the books used in the reading sessions, chi-square tests were performed.

It was found that the children's use of the different linguistic resources in English increased over the four-month period. It was also found that many of the increases were related to the particular books used. For example, although all seven books used in the study had a similar school theme and setting, the children used more utterances and talk management features in role-plays about two books in particular than they had for the other five books. Data from interviews with the children revealed that they found these books more enjoyable than the others. They reported that the books were funnier and more connected to their personal interests, and thus they were more willing to assume the roles depicted in these stories.

While these findings are interesting, what is important for our purposes is the value of microgenetic methods in allowing the researchers to understand the children's changing language behaviour in a way that more traditional 'snap-shot' methods cannot. The collection of repeated recordings of the children's language use over time, and data on the participants' perceptions of their involvement along with the use of both qualitative and quantitative analytic measures to document change, allowed the researchers to see not only whether change occurred, but what the behaviours looked like as they were undergoing change. Furthermore, they were able to link specific changes to specific books used in the reading sessions and to understand some of the basis for these links. In addition to documenting the learning of communicative resources, microgenetic methods are useful for studying other aspects of individual change such as identity formation and participation status (e.g. Penuel and Wertsch, 1995). A list of some recent readings about the microgenetic approach can be found in the following section.

Further reading on the microgenetic approach

Catan, L. (1986) The dynamic display of process: Historical development and contemporary uses of the microgenetic method. *Human development*, 29: 252–63. This article provides a brief, historical account of microgenetic methods in which the author argues for a slight but significant distinction between micro-*genetic* and micro-*developmental* methods for the study of behaviour.

Donato, R. and McCormick, D. (1994) A sociocultural perspective on language learning strategies: The role of mediation. *The Modern Language Journal*, 78(4): 453–64. This reports on a study of language learner development of learning strategies over the course of one semester. The authors used microgenetic methods to investigate the kinds of strategies the learners used, the shapes they took as the learners moved through the semester and the contextual conditions of their development.

Takahashi, E., Austin, T. and Morimoto, Y. (2000) Social interaction and language development in a FLES classroom. In J.K Hall and L.S. Verplaetse (eds), *Second and foreign language learning through classroom interaction* (pp. 139–59). Mahweh, N.J.: Lawrence Erlbaum. The authors report on a study of Japanese language learning among elementary school-aged children who were native speakers of English. Microgenetic methods were used to track changes over a two-year period in the children's participation patterns and language use in their interactions with the teacher.

Rojas-Drummond, S. (2000) Guided participation, discourse and the construction of knowledge in Mexican classrooms. In H. Cowie and G. van der Aalsvoort (eds), *Social interaction in learning and instruction: The meaning of discourse for the construction of knowledge* (pp. 193–213). Amsterdam: Pergamon. The research reported on here is concerned with interaction and learning in maths classrooms. Microgenetic methods were used in the investigation of the particular discursive strategies teachers used to guide students' participation in their instructional activities in and across classrooms.

Hall, J.K. (1998) Differential teacher attention to student utterances: The construction of different opportunities for learning in the IRF. *Linguistics and Education*, 9(3): 287–311. In this study, the author used micro developmental methods to investigate the shape of high school learners' of Spanish participation patterns in a particular instructional activity, changes in these patterns over one semester, and the consequences of these changes in terms of Spanish language development of four individual learners.

8.8 Summary

The six approaches presented in this chapter have informed a great deal of research in applied linguistics and I suspect they will continue to do so. Those who are new to the field, or at least new to research on language, culture and learning, are encouraged to seek out additional sources for guidance and information on these and other approaches. The more familiar we are with options for undertaking investigation, the more likely we are to formulate well-designed research plans whose methods can help to answer the questions we are asking.

_____

Chapter 9

Guidelines for doing research

_____

This chapter will ...

- present a set of guidelines for planning, carrying out and evaluating research projects.

9.1 Introduction: The research cycle

The research process is best understood as a cycle of six actions. These include identifying concerns and forming questions, choosing the most appropriate research approach for addressing the questions, gathering the data, analysing them, reflecting on the findings and deciding what to do based on what was found, and disseminating or in some way sharing what was learned with others. The process is cyclic in that each step leads to the next, with the findings from one project generating new concerns and questions for further investigation. The six steps, illustrated in Figure 9.1, are explained in greater detail below.

9.2 Identify concerns and develop research questions

The first step in the research process entails identifying particular concerns or issues arising from one's professional life as an applied linguist. For example, one's focus might centre on concerns with the larger social discourses that give shape to the institutions and activities comprising one's social or professional community. Alternatively, one's concerns may be with

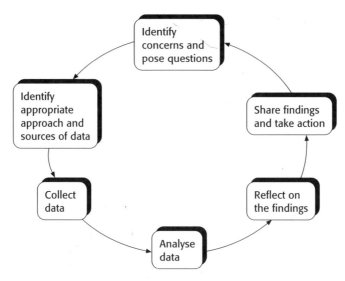

Figure 9.1   **Research cycle**

improving conditions for language learning in one's teaching context or with coming to a deeper understanding of an individual or group of individuals from a particular community with which the researcher is associated.

Once concerns have been generated, they can be prioritised according to their importance or significance to the researcher, and from this ranked list a specific topic for investigation can be identified. Once the researcher has decided on his or her specific focus, the next step is to generate a list of questions about it. For example, an interest in the more macro beliefs about a particular ethnic group embodied in a particular group's social institutions can lead to the following questions: What official documents produced by the social institution refer to or in some way deal with the ethnic group in question? What themes or topics related to the group characterise the documents? A concern with improving language pedagogy can lead to further questions, such as: What interaction patterns are typical of this learning context? What roles does the teacher play in constructing them, and what role do the students play? What kinds of linguistic actions are students becoming appropriated into via their participation in these patterns? And so on.

Once a set of questions on which to focus has been chosen, the researcher needs to consider whether they are reasonable in light of any constraints he or she may have in terms of time, and availability of resources. It may be, for example, that the question asked is both significant and of great interest to the researcher, but he or she lacks the resources needed to address it adequately. A final decision to be made before beginning to collect data is the intended outcome. That is, the researcher needs to consider what he or she plans to do with the findings. Perhaps, the goal is to present the findings at a peer-reviewed conference specifically for feedback on the study, with the ultimate aim of publishing a report of the study in a refereed journal and thereby contribute to professional discussions on that particular topic. Alternatively, one may wish to use the findings to help to justify changes to a particular instructional or organisational programme. Whatever the objectives, they will help to guide the implementation of the study, so it is important that they are clear to the researcher before commencing the study.

9.3   Identify research approach and sources of data

Once the research questions have been articulated, the next step is to formulate a plan for gathering data to help to answer them. This entails identifying the approach that the researcher considers to be the most appropriate, given the questions asked. Six of the more commonly used approaches to the study of language, culture and learning from a sociocultural perspective were presented in Chapter 8. The approach one chooses is, of course, very much tied to the questions one is asking. For example, if the concern is uncovering rhetorical patterns typical of a particular collection of oral or written texts, then a discourse analytic approach would be appropriate. If the concern is not only with uncovering points at which the use and interpretation of particular linguistic cues by participants in an interaction differ, but also with the effects the differences have on the subsequent unfolding of the communicative event, then an interactional sociolinguistic approach would be appropriate. It is also necessary at this point to identify the participants and setting of the study. These decisions are also based on the research questions in that they will lead the researcher in choosing a particular context and identifying members of that context. Once the setting and participants have been identified, the researcher must determine the particular sources of data.

It should be noted that while there are several possible sources of data, the sources one chooses are determined in part by the research approach taken. An ethnography of communication, for example, will require data from multiple sources, including, for example, videotapes of the communicative event of interest, field notes from long-term observations of the event, and collections of documents that are important to the accomplishment of the event. On the other hand, a micro-analysis of one communicative event may require less data from multiple sources collected over a period of time, and more finely tuned transcriptions of the event itself in order to capture the moment-to-moment movement of actions in the interaction. Some possible sources of data are discussed below.

9.3.1   Interviews and questionnaires

Interviews are conversations conducted with participants. They are usually audio- or video-recorded then transcribed for analysis. Interviews are typically of three types: *structured*, *semi-structured* and *open*. The purpose of *structured interviews* is to obtain specific kinds of information on a particular topic. The interview questions are compiled prior to the interview, leaving little opportunity for the interviewee to address other topics. This type of interview is helpful when one has a set of specific questions in mind and is interested in seeking answers to only those questions. The purpose of *semi-structured interviews* is also to get answers to specific questions and so here, too, the interviewer comes to the interview with a set of pre-formulated questions. However, unlike structured interviews, here the interviewee is afforded opportunities to elaborate upon his or her answers.

Open interviews are even less structured. Here the interviewer is free to direct the discussion as he or she wishes, expanding on some issues, raising others for discussion and so on. The interviewee also has more freedom to raise additional topics for discussion and in other ways move the conversation in various directions. An advantage to both semi-structured and open interviews is that one may end up with unanticipated perspectives on the research topic. They are particularly useful if one is interested in obtaining others' ideas on a general topic, or in uncovering others' understandings of particular concepts or terms. A disadvantage is that the interview data may be difficult to code and analyse, especially if each interviewee addresses a different aspect of the topic or decides to move the conversation towards different topics altogether.

Questionnaires are similar to interviews except that they ask for written responses from the participants. Like interviews, they can be structured, semi-structured or open. Structured and semi-structured questionnaires solicit specific kinds of information to be given in short answers or by choosing one response from several options. Questionnaires that are more open-ended ask participants to use their own words to provide opinions or information on a particular topic.

9.3.2   Think aloud protocols

This method of data collection involves asking individuals to verbalise their thoughts while engaged in a particular activity. The purpose of this method is to glean from individuals' comments the cognitive processes and strategies they are using to accomplish the task. This is a useful source of data if, for example, one is interested in gaining an understanding of an individual's perceptions of his or her involvement in a task. Think alouds are usually audio- or video-recorded, and later transcribed for analysis.

A variation of the think aloud protocols involves asking individuals to provide comments on their participation after the fact. This is often used when taking an interactional sociolinguistics approach, where participants are brought in to observe their taped participation in an event and asked to stop the tape wherever they thought their linguistic actions were being misunderstood by the other participants, or where they might have misunderstood those actions of their interlocutors. The researcher then begins his or her analysis of contextualisation cue difference at those points.

9.3.3 (Participant) observations and field notes

Observations require the researcher to be present for an extended period of time in the communicative event or context being studied. For example, if the researcher is interested in the activities that are of significance to a classroom community of language learners, he or she can choose to spend time in the classroom observing the activities. If, during the observations, the researcher decides to participate in the context, he or she is considered to be a *participant-observer*. One can decide to participate fully in the events, for example, acting either as an aide to the teacher in the classroom context or as the teacher. An advantage to full participation is that the presence of the researcher is likely to raise few concerns or questions among the other participants in that context. A major disadvantage is the difficulty one faces in trying to observe and collect data and at the same time be a fully involved participant. A more reasonable position may be to participate as an interested observer. In this case, the other participants are aware of the purpose of the researcher's presence but he or she does not have to be involved fully in all activities.

Written accounts, or *field notes*, are usually kept on these observations. These notes can be more or less structured, depending on the questions that have been asked. For example, prior to observing the classroom the researcher can make a list of behaviours in which he or she is particularly interested. While observing, the researcher can then use the list to note whether and how often the behaviours occur and the contexts of their occurrences. Alternatively, interest may be in documenting the myriad ways students participate in their classroom interactions, regardless of whether they conform to a particular list. In this case, the field notes become detailed descriptions of the different behaviours observed.

9.3.4 Video-recordings

Video-recordings of communicative events and activities are able to capture actions as they occur in real time. They allow the researcher to study the connection between (a) linguistic actions and spatial organisation,

(b) linguistic actions and body movements, including gestures, posture and facial movements and (c) communicative stability and change across time in ways that cannot be performed by any other means of data collection. Decisions about where to place recording devices, how many devices to use, and how often to record are important to the quality of the data collected. For example, placing one camcorder in the corner of a fairly small room may not permit all of the activity to be captured. Likewise, the single camcorder may not capture all the sounds of the classroom. For example, voices of individuals sitting in the far corner of the room may not be detected. Thus, it is important for the researcher to know the setting well enough to be able to set up devices in ways that will allow him or her to record all the sights and sounds particular to the context.

9.3.5   Personal reflection journals

Personal journals are documents produced by the researcher in which he or she records his or her feelings and reflections. They usually contain two parts. In the first, the researcher records detailed descriptions of incidents, readings, observations or other events considered significant to the research context. In the second, the researcher records personal feelings, opinions and reactions to the incidents, readings, observations and events. Journal recording is typically done according to some schedule – for example, at the end of each week of data collection. While journals are often written, they can also be kept as audio- or video-recordings. In addition to providing the researcher with additional documentation of events and activities taking place in the research context, the journals can help to make apparent whether and how the researcher might have influenced the collection and analysis of data.

9.3.6   Archives and other documents

Archives are collections of official documents that provide a historical record of a context. They can include written reports, records, tapes, newsletters, memoranda, physical artifacts and other materials that are typically stored in libraries, offices and other sites designated as official repositories. Such data can provide different viewpoints on a topic, and thus aid in comparative analyses across contexts. In addition, other documents and physical artifacts – some of which may not have official status but may be pertinent to a particular research setting – may be useful to identify and collect.

9.4 **Collect data**

Once the participants and sources of data have been identified, the next decision concerns the time period during which data will be collected. *When* one decides to collect data depends on one's research questions. If, for example, the researcher is interested in perceptions of newly arrived adult immigrants in a language programme of their language needs, then, clearly, the data need to be collected when the individuals first enter the programme. Likewise, if the researcher is interested in documenting his or her own development as an apprentice in a particular programme, or another individual's development as captured in personal reflections, then data should be collected over an extended period of time in order to produce enough data to be able to document any changes that occur.

One last point needs to be considered before the process of data collection can begin. No matter what questions are asked, what research approach is taken or what sources of data are used, the process of collecting data must be systematic. That is to say, decisions about the process of data collection should be clearly articulated, and methodical. If, for example, it is decided to ask adult language learners to generate a list of their perceived needs, all participants of the group should be involved. If, however, the researcher decides to ask just a few learners, he or she must be able to state the criteria used in selecting the individual respondents. For example, it may be decided to seek responses from females only, or from individuals with a particular first language. Likewise, if the researcher decides to videotape instances of a particular communicative event, the criteria for deciding when and how often to tape must be stated clearly, and the specific methods used to tape followed as systematically as possible for all recordings. Otherwise, as pointed out in Chapter 7, one runs the risk of collecting data that support one's own version of reality, whether or not it adequately reflects the reality of those whose contexts of experiences are the focus of study.

9.5 **Analyse the data**

Analysis of the data is the fourth step in the research process. This entails coding, or transforming the data into another form. How one codes depends on the kind of data collected and the larger research questions. For example, coding can involve identifying specific linguistic features of a set of verbal data and transforming them into numerical values, as with corpus-based analyses of texts. Alternatively, if one is working from transcriptions of videotaped interactions, and the concern is with patterns of interaction, the researcher may begin the analysis by coding utterances according to their functions as speech acts (e.g. coding the utterance 'what

did you say?' as a request for information) or according to the illocutionary force as determined by the role they play in the interaction (e.g.
coding the utterance 'what did you say?' as a statement of disapproval).
In other cases of interaction, the focus might be on finding specific communicative event boundaries, and coding the cues used by participants to
open and close them.

Often, the researcher will need to construct his or her own coding framework, although it is useful to draw on and, where possible, incorporate
coding schemes that others have used. Whatever coding framework the
researcher decides to use, it is important to define it clearly and to use it
consistently across similar sources of data. Once the data are coded, the
next step involves searching across datasets for regularities or patterns
of occurrence, and grouping and organising the regularities into larger
segments for subsequent qualitative and/or quantitative interpretation. In
terms of analysis across large datasets, the larger segments can function as
a framework with which to make systematic comparisons with subsequent
segments and to identify and interpret individual actions within them. As
Kasermann (1991) has noted, such a framework is useful in allowing for
systematic identification and comparison of both conventional and non-
conventional behaviour, at least as it pertains to a particular body of data.

A last step involves arranging the findings so that they fairly and accurately represent the data. Hymes's (1980) SPEAKING model, relevant to
an ethnography of communication approach and discussed in more detail
in Chapter 8, provides a useful framework for representing and comparing
findings from investigations of particular communicative events. Qualitative data can also be represented by transcriptions, diagrams, flow charts,
and pictures, in addition to written descriptions. In the case of quantitative
analyses, findings can be represented as numbers and displayed in the form
of tables, charts and graphs.

A chart such as the one provided as Figure 9.2 can help researchers conceptualise and organise their methods for collecting and analysing data.

Questions What do I want to know?	Data collection How will I get data to find answers?			Data analysis How will I examine data?
	Participants/ context	Source	When	
1. What are learners' perceived language needs?	15 newly arrived adult language learners	Individual interviews	1st class of language course	Thematic coding; frequency counts

Figure 9.2   **Matrix for organising methods for data collection and analysis**

9.6   Reflect on the findings

Once the data have been sufficiently analysed and the findings presented, the next step involves reflecting on the findings in relation to the questions originally asked and, where appropriate, identifying steps for using the findings to meet one's intended outcomes. Some questions to guide reflections on the findings include: What did you find? Of the findings, which ones did you anticipate and which ones were unexpected? Were your questions answered adequately or were there obstacles that prevented you from completing the project? Could the project have been done differently? How so? What new knowledge or understanding can you take from your study? What might your next steps be?

9.7   Share findings and take action where appropriate

The final step in the research process entails sharing what has been learned with others and, where appropriate, taking action. No matter what was found, there will be something worthwhile to report from which others can learn. Ways to share the new knowledge or understandings include more structured activities such as formal presentations of the findings to one's colleagues at a meeting arranged by a local, state, regional, national or international professional organisation. The researcher can also decide to submit a report for publication consideration to a professional journal or newsletter. Less formal means for sharing can include presenting the findings to others as part of a discussion group that takes place in real time, face-to-face interaction, or as part of an electronic chat room run by one's professional community. One can also decide to post the report to an electronic bulletin board or to one's own personal web page.

How and with whom the researcher shares information and findings from the project depends in part on the consequences he or she anticipates the project to engender, and the degree of support he or she believes is needed to help to ensure their realisation. In addition to enhanced understandings of a particular context, possible outcomes from engaging in research can include enhanced communication and collaboration between the researcher and his or her colleagues in a particular programme or organisation, or between the researcher and his or her students; enhanced self-awareness of one's professional role as an applied linguist; and increased awareness of one's larger social context and the role the researcher can play in facilitating change. Figure 9.3 lays out in detail the questions to be considered when planning, conducting and evaluating any kind of research project.

A. Introduction to problem

Is the stated problem clear and researchable?
- Is the rationale for the problem clearly presented?
- Has related background information been provided to support the need for this study?
- Is the research problem situated in a relevant theoretical framework?
- Are the research questions stated clearly?
- Is it clear what the study will contribute to existing understandings?

Is there a thorough review of literature?
- Are cited references relevant to the problem and up-to-date?
- Are the majority of sources primary?
- Are the results of cited studies compared and contrasted rather than summarised?
- Does the review make clear the relevance of the problem?

B. Methods

Did selection procedures identify participants and contexts appropriate to the problem?
- Are characteristics of participants and site described?
- Are reasons given for participant and site selection?
- Are selection and identification of participants ethical (e.g. informed, voluntary, confidential or anonymous)?

Are methods appropriate and adequate?
- Are sources of data adequately described and appropriate for answering the research questions?
- Are the methods for data collection appropriate for answering the research questions?
- Is it clear how, when, and by whom the data will be collected?
- Is there a theoretical rationale given for the particular methodology?
- Is it consistent with the theoretical framework of the research?
- Are procedures for analysis, including descriptions of coding procedures, fully described?
- Are they appropriate for the kinds of data that are collected?

C. Findings

Are results appropriate and clearly presented?
- Are the data reported clearly?
- Are the connections between the questions asked and the findings clear?
- Is enough evidence presented to support claims?
- Are all cases arising from the analysis fully accounted for?

D. Discussion

Do the results of the data analysis support the conclusions?
- Are explanations for the findings reasonable, appropriate and adequate?
- Does the argument made stay within the limitations of what the data allow?
- Are results grounded in the theoretical framework that motivated the research?
- Are findings compared to those of previous studies?
- Are conclusions supported by results?
- Have possible limitations of the study been discussed?
- Is the contribution this study makes to the field clearly stated, and appropriate?

Are there recommendations for future action?
- Are recommendations for future research given?
- Are the recommendations adequate and appropriate?

Figure 9.3   **Guidelines for planning, conducting and evaluating research projects**

9.8 Summary

Research is an essential component of the professional lives of applied linguists. In addition to being informed consumers of research, it is to our collective benefit as a field that we become skilled in conducting our own investigations. We must be able to ask relevant questions, choose appropriate methods for collecting and analysing data, be rigorous in the process, and be willing to reflect on the findings, making changes to our practices where appropriate, and share what we have learned with others.

In addition to enhancing our understandings of our worlds, engaging in research can help us to develop the skills we need to articulate more clearly concerns that are of significance to our particular circumstances, interests and needs as scholars and teachers of language and culture, their epistemological foundations, and both the theoretical and empirical questions these concerns give rise to. At the same time, the process affords us opportunities to move past what we already know and towards the development of new perspectives and different lenses for interpreting and understanding familiar surroundings.

Further reading

Denzin, N. and Lincoln, Y. (eds) (2000) *Handbook of qualitative research* (2nd edn). Newbury Park, CA: Sage. This collection of essays provides a guide to conducting research using qualitative methods. The volume is divided into six sections: locating the field; major paradigms and perspectives; strategies of inquiry; methods of collecting and analysing empirical materials; the art of interpretation, evaluation and presentation; and the future of qualitative research.

Gubrium, J. and Holstein, J. (eds) (2001) *Handbook of interview research: Context and method.* Thousand Oaks, CA: Sage Publications. The contributions to this book examine interviews as a means of collecting research data. The various chapters offer discussions on the conceptual, methodological and practical issues surrounding the use of interviews as an instrument for gathering data.

Johnstone, B. (2000) *Qualitative methods in sociolinguistics.* New York: Oxford University Press. This book provides a detailed discussion on the use of qualitative methods in research on language and society. It includes discussion of topics such as general theoretical and practical questions about research, and the principles of selecting, collecting, and analysing language use.

Lofland, J. and Lofland, L.H. (1995) *Analyzing social settings: A guide to qualitative observation and analysis* (3rd edn). Belmont, CA: Wadsworth Publishing Co. This is a comprehensive and practical guide to the collection and analysis of qualitative data. In their discussions, the authors include a wealth of illustrative examples. It is considered an exemplar of research methods texts.

Miles, M. and Huberman, A.M. (1994) *Qualitative data analysis: An expanded sourcebook.* Thousand Oaks, CA: Sage. The authors have created a practical sourcebook for researchers on how to design, and use qualitative data analysis methods. They describe several ways to display qualitative data including, for example, matrices and networks in addition to narrative text and provide practical suggestions for their adaptation and use.

Chapter 10

Contexts of research

This chapter will...

- describe a framework for conceptualising research contexts;
- offer suggestions for research projects for each dimension of the framework.

10.1 Introduction

In the preceding chapters, we have laid out some of the more significant assumptions about language, culture and learning embodied in a sociocultural perspective on human action, and we have reviewed how the concepts have informed teaching practices. In terms of research, we have discussed several issues related to the 'doing' of good research, discussed some of the more typical approaches that are currently being used by applied linguists to study language, culture and learning, and offered a set of guidelines for planning, conducting and evaluating research.

In this chapter we look at how we might identify topics and questions that are appropriate for empirical investigations. The discussion is framed around a conceptual map that arranges social activity into four dimensions. I discuss the characteristics and scope of each dimension, and for each I include suggestions for research projects. The suggestions are presented using the model of the research process described in Chapter 9. They are included as examples of how readers might plan and conduct studies of relevance to their professional contexts.

10.2   Contexts of research

As I have tried to make clear in this text, the general aim of research on language, culture and learning from a sociocultural perspective is on understanding our worlds, our varied identities and roles as social actors, and the varied consequences arising from our long-term involvement in our worlds. Since our communicative lives are complex and layered, understanding them involves unfolding or teasing apart the many layers of meanings. We need to understand not just how we act as individuals in any particular moment, but how, as individuals, we construct and are constructed in particular communicative activities. We also need to understand how these activities inform and are informed by the larger social institutions to which they are linked, and the larger beliefs, values and attitudes within which the institution are nested.

Figure 10.1, which is an adaptation of a map proposed by Layder (1993) for doing social research, presents a conceptualisation of the many layers involved in research on language and culture from a sociocultural perspective. As can be seen, the framework is composed of four overlapping dimensions: social structure, institutional contexts, communicative activities, including language socialisation practices, and the individual. Each of the four dimensions represents particular constellations of empirical characteristics that are typical of different levels of social activity.

Such a map is useful in that it 'tie[s] together the interpersonal world of everyday life with the more impersonal world of social institutions' (Layder, 1993: 206). That is, it makes apparent the interconnectedness of the more situated aspects of life to the more macro issues of social institutions, beliefs and ideologies. While the scope of the dimensions differs, the analysis we engage in for each is similar in that on each level we seek to describe what is going on and interpret the meanings of the activity from the perspective of those whose worlds we are investigating. We also seek to explain the activity by connecting what we have learned on one level to how the activity is constructed on other levels. This means, then, that uncovering the meanings of individual behaviour requires us to locate it in its larger contexts of action. Likewise, understanding social beliefs and attitudes entails connecting them to their instantiations in real-world contexts, in our language games.

Limiting our focus to only one level will constrain what we can see, and how we come to understand it. For example, suppose we look only at changes that occur in individual behaviour in classrooms and find that, over a period of time, the behaviours in question change only slightly. If we stay at this level, we may, perhaps wrongly, attribute the lack of change

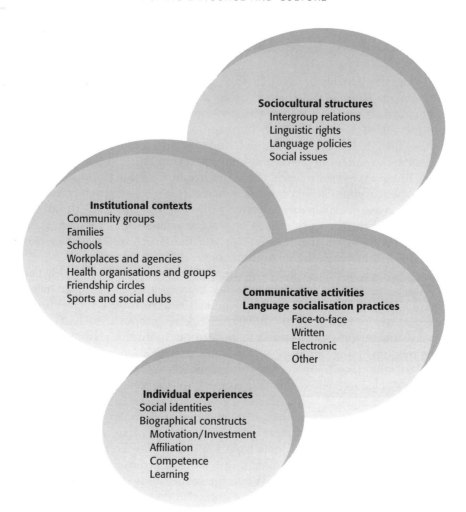

Figure 10.1   Contexts of research

to the individuals themselves, claiming individual inability or disinterest in making the changes. If we include an analysis of the classroom activities in which the individuals were involved, however, we may find that the opportunities for participation in the activities, at least for some individuals, were limited. This lack of opportunities may help to explain, in part, the lack of change in individual behaviour. And so on. The point is that without attempting to understand our findings in light of social activity on other levels, our understandings will remain incomplete.

> **Quote 10.1** Derek Layder on the interconnectedness of micro and macro elements
>
> ... [M]acro phenomena make no sense unless they are related to the social activities of individuals who reproduce them over time. Conversely, micro phenomena cannot be fully understood by exclusive reference to their 'internal dynamics', so to speak, they have to be seen to be conditioned by circumstances inherited from the past. In other words, micro phenomena have to be understood in relation to the influence of the institutions that provide their wider social context. In this respect macro and micro phenomena are inextricably bound together through the medium of social activity ...
>
> Layder (1993: 102–3)

A final point on our research concerns the kind of understanding of social activity we hope to achieve through our research endeavours. Remember, from a sociocultural perspective, that full understanding cannot be based on what something appears to be, no matter how detailed our analysis. Rather, it requires us to follow its development over time. This point was made about documenting language learning in Chapter 8, but in fact it holds for all social activity. If our aim is to understand social action, we must come to see it fully, in 'the cultural, institutional, and *historical* situations in which this action occurs' (Wertsch et al., 1995: 11; emphasis added). Thus, as Vygotsky (1978: 64–5) noted, 'the historical study of behavior is not an auxiliary aspect of theoretical study, but rather forms its very base'.

This means, then, that in addition to gaining a sense of what something *is*, we need to undertake a historical examination of *how it came to be*. This requires longitudinal investigations, that is, studies of activity – from the micro to macro levels – over time. From such analyses, we can discern the conventional or typical instantiations of the activity and the wider sociohistorical and political forces that have given shape to these instantiations. We can also discern how individuals gain or are afforded access to the activities, how it is that individuals attempt to use the resources towards their own ends, and how, through their evolving participation, they develop their particular strategies.

10.2.1   Sociocultural structures

This dimension is generally concerned with the large-scale, society-wide worldviews that are embodied within and both inform and are informed by the institutional contexts of a community, their communicative practices and the individuals situated within them (Layder, 1993). These worldviews encompass beliefs, values and attitudes towards social phenomena such as group identities (e.g. social class, gender and ethnicity) and intergroup relations. They also include understandings of social constructs such as personhood and freedom, and social issues such as linguistic rights and language policies, education and public policy, racism and discrimination.

A primary concern of research in this dimension is with explicating the worldviews embodied in particular public and other official documents, and documenting the linguistic and discursive means by which they are oriented to, distributed, and maintained, by those whose documents they are. The general aim of such research is to raise our awareness of how language is used to create particular viewpoints and particular representations of the world, and of how these views can persuade us to act in particular ways. In so doing, those engaging in such research hope to clear a pathway to social change. Sources of data can come from a range of genres, such as official written records and other public documents, news discourse, documentaries, and advertising. In addition, they can come from a range of fields such as medicine, law, public policy, education, labour markets and so on.

This macro dimension of sociocultural structure has been of particular interest to applied linguists. Two directions are evident in recent literature. In one, the concern is with bringing to the field's attention significant issues specific to language, such as linguistic rights, language policies, and language education. Tove Skutnabb-Kangas (1999, 2001), Robert Phillipson (1992, 2000), James Tollefson (1991, 2002) and Alastair Pennycook (1994, 1998), for example, are well known for their writings on these issues. In general, these writings provide insightful and even provocative viewpoints on ways the field might address these important language-related issues. However, they should not be confused with empirical investigations. That is, by and large, their concern is not with explicating the contextually situated meanings of these issues for particular individuals or groups. Rather, it is with framing the issues within larger social theories in order to better understand their complexities. If particular examples from the 'real world' are used, it is often to illustrate theoretical claims, not to make a case about particular 'real world' meanings.

A second direction recent literature has taken is towards the examination of context-specific ways language is used in official texts to create particular visions of social phenomena like gender and class, and social issues such as discrimination, democracy and so on. Here one finds the work of, to name a few of the more well-known writers, Norman Fairclough (1995a, 1995b, 2000), Teun van Dijk (1993a, 1993b), Roger Fowler (1991) and Ruth Wodak (1997; Reisigl & Wodak, 2001). The work undertaken by this second group is more aptly termed empirical in that their focus is on the interrogation of texts collected from specific institutional contexts.

While the goals of this research are in keeping with this dimension, some of the earlier studies have been criticized, and rightly so, for their lack of systematicity and rigour in explicating the criteria for choosing samples of texts to examine and in locating their interpretations of the meanings in the specific contexts of use, as realised by those whose texts they are (cf. Collins, 1997; Widdowson, 2000). As noted in Chapter 8 in relation to the analysis of data, if the methods are not clearly stated and systematically utilised, it raises the question as to whether the text samples are chosen to fit with the researcher's own viewpoint rather than to illustrate the particular worldviews embodied in the settings from which the samples are drawn. This point is not meant to steer one away from doing such broad-based research; it is only to call attention to the need for rigorous and systematically employed methods no matter what the scope of the investigation is.

I have included here, in Example 10.1, an illustration of the kinds of studies currently being done in applied linguistics concerned with the dimension of sociocultural structure. It is useful in that it illustrates both the weaknesses and strengths of current discourse analyses concerned with macro social issues. It is weak in that it lacks any explanation of criteria for choosing the texts and of methods for their analysis and thus raises questions about the legitimacy of the findings. At the same time, it illustrates the potential value such studies have for understanding the wider social, political and economic ideologies embodied in more micro contexts and social relations.

Example 10.1 Sociocultural structures

Lin, A.M. (1997) Analyzing the 'language problem' discourses in Hong Kong: How official, academic, and media discourses construct and perpetuate dominant models of language, learning, and education. *Journal of Pragmatics*, 28: 427–40.

Purpose: The purpose of Lin's analysis is to examine how the 'language problem' has been formulated in official public discourses in Hong Kong.

Data sources: Lin cites the following as sources for her data: government education policy document and reports, academic articles and reports, and public media such as 'influential newspapers' (p. 427). No other information is given on means for assuring that excerpts taken for analysis were representative of the larger corpus.

Data analysis: No specific means for analysing the collected data were given in the report, but it is surmised that a broad-based discourse analytic approach was taken.

Findings: According to Lin, the official documents she examined perpetuate particular conceptualisations of the notions of language, learning and education, including the following:

- The goal of education is to produce a labour force for businesses.
- Schools need to focus on development of learner proficiency in English and Chinese as a means to satisfy economic, political and other demands.
- Language learning goals should be defined by job-market needs.
- Teachers and students are considered 'sub-standard workers and learners' (p. 427).

According to Lin, these conceptualisations 'impose a labor-production model of education, denigrate the value of the child's mother tongue, impose a one-sided cognitive model of language and language learning, assume an ahistorical, non-sociocultural, computer-model of the social actor (e.g. the child, the learner)' (p. 438).

Conclusions: Current discourses are perilous to language learners as they cannot help in the development of effective educational programmes and practices. Official discourses must change to reflect views of language, learning and education that can lead to the development of educational programmes that meet learners' sociocultural needs and 'equip them with the necessary resources to survive and succeed in, as well as to contribute to, our society' (p. 439).

Suggestions for research projects

To recap, research on macro sociocultural structures involves the systematic collection and analysis of contextually situated oral and written texts for the purposes of uncovering the particular ideological assumptions embodied in their linguistic and discursive arrangements. Questions that can guide projects undertaken in this domain include the following: What social, cultural and ideological perspectives about the notions of language and culture are contained in a particular set of classroom texts for English language learners? What are the official language policies embodied in the standard practices of an educational or business organisation? How are these informed by beliefs about language and language users in the larger social context? What political ideologies about race and ethnicity are found in a particular professional organisation and how do they influence the kinds of practices found in that organisation? How do teachers construct learners' identities in their stories about their experiences in their classrooms? How do these constructions reflect the cultural and political ideologies of their educational institution?

Research project 10.1

Perspectives on the English-speaking culture(s) found in textbooks used in EFL classrooms

Identify concerns and pose questions
As we know, the resources and tools we use in our classrooms shape our learners' development in significant ways. Understanding what may be possible for their development in terms of, at the very least, social and cultural understandings requires in part that we understand the social and cultural meanings embodied in the tools and materials we make available to them. Thus, we are led to ask: What are the typical images and themes on culture that are found in one type of instructional tool common to EFL classrooms, textbooks.

Identify appropriate approach and sources of data
A discourse analysis would be the most appropriate approach for this study. Choose texts that are available for use in your classes. Make sure you are able to articulate the criteria you used to make your selections. Since examining every page would make the task unmanageable, choose specific sections from each text to examine. You may choose to look at every other chapter or a certain percentage of chapters from each text.

Collect data
Create a provisional analytic framework to use on which to note and classify the thematic content within each selection. Figure 10.2 is an example of one that can be used, or you can construct one that addresses your particular concerns.

Analyse data
Examine each selection, noting and classifying the content. Once you have examined each selection, look across datasets for recurring themes or concepts, or categories. Quantify the number of units that fit within each (as, for example, percentages) and choose the best, most representative examples for each theme, concept or category. You might construct a diagram to represent the semantic and other relations comprising a theme or

		Representations
	Words and phrases	Visual representations: Where appropriate, note demographics of individuals (e.g. socioeconomic status, gender, race, age), scene and location (e.g. geographical location, urban, rural) and so on.
Topical content Personal life Family life The community Sports Health and welfare Travel Education The workplace Current events Religion Arts, humanities Political systems Science Environment Other		

Figure 10.2   **Analytic framework for analysis of EFL texts**

category. Construct a set of statements about the data that you feel best represent what you found.

Reflect on the findings

What did you find out about the social and cultural content contained in the textbooks? Which findings did you anticipate? Which were most surprising? What might account for these meanings? How relevant are these meanings for your students? How might you add to or in some way change the tools and resources that students will use in the classroom?

Share findings and take action

It is likely that your findings will be of interest to those who teach similar courses. Thus, it would be worth while to share a summary of your findings with your colleagues, either as part of a faculty meeting, or as a posting to an electronic bulletin board for EFL teachers. In addition, you might send your review to a journal for publication consideration.

Research project 10.2

The representation of teenagers in the news

Identify concerns and pose questions

As we know, our social identities are constructed in part by the larger beliefs, practices and ideologies found in the wider social contexts in which we live. Through the various forms of media such as newspapers, television programmes, and magazines individuals are portrayed in certain ways, and these portrayals give shape to our understandings of individuals as social beings. The questions here then are: How are American (or other cultural group) teenagers portrayed in the media? More specifically: How do stories appearing in newspapers portray the lives and activities of teenagers?

Identify appropriate approach and sources of data

The most appropriate approach is discourse analysis. Choose the newspapers from which data will be collected. If you are interested in more local portrayals, then choose newspapers that are community-based. If the concern is with more global portrayals, then choose newspapers with a larger scope, i.e. that are geared to a regional or national market. Whatever choices are made, be sure you can articulate the rationale behind them. Specify the time period over which data collection will occur making sure that you will collect enough data to allow patterns to emerge (e.g. once a day vs once a week).

Collect data

Create a provisional analytic framework to use on which to note and classify the content of the news stories. Figure 10.3 is an example of one that can be used, or you can construct one that addresses your particular concerns.

Analyse data

Total the number of stories found from each newspaper for each collection period. Examine each selection, noting and classifying the content. Once you have examined each selection, look across datasets for recurring themes or concepts, or categories. Quantify the number of units that fit within each and choose the most representative examples for each theme, concept or category. Construct a set of statements about the data that you feel best represent what you found.

Reflect and reconsider

What topics were most frequently dealt with in the news stories? How were youths portrayed in these stories: e.g. Productive contributors to the community? Troublemakers? Sympathetic characters? Difficult to control? Celebrated? Did news stories vary by gender, race, or age? That is, were some groups represented in particular kinds of stories more than others? What

Topics	Demographics (e.g. age, SES*, race gender, ethnicity)	Tone of coverage (i.e. words used to create positive vs negative spin)

Educational issues
Sports,
Lifestyle
Crime (perpetrators/victims)
Accidents
Social health problems
  (e.g. drinking, smoking,
  drugs, eating disorders,
  teen suicide)
Race relations
Employment, workplace
Community activities
Other		

* Socioeconomic Status
Types of story
Illustrative (linking particular story to broader social context)
Event (relating account of a specific event with no link to some broader issue or concern)

Figure 10.3   **Framework for analysis of news stories**

can you conclude about the portrayal of teenagers in news stories? How might these images shape the everyday lives of teenagers in your community?

Share findings and take action
If you work for or are familiar with a youth community organisation, you might want to share your findings with them. Together you can discuss whether the representation of teenagers works to their advantage or disadvantage and together develop ways to enhance their public portrayals.

10.2.2   Institutional contexts

This dimension has to do with the institutional contexts constituting our social communities. These contexts are shaped by specific goals that are drawn from the larger worldviews in which they are nested. These goals, in turn, give shape to particular kinds of communicative activities and particular kinds of social roles and relationships in those contexts. Families, schools, churches, civic organisations, places of work, professional groups, friendship circles, neighbourhood and other social and special-interest clubs and associations are some of the more significant social institutions in which we hold memberships.

The general concern of research in this dimension is with explicating the communicative practices and activities that characterise particular institutional contexts, including the communicative resources and patterns of participation by which the social roles and role relationships within these activities are produced and regulated. That is, it seeks to make visible the socially constituted nature of the institution, the communicative activities comprising the institution, including their relationships to each other, and the communicative means by which individuals are appropriated into or assume particular social roles and role relationships as part of their involvement in these contexts.

The general approach to such studies is ethnographic. Sources of data typically include notes from long-term participant observations, audio- and video-recordings, interviews with participants whose contexts they are, and collections of official documents. Combining the use of the ethnography of communication framework with discourse and conversation analytic techniques to analyse the data allows us to see how more micro-social actions are connected to larger patterns of use, and how these patterns are embedded within and, on another level, help to constitute particular communicative meanings, beliefs and ideologies.

A sampling of research concerned with the institutional context was presented in Chapter 4. Remember the concern here was with documenting learners' communicative worlds outside the classroom with the aim of using them to transform the contexts of the learners' schools. As with research on the more macro issues, doing 'good' research here involves rigorous and systematic use of data collection and analysis methods. Because of the broad range, amount and type of data typically collected for these kinds of studies, it is sometimes easy for researchers to 'get lost' in their data. That is, they may 'lose sight of concrete communication in the sense of actual communities of persons. Forms of formalization, the abstract possibilities of systems, hoped-for keys to mankind as a whole, seem to overthrow the dogged work of making sense of real communities and real lives' (Hymes, 1974: 7). To ensure that the sense being made is reflective of those whose worlds are being studied, it is especially important for researchers to make clear how data were gathered, including the specific sources used, and how reflective of the entire corpus of data are the examples used in the research report.

I have included a short overview of a study of an elementary school programme, (Example 10.2) as an example of the kinds of studies currently being done in applied linguistics concerned with the dimension of institutional context. Like the earlier example, it has both strengths and weaknesses. While it explains more clearly its sources and means of collecting data, it does not make clear how the data were analysed, how the different sources of data were analysed in relation to each other, and how reflective the samples are of the whole body of data. It is useful, however, in demonstrating the links between the members' social actions and the shapes that the communicative worlds in their schooling community take.

Example 10.2 Institutional contexts

Toohey, K. (2000) *Learning English at school: Identity, social relations and classroom practice.* Clevedon: Multilingual Matters.

Purpose: The multipurpose of Toohey's study is to uncover: (a) the specific communicative practices by which a group of language-minority children engage with their teachers and each other over the course of their primary schooling, from kindergarten to grade 2; (b) how these practices distribute and regulate the kinds of social identities and roles the children are socialised into; and (c) the consequences in terms of opportunities for learning afforded by these practices.

Participants: With the help of the kindergarten teacher, Toohey identified six language-minority children attending primary school in a large suburban school district in Canada to follow over the duration of the study. The children represented three different language groups, and for each group, one male and one female child were chosen.

Data sources: Toohey used a variety of sources typical of a broad-based ethnography from which to collect data over a three-year period. For example, she and her research assistants kept field notes while participant-observers in the setting. They also audio- and video-recorded regularly scheduled sessions, and interviewed the teachers and parents of the children several times over the duration of the project.

Data analysis: Little explicit mention is made of the analytic techniques used, but it is surmised that a discourse analysis of the transcribed recordings, interview data and field notes was the primary approach.

Findings: The general finding arising from this longitudinal, ethnographic study is this: the children's opportunities for learning were enhanced in situations where they were given the chance to take on desirable and powerful positions in the situations, when they had access to their peers' expertise, and when they were allowed to play, and use English, with their peers. Influencing the availability of these opportunities were seating arrangements (e.g. *where* children were made to sit for certain activities, and who their seat neighbours were), and the kinds of participation structures afforded by the instructional practices (e.g. teacher-whole group, small group work, individual seat work, and so on).

Conclusion: The kinds of learning opportunities afforded to language-minority children shape their success as learners. Improving language-minority children's learning opportunities involves minimally making teachers aware of how schooling practices shape, in fundamental and consequential ways, these learners' possibilities for success.

Suggestions for research projects

As noted above, the general concern of research in this dimension is with explicating the communicative practices and activities, including participant roles and role relationships, embodied in particular social institutions. Questions to guide research projects in this domain include the following: What communicative practices and activities comprise a particular institution? What beliefs and assumptions about language and culture are embodied in them? Whose interests do these serve? How compatible are the activities within institutions and how do they compare across institutions?

Research project 10.3

Students' funds of knowledge

Identify concerns and pose questions

As we know, students come to school with rich reservoirs of cultural and linguistic knowledge developed in the context of their families upon which teachers can build to create a more meaningful learning environment in the classroom. To uncover some of the knowledge and skills your students already possess, you can conduct a funds of knowledge project, based on the work done by Luis Moll and his associates and described in Chapter 4. A question that can guide your research is: What funds of knowledge and resources do students bring with them from their home contexts?

Identify appropriate approach and sources of data

One approach appropriate for this study is discourse analysis. A primary means for collecting data can be through interviews and questionnaires with your students and their families. In addition to being primary sources of data, students can also be involved as co-investigators and asked to conduct interviews or complete questionnaires with their family members. They can also be asked to create portfolios in which they include written, visual, graphic, audio, video and other kinds of materials that they feel best represent their home communities.

Collect data

Together with the students develop an interview protocol or questionnaire they can use with their family members. Develop a time line for conducting the interviews and completing the questionnaires. Since the findings are to be used to transform your classroom environment, it is advisable to conduct the study early in the school year. Provide students with guidelines for creating home portfolios along with a deadline for completing them.

Analyse data

Together with students, read the transcribed interviews and completed questionnaires, noting recurring themes and topical patterns. Follow the same procedure for the portfolios. Summarise and arrange the findings from the interviews, questionnaires and student portfolios into particular funds of knowledge.

Reflect on the findings

What funds of knowledge do students bring with them to school? How similar or different are they across students? How do they compare with the school's funds of knowledge as represented in the curricular and instructional practices and policies? What do they tell you about the needs, interests, and abilities of your students? How do they compare with the funds of knowledge you bring from your home context? How might they be incorporated into your classroom learning community?

Share findings and take action

Together with the students, design means for sharing what you have learned with the larger school community. You might also create a web site and invite other school communities to do similar kinds of project. Also consider presenting your findings to a professional group of teachers. What you have learned may help them to decide to make changes to their own classroom communities.

Research Project 10.4

Family literacy practices in multilingual environments

Identify concern and pose questions

While we know that many families arriving to our communities come with many languages, often within the same family, we know far less about how families with multiple languages manage their communicative experiences, and more particularly their literacy practices. Thus, the question guiding this project is: What are the literacy practices of one multilingual family?

Identify appropriate approach and sources of data

The approach to take here is broadly ethnographic, including methods typical of an ethnography of communication to capture the range and scope of literacy practices, and discourse analytic methods for analysis of written documents that include transcriptions of taped conversations and interviews with participants, and the materials they use in their literacy practices (e.g. books, newspapers, lists, letters, etc.). Given the range of data to be collected, it is most feasible to begin with one family. The findings here can lead to new questions for exploration with additional multilingual families.

Collect data

Collecting data involves long-term participation with the group of participants. It can include regular conversations with the family to discuss literacy practices and their perceptions of them; observations of the individual family members as they go about their daily lives to uncover the ways that literacy practices enter into and are used by the individuals to construct their worlds; and collection of materials that are important to the group in terms of what they read and what they write.

Analyse data

Transcribe the videotapes and identify the common features of the literacy practices. Use Hymes's SPEAKING model as a beginning framework. Describe the patterned uses of print, the codes of language they involve, and interpret the conventional meanings in light of how they are used by the family. In addition, analyse your field notes and participant interviews for recurring themes and use them to help explain the literacy activities in light of the larger social and cultural contexts.

Reflect on the findings

What literacy practices are most commonly engaged in by this family? Do they vary by language? What do the practices mean to the family? Do the meanings vary by family role (e.g. parent vs child)? How important are they to maintaining their identities as multilinguals? How closely are they supported by the larger social community?

Share findings and take action

Your findings will have much to offer teachers and administrators in K-12 schools and adult education programmes, and both local and state policy makers. You might consider offering workshops on your findings for these groups. You might also see if there is interest among families in your community who have similar multilingual backgrounds in organising and participating in literacy-based clubs.

10.2.3   Communicative activities

This third dimension is concerned with the identification and characterisation of the communicative activities sustaining, and sustained by, a particular institutional context. In addition to everyday activities by which institutional members of particular communities live their lives, attention is also given to those practices by which novice members or newcomers are apprenticed into the institution's activities and the specific means by which they are assessed or evaluated as bona fide members. Communicative activities include oral and written events as well as those accomplished with electronic means, such as e-mailing and electronic bulletin board postings.

The aim of research in this dimension is to identify, describe, interpret and ultimately explain the locally situated meanings of the communicative actions by which individuals jointly produce their encounters. The focus here is not on individuals within their activities, but on the particular activities that shape and are shaped by individual involvement.

Several approaches can be used to accomplish the goals of this dimension. Ethnographies of communication are typically used to uncover the conventional linguistic patterns of participation and communicative plans shared by group members and by which they accomplish their activities. If the activity is accomplished through face-to-face interaction, conversation analysis is sometimes combined with the more general ethnographic analyses to uncover the particular interactional features oriented to by the participants to produce order in the conversation. Studies like that by Jacoby and Gonzales (1991) and Capps and Ochs (1995), noted in Chapter 2, are good examples of how to combine ethnography of communication methods with more detailed analyses of conversation.

Studies can also take an interactional sociolinguistic approach to examine points of *mis*-communication to uncover differences in meanings attributed to particular cues. Examples of such studies were presented in Chapters 2 and 8. Finally, discourse analysis can be used to uncover particular linguistic cues used to index larger contextual meanings. Examples of studies taking a discourse analytic approach were presented in Chapter 8.

Similar to the studies undertaken in the other two dimensions, in addition to audio- and video-recordings of the encounters, data sources include field notes taken from participant-observations, and interviews with the participants themselves. The sampling of studies of communicative activities cited in Chapter 1, the language socialisation practices reviewed in Chapter 3, and the review of communicative activities particular to classrooms reviewed in Chapter 5, are examples of the kinds of studies typical of this dimension. In addition, I have included a short overview of a study (Example 10.3) which examines one particular activity, testing routines, as instantiated in the classroom practices of three different teachers. It is notable that in her report, the author provides details on her sources of data, and the methods she used to gather and analyse them. As pointed out earlier, such information helps the reader to make sense of and evaluate how well the findings represent the larger corpus of collected data.

Example 10.3 Communicative activities

Poole, D. (1994) Routine testing practices and the linguistic construction of knowledge. *Cognition and Instruction*, 12 (2): 125–50.

Purpose: The purpose of Poole's study is to examine how routine classroom testing events are linguistically encoded, and within these events how curricular knowledge is encoded.

Data source: The data were gathered over a four-month period from the classrooms of three teachers each from a different junior high school, all located in an urban area of southern California. They included field notes taken during observations of 50 class hours, audio- and video-recordings of 39 of these class hours, informal discussions with the teachers, and more structured interviews at the end of the data collection period. Data selected for analysis included the following identified activities: two pre-test reviews, six post-test reviews, and the written tests which constituted the focus of the reviews.

Data analysis: Poole used modified conversation analytic techniques to transcribe the recordings of the pre- and post-test reviews, and used an ethnography of communication approach to identify, describe and interpret the meanings of the recurring patterns in the conversations, including speech acts and speech act sequencing.

Findings: One of the findings that emerged from Poole's analysis revealed that the curricular content in these sessions was encoded primarily through IRE sequences 'that take the form of *"test-questions"* or incomplete sentence frames' (p. 130). The questions themselves were largely display or known-answer questions such as 'Where was the Whiskey Rebellion?' and 'What did the immigration act of 1924 do?' Moreover, the questions asked in the pre- and post-test reviews reflected the kinds of questions found on the written tests. For example, the question above asked by the teacher about the immigration act appeared in this exact form on the written test. Student responses, both in the reviews and on the test, were primarily limited to short noun-phrases.

Conclusion: The kinds of questions asked in the pre- and post-test reviews, and again on the written texts, as well as the student responses such questions led to, constituted knowledge as 'objectifiable, seemingly value-free form of knowledge presentation' (p. 143). Poole argues that long-term engagement of the learners in such events socialises them into a limited, constraining understanding of knowledge as discrete, isolatable display of facts. She calls for alternative forms of assessment in which 'school-valued knowledge can be assessed in a more complex form' (p. 144).

Suggestions for research projects

As noted above, this dimension is concerned with identifying, characterising and explaining the meanings of the particular communicative tools and resources used by individuals to produce their communicative activities. Also of concern are the means by which newcomers or novices are socialised into full, competent participation. The focus here is not so much on individuals within their activities, but on the particular activities that shape and are shaped by individual engagement. Research projects seek answers to such questions as: What are the communicative means and plans constitutive of a communicative activity determined to be significant to the lived experiences of the members of a particular institutional context? What social identities and role relationships are made available to the participants in the activity? How are newcomers and other novices oriented to and appropriated into legitimate participation? Where does long-term use of the activity's mediated means lead the participants in terms of what they learn and how they learn it?

Research project 10.5

Social activity in a retirement community

Identify concern and pose questions

Communicative activities are important means by which individuals and groups enact and construct their everyday worlds. While there has been much recent work on activities of youths and schooling communities, far fewer studies have been done on adults, and in particular, on adults living in retirement communities. Those interested in this population might be interested in conducting a project that examines this group more closely. One question to guide the project is: What is one communicative activity that is important to creating and maintaining social affiliation in a retirement community?

Identify appropriate approach and sources of data

Ethnography of communication would be an appropriate approach. The choice of a particular community depends on your professional and practical interests. The choice of particular activity should be determined after you have spent time with the community.

Collect data

This study requires long-term involvement in the community as an observer or participant-observer. In addition to making multiple video-recordings of the activity of interest, keep field notes of your own observations and experiences, interview the participants for their reflections and observations, and collect all related materials, artifacts, documents and written records.

Analyse data

Transcribe the videotapes and identify the features important to the accomplishment of the activity. Construct a framework of the conventional or typical sequence of communicative actions as they unfold in the activity. Describe the patterned uses of language and interpret their conventional meanings in light of how they are used by the participants to take action.

The SPEAKING framework would be useful here in describing the activity. In addition, analyse your field notes and participant interviews for recurring themes and use them to help to explain the activity in light of the larger social and cultural contexts it helps to (re)create in the community.

Reflect on the findings

What did you find about the particular communicative activity? How is it typically enacted? What functions does it play in the larger community? Whose interests does it seem to serve? How do participants feel about it? What new knowledge or understanding about this community can you take from your study? What might your next steps be?

Share findings and take action

Depending on your professional role, you can decide to share your findings with those who work in or aspire to work in retirement communities. You can also present your findings to a professional organisation concerned with ageing and language use. More informally, you can post your findings to a professional electronic bulletin board.

Research project 10.6

Classroom discourse and language learning

Identify concern and pose questions

As discussed in Chapter 5, the discourse of classrooms is consequential to learners' development in that it helps to shape both the processes and products of learning. If you are concerned with improving classroom conditions for foreign language learning, one place to begin is by examining the discourse of these classrooms. A basic question to guide this project is: what are the intellectual and practical activities that teachers and students construct in and through their discourse in a foreign language classroom?

Identify appropriate approach and sources of data

Ethnography of communication would be an appropriate approach to uncovering the communicative activities comprising the discourse of a classroom community. The level and grade of the foreign language classroom will depend on your own professional interests.

Collect data

To get a sense of the conventional practices constituted in the classroom discourse requires long-term involvement in the community. How often you visit the classroom depends on how long the course runs. If, for example, it runs for an entire academic year, you might decide to collect data once a week. If it is much shorter, say an 8-week course, you should probably plan on collecting data a few times a week. In addition to audio- and video-recording the classroom activities, keep field notes, collect related materials and artifacts, and plan to interview the teacher and students for their perceptions.

Analyse data

The first step of the analysis involves transcribing the recordings. The second involves coding the discourse into its constituent activities. You might consider involving the teacher in constructing the official coding scheme. On the transcriptions, ask her to indicate what was happening, i.e. the purpose(s) directing the interaction, and label the various activities embedded in the talk accordingly. She might use labels such as 'transitioning', 'disciplining a student' and 'drilling subject/verb agreement'. She can also be asked to indicate points in the talk where these activities began and ended, and where she was unsure of what was going on. Hymes's SPEAKING model would be helpful as a descriptive framework. Another step involves constructing a framework of the conventional or typical sequence of utterances as it unfolded in a particular activity. In addition, analyse your field notes and participant interviews for recurring themes and use them to help explain the significance of the activities to the classroom community.

Reflect on the findings

What kinds of activities are typical of the discourse of this foreign language community? Were any a surprise to you? To the teacher? What kinds of communicative activities and understandings of language are students being socialised into?

Share findings and take action

Together with the teacher, you might consider how to change or enhance the classroom discourse so that it provides more opportunities for student involvement and for their using language that is communicatively rich. You might also co-present your findings at a meeting of foreign language educators.

10.2.4   Individual experiences

The final dimension focuses on the 'intersection of biographical experience and social involvements' (Layder, 1993: 9). That is, the concern is
with individuals' experiences within their communicative worlds. This
focus differs from a concern with communicative activities, described
above, in that it gives attention to 'the way individuals respond to, and
are affected by, their social involvements as against a focus on the *nature*
of the social involvements themselves' (ibid.: p. 74; emphasis in the
original).

Such a focus includes concerns with how individuals use the cues
available to them in their communicative encounters to both index and
construct their everyday worlds. It focuses, in particular, on the ways
individuals index and construct their social identities and roles and those
of others in light of the kinds of identities and roles into which they have
been ascribed or socialised. In addition, attention is given to the ways that
individuals use language in the construction of concepts such as motivation, voice, affiliation, agency and competence. Remember, as with social
identities and roles, these constructs are considered to be fundamentally
social, developed within and thus contingent on individuals' particular
experiences in their social worlds.

Like studies of communicative activities, studies here can take different
approaches. Sources of data typically include field notes from participant-
observations of individuals' biographical experiences, and interviews
and conversations with the individuals, in addition to audio- and video-
recordings of their experiences. The conventions of language use uncovered by ethnographies of communication can allow closer inspection of
how individuals orient to their conventionality. The study by Hall (1993c)
mentioned in Chapter 1, for example, provides a microscopic look at how
one individual manipulated in creative ways a particular convention associated with the activity of gossiping – an activity that had much social
significance to the individual's social community – to raise her status as a
participant in the activity.

Both interactional sociolinguistics and discourse analytic approaches
also permit a focus on individual use of language. Shea's (1994) study of
a non-native English speaker's experiences with two different academic
advisers, discussed earlier in Chapter 2, is an example of a study that used
IS to reveal how an individual's competence in accomplishing a goal was
constructed in part by his interlocutor's willingness to participate in the
encounter. Rampton's (1995) study, also discussed in Chapter 2, takes a
discourse analytic approach to the study of how individuals communicatively experience their social worlds. Remember, his study was concerned
with the varied ways that adolescents living in multi-ethnic communities
used the linguistic resources available in their communities to stake out

their positionings in particular interactions and create particular social identities. Chapter 2 discussed some additional studies concerned with language use at the level of the individual. Finally, microgenetic methods are particularly useful for investigating change on the level of the individual. An extended example of such a study by Kim and Hall (2002) was presented in Chapter 8.

I have included a short overview of a study by Betsy Rymes, in Example 10.4, on the linguistic cues used by a group of students to construct themselves as particular kinds of individuals in stories they tell about their experiences of dropping out of school. Similar to Poole, Rymes provides needed detail on the sources of the narratives, and the means by which she collected and analysed them. While the analysis remains at the interpretive level, it is useful nonetheless in demonstrating how linguistic resources are used to index agency in even the most mundane of narratives.

Suggestions for research projects

To recap, the concern of this dimension is with individuals' experiences within their communicative worlds and, in particular, with how they use the cues available to them to both index and construct their everyday worlds, and their social identities and roles and those of others in light of the kinds of identities and roles into which they have been ascribed or socialised. In addition, attention is given to the ways that individuals use language in the construction of socially mediated concepts such as motivation, voice, affiliation, accommodation, agency and competence. Questions that studies in this dimension seek to answer include: How are the communicative resources of a practice used by participants to index their individual, social and cultural identities? How do individuals position themselves linguistically and otherwise in terms of the kinds of identities and role relationships made available to them in their communicative practices? Which voices seem more privileged or engender more authority, and which social identities are being made relevant? How are these identities reshaped by individuals as they make their way in their activities and with what communicative means? How do the participants appropriate the resources of others for their own purposes? What are the different means by which individuals accommodate to, resist, or actively oppose their involvement in particular communicative activities? What are the social, cognitive, linguistic and other consequences arising from an individual's long-term participation in particular communicative activities? What do individuals believe about their roles as participants and how, if at all, do these beliefs shape what they do?

Example 10.4 Individual experiences

Rymes, B. (2001) *Conversational borderlands: Language and identity in an alternative urban high school*. New York: Teachers College Press.

Purpose: One of the purposes of Betsy Rymes' study of a short-lived charter school in California is to describe the linguistic resources used by a group of students from the school to tell their stories of 'dropping out' of traditional public schools. She looks in particular at how they construct themselves as moral agents in these stories.

Data source: Her analysis is based on 12 video-recorded narratives told by eight Latino students between the ages of 15 and 18, four of whom are men and four of whom are women.

Data analysis: Rymes combines ethnographic data with a discourse analytical approach to describe and interpret the meanings of the particular resources used by the students in their stories.

Findings: Rymes found that these students render their leave-taking from traditional schools as reasonable and honourable responses to the difficult situations in which they found themselves through the use of several grammatical cues. One cue for doing so involved the use of progressive aspect to signal the durative nature of troublesome, or unmanageable actions in these situations. In describing the atmosphere of the school from which she eventually dropped out, for example, one student stated, 'if they want you bad *they'll be waiting for you*' (p. 43; emphasis in the original). Another student marked an enduring antagonistic relationship with a teacher as her reason for dropping out, stating, 'and *he was looking for me* that's why I couldn't go there anymore 'cause I knew if I would go there I would get in trouble.' (p. 44; emphasis in the original).

Another grammatical cue used by these students to evoke an ongoing antagonistic atmosphere was through the use of the non-referential or exist-ential 'it' and 'there' as in 'it's rough' and 'there's a lotta gangs' (p. 45) to describe their situations. According to Rymes, these forms 'convey a general presence, an atmospheric surround within which "the problem starts"' (p. 50). In these same narratives, the students use particular means to con-struct their involvement in the events leading up to their dropping out in such a way as to engender the sympathy of their interlocutors. They often use the pronouns 'they', 'everybody' and 'everyone' as agents and position themselves as involuntary objects of these agents' actions as in the following: "cause *they got me* from the back boom boom boom', 'everybody rushed me', and 'everybody was socking me hitting me' (pp. 54–5; emphasis in the original).

Conclusion: Rymes concludes that the study of the use of particular gram-matical cues in individual narratives can reveal the intricate ways that indi-viduals position themselves in their worlds.

Research project 10.7

Perceptions of identity and agency in narratives of bilingual speakers

Identify concerns and pose questions
The ways in which we use language in our communicative activities depend in part on our notions of identity and agency, that is, who we perceive ourselves to be, how we think others see us and how we would like others to perceive us. Understanding the everyday worlds of bilingual speakers requires in part our coming to understand their own understandings of themselves as language users. The question guiding this project is: How do a group of adult bilingual speakers perceive themselves as language users, and how do they construct their identities in the stories they tell about themselves?

Identify appropriate approach and sources of data
Narrative analysis would be an appropriate approach. The sources depend on the group you are interested in. If you are a teacher, you might want to gather narratives from a group of students. If your interest is the workplace, consider gathering narratives from bilingual individuals who hold positions in your field. The number of narratives collected depends on the context in which you are conducting your study and the kinds of claims you hope to make.

Collect data
Ask participants to provide written personal narratives. You can provide prompts such as 'How did you learn your two languages?' or 'How important are they to you?' rather than simply asking them to 'Write about yourself'. In a class situation, you might first read and discuss narratives written by other bilingual speakers, such as *Hunger for Memory* by Richard Rodriguez to get them thinking about the issues of identity and language.

Analyse data
First, decide on the features you wish to examine. They can include, for example, themes and topics, and use of pronouns and other linguistic markers to index in-group vs out-group identities, or to create themselves as characters in plots of their stories. You can also examine words they use to describe and thus construct themselves and others as certain kinds of individuals in relation to particular contexts or events and the particular languages they speak. You might choose to quantify the number of units that fit within each feature. Next, identify, describe and interpret the meanings of the patterned uses of the features. Construct a set of statements about the data that you feel best represent what you found.

Reflect on the findings

How do these individuals perceive themselves as language users? What identities are relevant to them? How do they position themselves in relation to others in their worlds? To the social contexts they consider significant? How do their perceptions compare across the group?

Share findings and take action

There are several electronic websites devoted to bilingualism where you can post your findings. If your participants were also your students, you might discuss the implications of the findings with them.

Research project 10.8

A bilingual child's use of language in play activities

Identify concern and pose questions

While there is much evidence on the linguistic features of child bilingual development, less is known about their communicative development in specific contexts of language use. In order to understand more fully the directions the language development of children who are raised as simultaneous bilinguals can take, these contexts need closer examination. Thus, a question to guide this research project is: How does a child being raised bilingually use her two languages to constitute her involvement in play?

Identify appropriate approach and sources of data

A microethnographic analysis of play events is an appropriate approach. Because of the detailed focus on language use, the number of participants can be small. In this case, one focal child and her involvement in play events with her adult caregivers can be used. If each caregiver interacts with the child in one of the two languages (e.g. mother interacts in English, the father in German), the dataset should include an equal number of play events for each language.

Collect data

Set up a video-recorder in the room where the child plays and record the play events as they take place. Decide on a time period for collecting the data. You should have enough data to be able to justify claims about the typicality of the child's language use in her play events.

Analyse data

After first transcribing the recordings, code each utterance according to language code (i.e. German or English). Utterances containing morphological or lexical items from both languages should be coded as mixed. Also code each utterance for its communicative intent (e.g. agreeing, confirming, directing, requesting). Quantify codings for each event, and search across datasets for regularities or patterns in terms of language code use and function and choose examples from the data that best illustrate the patterns found. Construct a set of statements about the data that you feel best represent them.

Reflect on the findings
What languages did the child use in her interactions with the adult caregivers? How closely did her code use correspond to the language used by each interlocutor? What functions typify her utterances? Do they vary by code use? By interlocutor? By play event? How might you characterise the child's involvement with each interlocutor? What conclusions can you draw about the child's communicative development in the two languages?

Share findings and take action
Consider writing up your report of the study and submitting to a journal concerned with bilingualism and child development.

10.3 Summary

The ideas presented in this chapter are meant to help newcomers to the field and others who are not familiar with a sociocultural perspective to get some idea of the range of possibilities for exploration. The framework highlighting the multiple dimensions of research contexts not only helps us to conceptualise the multiple layers of our social worlds, it also provides a guide for identifying possible topics and questions for undertaking research. While the possibilities are unlimited, the focus of any investigation depends on one's particular circumstances, interests and needs.

Without a doubt, conducting research on language, culture and learning from a sociocultural perspective is both labour and time intensive, and thus, requires a fairly strong commitment to engaging in 'the dogged work of making sense of real communities and real lives' (Hymes, 1974: 7). Such work is typically not for those who are looking for quick studies, with simple answers. Rather, it is for those who enjoy exploring, who are not discouraged by what can sometimes seem to be unruly ways of living, and who are willing to persevere despite the bumps and obstacles they are likely to encounter in their journeys. Chapter 11, the last chapter, contains lists of relevant journals, professional organisations and websites where readers can find additional materials, resources and tools to aid them in their explorations.

IV Resources for teaching and researching language and culture

Resources for teaching and researching language and culture

This chapter will . . .

- provide a list of journals that publish studies on language and culture;
- provide a list of professional organisations for applied linguistics;
- provide a list of web-based resources for teaching and researching language and culture.

11.1 Introduction

Increased world-wide access to electronic network capabilities such as the World-Wide Web has changed the ways in which we stay in touch with current practices in the field and communicate and connect with others. We can now gain entry to myriad research and teaching sites, connect with colleagues around the world, and both present and respond to innovations almost as quickly as they are developed. The purpose of this chapter is to provide some web-based resources to get readers started in their own explorations in the teaching and researching of language and culture. The information here is in no way meant to be comprehensive. Rather, the intent is to provide an initial chart of possible connections and linkages that readers can pursue according to their interests and needs. No doubt readers will uncover additional sites on their journeys.

Presented first is an annotated list of journals that publish articles on matters related to teaching and researching language and culture. Included for each is the website address where additional information, including submission and subscription guidelines, can be found. Also included is an annotated list, including website addresses, of some of the major professional organisations for applied linguists. Membership information and other material can be found at each organisation's website. Finally, the chapter includes an annotated list of web-based resources pertinent to teaching and researching language and culture. Each site contains fairly extensive sets of links to a variety of topics that, for the most part, are geared specifically to applied linguists.

11.2   Journals

Included here is an abridged annotated list of journals where the reader is likely to find articles that treat the topics discussed in the text.

Annual Review of Applied Linguistics
[http://uk.cambridge.org/journals/apl/intro.htm]
This journal, published once a year, provides a comprehensive, up-to-date review of research in key areas in the broad field of applied linguistics. Each issue is thematic, covering the topic by means of critical summaries, overviews and bibliographic citations.

Anthropology & Education Quarterly
[http://new.aaanet.org/cae/aeq/]
This peer-reviewed journal publishes scholarship on schooling in social and cultural contexts and on human learning both inside and outside schools. Articles rely primarily on ethnographic research to address immediate problems of practice as well as broad theoretical questions. It is the journal of the Council on Anthropology and Education, a professional association of anthropologists and educational researchers and a section of the American Anthropological Association.

Applied Linguistics
[http://www3.oup.co.uk/jnls/list/applij/]
This quarterly journal publishes research on language with relevance to real world problems. It encourages principled and multidisciplinary approaches to research on language-related concerns and welcomes contributions that reflect critically on current practices in applied linguistic research.

Canadian Modern Language Review
[http://www.utpjournals.com/cmlr/cmlr.html]
This quarterly journal publishes peer-reviewed articles on all aspects of language learning and teaching. Article topics range from ESL, to French immersion, to international languages, to native languages. The journal's issues include reviews of relevant books and software, along with helpful teaching techniques and plans.

Discourse & Society
[http://www.sagepub.co.uk/journals/details/j0115.html]
This is a multidisciplinary journal that publishes research at the boundaries of discourse analysis and the social sciences. It focuses in particular on the discursive dimensions of social and political issues and problems, and encourages contributions that relate the situational micro-context of verbal interaction, discourse and communication to the macro-context of social, political and cultural structures.

The ELT Journal
[http://www3.oup.co.uk/eltj/scope/]
This quarterly publication is for those in the field of teaching English as a second or foreign language. Its goal is to provide an interdisciplinary forum for discussion of the pedagogical principles and practices that shape the ways in which the English language is taught around the world.

International Journal of Bilingualism
[http://www.ncl.ac.uk/speech/research/ijb.htm]
This journal is for the dissemination of research on linguistic, psychological, neurological, and social issues emerging from language contact, with particular interest in the language behaviour of bi- and multilingual individuals.

International Journal of Bilingual Education and Bilingualism
[http://www.multilingual-matters.co.uk/multi/journals_info.asp]
The focus of this journal is on international developments, initiatives, ideas and research related to bilingualism and bilingual education.

Issues in Applied Linguistics
[http://www.humnet.ucla.edu/humnet/teslal/ial/]
Started in November of 1989, this refereed journal is managed, edited and published by graduate students of the UCLA Department of Applied Linguistics. Published twice a year, its aim is to publish outstanding research from students, faculty and independent researchers in the broad areas of discourse analysis, sociolinguistics, language acquisition, language analysis, language assessment, language education, language use and research methodology.

Journal of Language, Identity and Education
[http://www.asu.edu/educ/epsa/JLIE.htm]
The focus of this peer-reviewed quarterly journal is on rigorous research and critical scholarship that helps to define and promote inquiry concerned with broad educational issues related to language and identity. They seek contributions that reflect diverse theoretical and methodological frameworks and deal with areas such as educational policy regarding cultural and linguistic diversity, research on schooling practices for linguistically and

culturally diverse student populations, multilingualism and multiliteracy, and the role of indigenous languages and language varieties in education.

Journal of Multilingual and Multicultural Development
[http://www.multilingual-matters.co.uk/multi/journals_info.asp]
This journal publishes articles on the many aspects of multilingualism and multiculturalism, including theoretical essays, reports of research studies, descriptions of educational policies and systems, and accounts of teaching and assessment procedures.

Language and Communication
[http://www.elsevier.nl/inca/publications/store/6/1/6/]
This peer-reviewed journal provides a forum for the discussion of topics and issues in communication by publishing contributions from researchers in all fields relevant to the study of verbal and non-verbal communication.

Language, Culture and Curriculum
[http://www.multilingual-matters.com/multi/journals_lcc.asp?TAG
=BX165X8X687879961UTDAJ&CID=]
This journal publishes articles that discuss the myriad social, cultural, cognitive and organisational factors relevant to the formulation and implementation of language curricula. Second languages and minority and heritage languages are a special concern.

Language & Intercultural Communication
[http://www.multilingual-matters.com/multi/journals_laic.asp?TAG
=BX165X8X687879961UTDAJ&CID=]
The goal of this journal is on promoting an understanding of the relationship between language and intercultural communication that can lead to personal development and international understanding, dialogue and cooperation. It seeks publications that explore new ways of understanding intercultural relationships, the linguistic and communicative aspects of intercultural communication, and the pedagogical implications of these strands of research.

Language in Society
[http://uk.cambridge.org/journals/lsy/intro.htm]
This international journal is concerned with all branches of speech and language as aspects of social life. Published quarterly, the journal includes empirical articles of general theoretical, comparative or methodological interest. In addition to original articles, the journal publishes numerous reviews of the latest important books in the field.

Linguistics and Education
[http://peabody.vanderbilt.edu/depts/tandl/faculty/Bloome/
Linguisticsed.html]
The purpose of this journal is to disseminate research and other scholarly works, and to facilitate discussion and inquiry on all topics related to

linguistics and education, broadly defined. Such topics include classroom interaction, language diversity in educational settings, language policy and curriculum, written language learning and the application of discourse analysis, social semiotics, conversational analysis, and ethnomethodology to educational issues.

Mind, Culture and Activity
[http://lchc.ucsd.edu/MCA/Journal/moremca.html]
Published quarterly, this journal publishes articles that address the relationship among mind, culture and activity. Readership is quite broad and includes anthropologists, psychologists, linguists, sociologists and educators.

Modern Language Journal
[http://polyglot.lss.wisc.edu/mlj/about.mlj.htm]
This quarterly refereed journal is devoted to questions and concerns about the learning and teaching of foreign and second languages. It publishes articles, research studies, editorials, reports, book reviews and professional news and announcements pertaining to modern languages, including TESL.

Pragmatics
[http://ipra-www.uia.ac.be/ipra/]
This is the quarterly publication of the International Pragmatics Association. In addition to regular scientific articles, research reports and occasional discussions, it contains a bulletin section with book notices, the annual list of members, and occasional announcements.

Research on Language and Social Interaction
[http://www.erlbaum.com/Journals/journals/RLSI/rlsi.htm]
This journal publishes research about language and other social codes that are consequential for interaction; and the structure, dynamics, or functions of social interaction. It welcomes studies of talk in interaction; linguistic pragmatic work; strategic analyses of discourse; investigations of the relationship between speech communities and language-related behaviours; and research on the values and motives, and practices and constraints on interaction. Research may involve conversation analysis, discourse analysis, quantitative coding, interviewing, and analyses of observational, document or archival data.

TESOL Quarterly
[http://www.tesol.org/pubs/magz/tq.html]
Published by the TESOL organisation, *TESOL Quarterly* is a professional, refereed journal that publishes contributions on topics of significance to the broad field of English language teaching. It seeks articles that draw from research into linguistic anthropology, communication, applied linguistics and education and address pedagogical implications of the research.

11.3   Professional organisations

Listed here are a few of the many organisations for applied linguists. Readers who are interested in locating and joining a national or regional organisation specifically for applied linguists should consult the web site of AILA, the International Association of Applied Linguistics, for a list of world-wide affiliates.

AILA –
[http://www.aila.ac/]
Founded in 1964, AILA (International Association of Applied Linguistics/ Association Internationale de Linguistique Appliquée) is the premier international association for applied linguists world wide linking 37 national and regional applied linguistics associations. Its purpose is to promote research, scholarship and practice in applied linguistics, to foster language pluralism and ensure equal access to all members. It holds a triennial world congress of applied linguistics, supports the research of more than 20 scientific commissions, and collaborates with other organisations with related objectives and goals. Some of the major national and regional associations of applied linguists include American Association for Applied Linguistics (AAAL), the Applied Linguistics Association of Australia (ALAA) and the British Association for Applied Linguistics (BAAL).

American Association of Applied Linguistics
[http://www.aaal.org]
Founded in 1977, the American Association for Applied Linguistics (AAAL) promotes principled approaches to language-related concerns, including language education, acquisition and loss, bilingualism, discourse analysis, literacy, rhetoric and stylistics, language for special purposes, psycholinguistics, second and foreign language pedagogy, language assessment, and language policy and planning.

Applied Linguistics Association of Australia
[http://www.arts.usyd.edu.au/Arts/departs/langcent/alaa/]
Established in 1976, the Applied Linguistics Association of Australia (ALAA) includes both national and international members. ALAA organises an annual conference, produces the journal *Australian Review of Applied Linguistics*, edits occasional papers in applied linguistics, provides scholarships for high-quality student research in areas of applied linguistics, jointly sponsors the Australian Linguistics Institute with the Australian Linguistic Society, and more recently has established an online discussion group, APPLIX, which is open to anyone interested in the area of applied linguistics.

British Association of Applied Linguistics
[http://www.baal.org.uk/]
The British Association of Applied Linguistics is a professional association
of applied linguists based in the UK. In addition to organising regularly
scheduled scientific meetings, BAAL publishes a newsletter and conference proceedings, and awards an annual Book Prize.

The International Society for Cultural and Activity Research
[http://www.iscrat.org]
The International Society for Cultural and Activity Research theory (ISCAR)
brings together researchers in both Eastern and Western European countries whose interests are tied to a cultural–historical approach to human
development. The organisation sponsors world congresses, held every four
years, which bring together scholars from disciplines such as psychology,
education, anthropology, linguistics, philosophy, semiotics and communication to foster interdisciplinary cooperation and discussion.

The International Society for Language Studies
[http://137.99.89.70:8002/isls/]
This association is for those interested in critical discourse and research in
language matters, broadly conceived. Established in 2002, the association
hosts a website and produces a web-based newsletter.

International Pragmatics Association
[http://ipra-www.uia.ac.be/ipra/]
The International Pragmatics Association (IPrA) is an international
scientific organisation devoted to the study of language use. Established
in 1986, it now has over 1,000 members in over 60 countries world wide.
It is a recognised member of the Consortium of Affiliates for International
Programs of the American Association for the Advancement of Science.

Linguistic Society of America
[www.lsadc.org]
The purpose of the Linguistic Society of America is the advancement of
the scientific study of language. Its website contains links to the organisation's calendar of events, including information on their annual conference
and the annual summer institute. It also has links to its publications,
including the journal *Language*.

SIETAR
[http://www.sietarinternational.org/]
Founded in 1974, the Society for Intercultural Education, Training and
Research (SIETAR) is the world's largest interdisciplinary association
devoted to intercultural communication. Its primary goal is to encourage
and support the development and application of values, knowledge and
skills that promote beneficial and long-lasting intercultural and interethnic

relations at the individual, group, organisation and community levels. SIETAR is affiliated with the Council of Europe and holds Non-Governmental Organisation (NGO) status with the United Nations.

TESOL
[www.tesol.org]
Teachers of English to Speakers of Other Languages, Inc. (TESOL) is an international education association, with over 10,000 members. In addition to sponsoring an annual convention, the association offers seminars and workshops on topics of interest to teachers. It also produces several publications including *TESOL Quarterly*, a scholarly journal, *TESOL Journal*, a practical magazine, *TESOL Matters*, the association's newspaper and several published books and materials on a wide range of topics.

11.4   Web-based resources for teaching and researching language and culture

Included here is a list of web-based repositories containing an extensive range of links to resources, materials and tools useful for teaching and researching language and culture.

Action Research
[http://carbon.cudenver.edu/~mryder/itc/act_res.html]
This site, maintained by the University of Colorado at Denver School of Education, provides links to overviews, articles, projects and resources on action research.

Center for Applied Linguistics (CAL)
[http://www.cal.org/]
CAL is a private, non-profit organisation for scholars and educators interested in how findings from linguistics and related sciences are being used to address language-related problems. The site includes links to a wide range of topics including research, teacher education, design and development of instructional materials, technical assistance, programme evaluation and policy analysis.

Child language data exchanges system (CHILDES)
[http://childes.psy.cmu.edu/]
CHILDES provides tools for studying conversational interactions. These tools include a database of transcripts, programmes for computer analysis of transcripts, methods for linguistic coding, and systems for linking transcripts to digitised audio and video.

Communication Institute for Online Scholarship (CIOS)
[http://www.cios.org/www/CIOS.htm]
CIOS online services provide access to thousands of files in the resource
library as well as dozens of scholarly conferences enrolling over 4,000 professionals and students. Also available is the online journals index database
indexing more than 36,500 bibliographic references from 78 communication journals and electronic white pages for more than 5,000 professionals
and students in the communications field.

The Cooperative Learning Center
[http://www.clcrc.com/]
This is the website for the Cooperative Learning Center, a research and
training centre on cooperative learning methods and techniques at the
University of Minnesota and directed by David and Roger Johnson. The
site includes links to essays on cooperative learning and lists of resources.

The Educational Resources Information Center (ERIC)
[http://www.accesseric.org/]
Supported by the US Department of Education, Office of Educational
Research and Improvement and the National Library of Education, ERIC
is an information system providing users with access to an extensive corpus
of literature on language education.

Electronic Statistics Textbook
[http://www.statsoft.com/textbook/stathome.html]
This site hosts the *Electronic Statistics Textbook*, which offers training in
understanding and using statistics in research. It provides an overview of
relevant concepts and methods, and discussions on how to apply them in a
variety of disciplines, including social science research. It also provides a
glossary of statistical terms.

Language & Education Links
[http://www.ncbe.gwu.edu/links/index.htm]
Sponsored by the National Clearinghouse for English Language Acquisition & Language Instruction Educational Programs, this site provides links
to a variety of web resources concerned with language, culture and education. Specific topics include bilingualism and bilingual education, languages of English language learners in the United States, and technology.

The Language Varieties Web Site
[http://www.une.edu.au/langnet/index.html]
This site contains information on varieties of languages world wide including Creoles, regional and minority dialects, and indigenous varieties that
differ from the standard varieties that are typically used in the media and
taught in schools. It is sponsored by the School of Languages, Cultures
and Linguistics at the University of New England in Australia and the
Association for Supervision and Curriculum Development.

The Linguistic Data Consortium
[http://morph.ldc.upenn.edu/]
Hosted by the University of Pennsylvania, the Linguistic Data Consortium is an open association of universities, companies and government research laboratories. Its purpose is to create, collect and distribute speech and text databases, lexicons, and other tools and resources for language-related research and development purposes.

Mind, Culture, and Activity Homepage
[http://lchc.ucsd.edu/MCA/]
This site provides an interactive forum for those interested in the study of human mind in its cultural and historical contexts. It is hosted by the Laboratory of Comparative Human Cognition (LCHC) at the University of California, San Diego, which also publishes the journal *Mind, Culture and Activity*. On the homepage are links to current and past issues of the journal, online discussions from the XMCA mailing list, and links to other related sites.

Network for Researchers in Conversation Studies (NorFA)
[http://www.nordiska.uu.se/convnet/]
NorFA is a forum for researchers working with various aspects of talk-in-interaction in Scandinavia and the Baltic countries. The network is designed to provide for cross-disciplinary contacts and involves researchers from language studies and linguistics, sociology and social psychology, communication studies, and media studies.

The Open Language Archives Community (OLAC)
[http://www.language-archives.org/]
OLAC is an international partnership of institutions and individuals who are creating a world-wide virtual library of language resources by developing consensus on best current practice for the digital archiving of language resources, and developing a network of interoperating repositories and services for housing and accessing such resources.

Research Methods Knowledge Base
[http://trochim.human.cornell.edu/kb/]
The *Research Methods Knowledge Base* is a comprehensive web-based textbook by William M. Trochim of Cornell University. The text addresses all of the topics in a typical introductory undergraduate or graduate course in social research methods.

Research Methods Resources
[http://www.slais.ubc.ca/resources/research_methods/default.htm]
This site was originally created by Mary Sue Stephenson, Coordinator of Information Technology in the School of Library, Archival and Information Studies at the University of British Columbia. It contains a range of

links to discussions on and tools for using both quantitative and qualitative research methods.

Resources for Teaching Intercultural Communication and Multicultural Awareness
[http://www.geocities.com/~wilson_pam/culture/.]
This site is a repository of resources for developing cultural and intercultural competence, multicultural awareness, and skills for intercultural communication. It is addressed to both academic and business communities and is maintained by Pam Wilson, a faculty member in the Department of Communications at Robert Morris College in Pennsylvania, USA.

Socio-Cultural Theory
[http://carbon.cudenver.edu/~mryder/itc_data/soc_cult.html]
Sponsored by the University of Colorado School of Education, this site offers a comprehensive set of links to articles and books on Vygotsky and his work, and to sociocultural theory more generally.

The Subject Centre for Languages, Linguistics and Area Studies
[http://www.lang.ltsn.ac.uk/index.html]
The Subject Centre for Languages, Linguistics and Area Studies is part of the UK-wide Learning and Teaching Support Network. The mission of the centre is to act as a repository of information and service and to promote high-quality learning and teaching of languages, linguistics and area studies across higher education institutions in England, Northern Ireland, Scotland and Wales.

Teaching Library Internet Workshops
[http://www.lib.berkeley.edu/TeachingLib/Guides/Internet/About.html]
Designed by the UC Berkeley library, this web-based tutorial offers instructions on how to locate up-to-date resources on the World Wide Web for those doing, or interested in doing, research.

Terralingua
[http://www.terralingua.org]
Formed in 1996, Terralingua is an international, non-profit organisation concerned about the future of the world's biological, cultural and linguistic diversity. It contains links supporting the perpetuation and continued development of the world's linguistic diversity and the exploration of connections between linguistic, cultural and biological diversity.

Xrefer
[http://www.xrefer.com/]
This is the free home of an electronic reference site containing encyclopaedias, dictionaries, thesauri, books of quotations and reference works covering a wide range of subjects. All topics are cross-referenced.

Glossary

agency One's socioculturally negotiated ability or willingness to act within specific sociocultural contexts.

appropriation Term usually used to describe the process by which children or novice members of an activity or event move from their roles as less expert participants to more expert participants. In the process, they borrow or model other, more expert members' ways of participating. Eventually, the novices take on these ways as their own, transforming them into ways that are specifically theirs.

classroom discourse The language of the classroom, used by teachers and students to create and participate in their classroom communities. See *discourse*.

co-construction The joint creation of a culturally meaningful reality between two or more individuals.

communicative competence Term first proposed by Dell Hymes in response to Chomsky's notion of linguistic competence. It comprises the knowledge and ability one needs to understand and use linguistic resources in ways that are structurally well formed, socially and contextually appropriate, and culturally feasible in communicative contexts constitutive of the different groups and communities of which one is a member.

communicative event A communicative activity recognised as a bounded unit of socioculturally significant activity by members of a particular speech community. It is a central unit of analysis in an ethnography of communication approach to the study of language use.

communicative plans Socially shared understandings about the conventional nature of communicative activities – and the means for participating in them – that are of sociocultural significance to the groups to which we belong.

communities of practice Groups of individuals who come together with shared purposes structured around professional, social, community, religious or other type of goals.

communities of inquiry Particular *communities of learners* in which classroom activities are organised around the open-ended, exploratory study of questions or topics that are generated from real experiences of the group members and thus are of genuine interest to them.

communities of learners Particular *communities of practice* that include expert and novice members, and who share goals centred on moving learners from limited participatory roles as novices to full participatory roles as experts in activities and practices determined to be of significance to the communities.

consciousness-raising tasks Instructional activities whose purpose is to help learners to become aware of particular gaps in their linguistic knowledge. Such awareness-raising is thought to help learners to access and eventually internalise linguistics forms. It is based on a traditional perspective of language and learning.

contextualisation cues Symbolic resources imbued with contextually significant meaning. They provide individuals with recognisable markers for signalling and interpreting *contextual presuppositions*. See *interactional sociolinguistics* and *linguistic indexes*.

contextual presuppositions Foregrounding-information or understandings used by individuals to interpret and respond appropriately to communicative interactions with other social group members.

conversation analysis An approach to the study of talk-in-interaction. Its focus is on uncovering the socially constituted means or mechanisms by which social order is produced in interaction.

conversation regularities Regular patterns of talk-in-interaction as practised by particular speech community members, which make it possible for us to come to each other's talk-in-interaction with particular dispositions and expectations. Conversation regularities are culture-specific and a main interest of ethnography of communication.

cooperative agent An individual who works cooperatively towards the achievement of mutually negotiated goals with other interlocutors.

cooperative learning An approach to pedagogy that has as a primary goal the fostering of cooperation among learners to accomplish shared goals in supportive learning environments.

critical discourse analysis An approach to the study of language use. Its main concern is with how language use is shaped by relations of power and ideologies, and how such relations affect individuals' understandings of themselves, of others, and of their larger social worlds. See *discourse analysis*.

critical framing   One of four types of learning opportunities associated with the *multiliteracies pedagogy*, whose aim is to help learners to understand the historical, social, cultural, political and ideological dimensions of their communicative activities. See *situated practice*, *overt instruction* and *transformed practice*.

critical pedagogy   A general approach to education that focuses centrally on the issue of power in teaching and learning contexts. It considers the ideal goal of education to be emancipatory.

dialogicality   Refers to the relational character of meaning whereby meaning is defined as emerging from the (non-static or fluid) interrelationship between the use of a linguistic resource at a locally situated moment and its historical/conventional use, not purely from any one source.

discourse   Extended verbal communication that is shaped by and, in turn, gives shape to its linguistic resources, and particular purposes or functions and contexts of use.

discourse analysis   A broad approach to the study of language use whose focus is on uncovering the contextually based meanings of linguistic resources.

discourse-historical methodology   A variation of *critical discourse analysis*. Its focus is on studying how oral and written texts reflect particular power systems and ideologies from a historical perspective, and exploring the ways in which they change through time.

discursive space   The communicative dimension in which culture is articulated, negotiated, and redefined in the use of language.

emergent grammar   A view on language in which grammar is understood as arising from regularities in language use rather than existing as a set of *a priori* mental categories.

encode   To arrange or transform thoughts into a code such as language.

ethnography of communication   An approach to the study of language use developed by linguistic anthropologist, Dell Hymes. Its focus is on capturing patterns of language use and understandings conventionally associated with sociocultural events and activities typical of particular sociocultural groups and contexts.

funds of knowledge   Historically developed, significant sociocultural practices, activities, skills, abilities, beliefs, and bodies of knowledge embodied in households. It is a key concept of a pedagogical innovation in which learners' funds of knowledge are used to transform curricular and instructional practices.

habitus The sets of beliefs, knowledge and skills that predispose one's way of being – i.e. behaving, believing, thinking, feeling, interacting with others, etc. One's habitus is largely determined by one's sociocultural environments (i.e. economic status, ethnicity, religion and groups or communities to which one belongs).

indexicality The process by which particular (contextual) meanings are assigned to forms.

input enhancement Instructional means of priming the linguistic input available to language learners so that the learners can take in and assimilate more easily target language forms. It is associated with a traditional perspective of language and language learning.

interactional sociolinguistics An approach to the study of language use, the development of which is most often attributed to John Gumperz. A primary aim is to uncover differences in use of cues to signal and interpret meaning in particular contexts of interaction.

intercultural communicative competence The knowledge, skills and abilities needed to participate in activities where the target language is the primary or preferred communicative code. It comprises four components:

- *Savoirs*: General knowledge about the target language and culture
- *Savoir-apprendre*: The ability to use savoirs
- *Savoir-faire*: The skills to identify and negotiate communication problems
- *Savoir-être*: General attitudinal dispositions towards or willingness to be involved with culturally different others.

interpretive framework Theoretical framework or perspective by which one understands and explains particular phenomena.

intersubjectivity The achievement of shared communication between or among individuals.

IRE Three-part interactional pattern typical of *classroom discourse*. It involves a teacher-initiated question (I), followed by a student response (R), followed by a teacher evaluation of the response (E). See *IRF*.

IRF Variation of the three-part interactional pattern of classroom discourse. It involves a teacher-initiated question (I), a student response (R), and a teacher follow-up to the response in the form of, for example, a comment, an elaboration, or a request for additional information (F). See *IRE*.

language awareness curriculum A curricular component whose purpose is to enhance individuals' awareness of or sensitivity to linguistic variations. An example of such a component is dialect education where learners from non-mainstream language backgrounds explore the structural and communicative features of their own varieties.

language games Established, conventionalised patterns of action, ways of knowing, valuing and experiencing the world, agreed upon and shared in by members of a culture group. The term is most often associated with the writings of Ludwig Wittgenstein.

language socialisation practices *Communicative events* or activities that are realised primarily through language, by which individuals are socialised into roles as legitimate members of particular communities.

legitimate peripheral participation Process of providing increased opportunities to individuals recognised as bona fide novice members of a community or sociocultural group for developing expertise they need in order to be considered accomplished, expert members in the community or group. See *communities of practice*.

linguistic indexing The act of indexing or invoking meanings conventionally associated with particular linguistic forms.

linguistic indexes or indexicals Linguistic resources whose uses index or invoke particular contextual meanings. See *contextualisation cues*.

linguistic relativity A core concept of the Sapir–Whorf hypothesis. Its basic assertion is that language is a social system based on agreement among speech community members. Since members perceive the world using the resources of their systems, people who live in different linguistic systems see the world differently to the extent that their linguistic systems are different.

literacy practices Communicative activities involving the skills of reading and writing and oriented to by members of a group or community as socioculturally meaningful activities.

microgenetic approach An approach to the study of language development, the focus of which is on tracking changes in behaviour as they occur over the duration of a particular event in specific settings.

micro-ethnography An approach to the study of language use, the focus of which is on the close analysis of one communicative event with particular interest in the specific means by which the event is jointly constructed.

multiliteracies pedagogy A general approach to pedagogy developed by an international group of scholars, the goal of which is to develop in learners the knowledge, skills and abilities that will expand their communicative options for bringing their cultural worlds into existence, maintaining them, and transforming them for their own socially meaningful purposes. See *situated practice, overt instruction, critical framing* and *transformed practice*.

natural approach   Instructional approach to language learning most often associated with Stephen Krashen and Tracy Terrell, and based on their 1983 book. Based on a traditional notion of language, its primary focus is on the development of basic interpersonal communication skills.

non-parametric measures   Typically used in studies where the parameters of the variables of interest in the population are unknown. They are most appropriately used when the sample sizes are small.

overt instruction   One of four types of learning opportunities associated with the *multiliteracies pedagogy*, the aim of which is to provide opportunities for learners to focus on, practice and take control of the various linguistic and other relevant conventions needed for competent engagement in their communicative activities. See *situated practice, critical framing* and *transformed practice*.

participant-observation   A method for collecting data in a qualitative approach to research. The researcher collects data at the same time that he/she participates in and observes the target contexts or communicative activities.

participatory pedagogy   A general approach to language education that draws on the work of Brazilian educator Paulo Freire. Its general aim is to help learners to develop their own voices in response to their local conditions and circumstances and, in so doing, transform their lives in socially meaningful ways.

register   Configurations of semantic options available to individuals in particular communicative situations in terms of field, tenor and mode, which are externalised into linguistic forms (i.e. grammatical or lexical properties).

savoirs   See *intercultural communicative competence*

savoir-apprendre   See *intercultural communicative competence*

savoir-faire   See *intercultural communicative competence*

savoir-être   See *intercultural communicative competence*

situated practice   One of four types of learning opportunities associated with the *multiliteracies pedagogy*, the purpose of which is to afford learners the possibility to develop a familiarity, or a 'feel' for communicative activities in which it is considered important for learners to become active, legitimate members. See *overt instruction, critical framing* and *transformed practice*.

social identity   The social roles, positions, relationships, reputations and other dimensions of social character as related to our various group memberships, along with the values, beliefs and attitudes associated with them.

sociolinguistic relativity   Hymes's reformulation of Whorf's notion of *linguistic relativity*, in which primacy is given to language use and function rather than linguistic code and form. In other words, in the notion of sociolinguistic relativity, context-embedded use of language replaces the notion of linguistic system.

SPEAKING   Analytic framework proposed by Dell Hymes for describing systematically the links between the use of language forms and context in a communicative event. Each letter stands for one component of the communicative event to be described.

structuration   The process by which social structures or systems – i.e. conventionalised ways of doing things – are established. Once established, social structures give shape to individual actors' *communicative events* or activities, and at the same time are reproduced through them.

systemic functional linguistics   A theory of language formulated by Michael Halliday, which posits that meanings of language forms are located in their systematic connections between their functions and the contexts of use.

task-based language teaching (TBLT)   An instructional approach to language learning in which the focus is on engaging learners in tasks where they are compelled to negotiate meaning with their interlocutors. The negotiations lead to input that is more attuned to the learners' levels of linguistic competence, which, in turn, helps learners to take notice of and ultimately acquire new syntactic forms. *Consciousness-raising tasks* are an example of the kinds of tasks that are used in this approach.

transformed practice   One of four types of learning opportunities associated with the *multiliteracies project*, the purpose of which is to provide learners with opportunities to take the lead in their own learning. See *situated practice*, *overt instruction* and *critical framing*.

turn-taking patterns   Regularities in ways that turns are taken in interaction. In some events, turns are self-selected in that anyone who wants to talk, can. In others, individuals must bid for turns, as in the case of classrooms where students often raise their hands to request turns from the teacher.

utterance   A complete meaningful unit of language use. It is a fundamental unit of analysis in research on language from a sociocultural perspective.

References

Abrahams, R. (1976) *Talking black*. Rowley, MA: Newbury House.

Adger, C., Christian, D. and Taylor, O. (eds) (1999) *Making the connection: Language and academic achievement among African American students*. McHenry, IL: Delta Systems.

Ahearn, L. (2000) True traces: love letters and social transformation in Nepal. In D. Barton and N. Hall (eds), *Letter writing as social practice* (pp. 199–207). Amsterdam: John Benjamins.

Ahearn, L. (2001) Language and agency. *Annual Review of Anthropology*, 30: 109–37.

Allport, G. (1954) *The nature of prejudice*. Cambridge: Addison Wesley.

Altieri, C. (1994) *Subjective agency*. Cambridge, MA: Blackwell.

Andrews, L. (1998) *Language exploration and awareness*. Mahwah, NJ: Lawrence Erlbaum Associates.

Aronson, E. and Yates, S. (1983) Cooperation in the classroom: The impact of the jigsaw method on inter-ethnic relations, classroom performance and self-esteem. In H. Blumberg and P. Hare (eds), *Small groups*. London: John Wiley & Sons.

Aronson, E. and Thibodeau, R. (1992) The jigsaw classroom: A cooperative strategy for reducing prejudice. In J. Lynch, C. Modgil and S. Modgil (eds), *Cultural diversity in the schools*. London: Falmer Press.

Aronson, E. and Patnoe, S. (1997) *The jigsaw classroom: Building cooperation in the classroom* (2nd edn). New York: Addison Wesley Longman.

Au, K.H. (1980) Participation structures in a reading lesson with Hawaiian children: Analysis of a culturally appropriate instructional event. *Anthropology and Education Quarterly*, 11 (2): 91–115.

Au, K.H. and Mason, J.M. (1983) Cultural congruence in classroom participation structures: Achieving a balance of rights. *Discourse Processes*, 6: 145–67.

Auerbach, E.R. (1991) *Making meaning, making change: Participatory curriculum development for adult ESL literacy*. Washington, DC: Center for Applied Linguistics.

Auerbach, E.R. (1998) Designer literacy: Reading the labels. *Bright Ideas*, 7 (4). [On line at http://www.sabes.org/b2auerba.htm]

Auerbach, E. (2000) Creating participatory learning communities: Paradoxes and possibilities. In J.K. Hall and W. Eggington (eds), *The sociopolitics of English language teaching* (pp. 143–63). Clevedon: Multilingual Matters.

Auerbach, E.R. (2001) 'Yes, but': Problematizing participatory ESL pedagogy. In B. Burnaby and P. Campbell (eds), *Participatory approaches in adult education.* Mahwah, NJ: Lawrence Erlbaum.

Auerbach, E.R. and Wallerstein, N. (1987) *ESL for action: Problem-posing at work.* Reading: Addison-Wesley.

Bachman, L.F. (1990) *Fundamental considerations in language testing.* Oxford: Oxford University Press.

Bachman, L.F. and Palmer, A.S. (1996) *Language testing in practice.* Oxford: Oxford University Press.

Bakhtin, M.M. (1981) *The dialogic imagination* (C. Emerson and M. Holquist, trans.). Austin: University of Texas Press.

Bakhtin, M.M. (1986) *Speech genres and other late essays* (C. Emerson and M. Holquist, eds; V.W. McGee, trans.). Austin: University of Texas Press.

Bakhtin, M.M. (1990) *Art and answerability* (M. Holquist and V. Liapunov, eds). Austin: University of Texas Press.

Barnes, D. (1992) *From communication to curriculum.* Portsmouth, NH: Boynton/Cook.

Barton, D. (1991) The social nature of writing. In D. Barton and R. Ivanic (eds), *Writing in the community* (pp. 1–13). Newbury Park: Sage.

Barton, D. and Hamilton, M. (1998) *Local literacies: Reading and writing in one community.* London: Routledge.

Baugh, J. (1983) *Black street speech: Its history, structure, and survival.* Austin: University of Texas Press.

Baugh, J. (1999) *Out of the mouths of slaves: African American language and educational malpractice.* Austin: University of Texas Press.

Bauman, R. (2000) Language, identity, performance. *Pragmatics,* 10 (1): 1–5.

Begay, S., Dick, G.S., Estell, D.W., Estell, J., McCarty, T. and Sells, A. (1995) Change from the inside out: A story of transformation in a Navajo community school. *The Bilingual Research Journal,* 19 (1): 121–39.

Bergvall, V.L., Bing, J.M. and Freed, A.F. (eds) (1996) *Rethinking language and gender research: Theory and practice.* London: Longman.

Berkowitz, S. (1997) Analyzing qualitative data. In J. Frechtling and L. Westat (eds), *User-friendly handbook for mixed method evaluations.* Washington, DC: Division of Research, Evaluation and Communication, National Science Foundation. [On line at: http://www.ehr.nsf.gov/EHR/REC/pubs/NSF97–153/CHAP_4.HTM].

Berman, R. and Slobin, D. (1994) *Relating events in narratives: A crosslinguistic developmental study.* Hillsdale, NJ: Lawrence Erlbaum Associates.

Bhabha, H. (1994) *The location of culture.* London: Routledge.

Bixler-Márquez, D.J. and Ornstein-Galacia, J. (eds) (1988) *Chicano speech in the bilingual classroom.* New York: Peter Lang.

Bourdieu, P. (1977) *Outline of a theory of practice.* Cambridge: Cambridge University Press.

Bourdieu, P. (1980) *The logic of practice.* Stanford: Stanford University Press.

Bourdieu, P. (2000) *Pascalian meditations.* Stanford: Stanford University Press.

Bowerman, M. (1996) The origins of children's spatial semantic categories: Cognitive vs. linguistic determinants. In J.J. Gumperz and S.C. Levinson (eds), *Rethinking linguistic relativity* (pp. 145–76). Cambridge: Cambridge University Press.

Bowerman, M. and Choi, S. (2001) Shaping meanings for language: Universal and language-specific in the acquisition of spatial semantic categories. In M. Bowerman and

S.C. Levinson (eds), *Language acquisition and conceptual development* (pp. 475–511). Cambridge, UK: Cambridge University Press.

Bowerman, M. and Levinson, S. (2001) Introduction. In M. Bowerman and S.C. Levinson (eds), *Language acquisition and conceptual development* (pp. 1–18). Cambridge: Cambridge University Press.

Boxer, D. (2002) *Applying sociolinguistics*. Amsterdam: John Benjamins.

Boxer, D. and Cortés-Conde, F. (2000) Identity and ideology: Culture and pragmatics in content-based ESL. In J.K. Hall and L.S. Verplaetse (eds), *Second and foreign language learning through classroom interaction* (pp. 203–20). Mahwah, NJ: Lawrence Erlbaum.

Boyd, M. and Maloof, V.M. (2000) How teachers can build upon student-proposed intertextual links to facilitate student talk in the ESL classroom. In J.K. Hall and L.S. Verplaetse (eds), *Second and foreign language learning through classroom interaction* (pp. 163–82). Mahwah, NJ: Lawrence Erlbaum.

Bryman, A. (1984) The debate about quantitative and qualitative methods: A question of method or epistemology? *British Journal of Sociology*, 35: 75–92.

Bucholtz, M., Liang, A.C. and Sutton, L.A. (eds) (1999) *Reinventing identities: The gendered self in discourse*. New York: Oxford University Press.

Byram, M. (1997) *Teaching and assessing intercultural communicative competence*. Clevedon: Multilingual Matters.

Byram, M. and Fleming, M. (eds) (1998) *Language learning in intercultural perspective: Approaches through drama and ethnography*. Cambridge: Cambridge University Press.

Byram, M. and Zarate, G. (eds) (1997) *The sociocultural and intercultural dimension of language learning and teaching*. Strasbourg: Council of Europe.

Calderon, M., Hertz-Lazarowitz, R. and Slavin, R.E. (1998) Effects of bilingual co-operative integrated reading and composition on students making the transition from Spanish to English reading. *Elementary School Journal*, 99: 153–65.

Canagarajah, A.S. (1993) Critical ethnography of a Sri Lankan classroom ambiguities in student opposition to reproduction through ESOL. *TESOL Quarterly*, 27 (4): 601–26.

Canale, M. (1982) From communicative competence to communicative language pedagogy. In J.C. Richards and R. Schmidt (eds), *Language and communication* (pp. 2–27). London: Longman.

Canale, M. and Swain, M. (1980) Theoretical bases of communicative approaches to second language teaching and testing. *Applied Linguistics*, 1: 1–47.

Candlin, C.N. (1987) Beyond description to explanation in cross-cultural discourse. In L. Smith (ed.), *Discourse across cultures: Strategies in World Englishes* (pp. 22–35). New York: Prentice Hall.

Capps, L. and Ochs, E. (1995) *Constructing panic: The discourse of agoraphobia*. Cambridge, MA: Harvard University Press.

Cazden, C. (1988) *Classroom discourse*. Portsmouth, NH: Heinemann.

Cazden, C. (1993) Vygotsky, Hymes and Bakhtin: From word to utterance. In E. Forman, N. Minick and C.A. Stone (eds), *Contexts for learning* (pp. 197–212). New York: Oxford University Press.

Cazden, C. (1996) *Communicative competence (1966–1996)*. Paper presented at the Annual Meeting of the American Association for Applied Linguistics, Chicago, IL.

Celce-Murcia, M. (1991) Grammar pedagogy in second and foreign language teaching. *TESOL Quarterly*, 25 (3): 459–80.

Celce-Murcia, M., Domyei, Z. and Thurrell, S. (1995) Communicative competence: A pedagogically motivated model with content specification. *Issues in Applied Linguistics*, 6 (2): 5–35.

Chaiklin, S. and Lave, J. (eds) (1993) *Understanding practice: Perspectives on activity and context*. New York: Cambridge University Press.

Chapelle, C. (1998) Some notes on systemic-functional linguistics. [On line at www.public.iastate.edu/~carolc/LING511/sfl.html]

Chomsky, N. (1957) *Syntactic structures*. The Hague: Mouton.

Chomsky, N. (1965) *Aspects of the theory of syntax*. Cambridge, MA: M.I.T. Press.

Chomksy, N. (1966) *Topics in the theory of generative grammar*. The Hague: Mouton.

Christian, D., Wolfram, W. and Dube, N. (1988) *Variation and change in geographically isolated communities: Appalachian English and Ozark English*. Tuscaloosa, AL: University of Alabama Press.

Christie, F. and Unsworth, L. (2000) Developing socially responsible language research. In L. Unsworth (ed.), *Researching language in schools and communities: Functional linguistic perspectives* (pp. 1–26). London: Cassell.

Civil, M., González, N. and Andrade, R. (1998) *Talking Leaves*, 3 (2): 3–4.

Cohen, E. (1994) *Designing groupwork: Strategies for heterogeneous classrooms* (2nd edn). New York: Teachers College Press.

Cole, M. (1996) *Cultural psychology*. Cambridge: Harvard University Press.

Collins, C. (1997) Foregrounding language in housing and urban research: What's this for and how do we do it anyway? Paper presented for the seminar, '*Discourse and urban change: foregrounding language in housing and urban research*', presented at the Centre for Housing Research and Urban Studies, University of Glasgow, Scotland.

Consolo, D. (2000) Teachers' action and student oral participation in classroom interaction. In J.K. Hall and L.S. Verplaetse (eds), *Second and foreign language learning through classroom interaction* (pp. 91–108). Mahwah, NJ: Lawrence Erlbaum.

Cook, V. (1999) Going beyond the native speaker in language teaching. *TESOL Quarterly*, 33 (2): 185–209.

Cope, B. and Kalantzis, M. (2000) Multiliteracies: The beginnings of an idea. In Cope, B. and Kalantzis, M. (eds), *Multiliteracies: Literacy learning and the design of social futures* (pp. 3–8). London: Routledge.

Cope, B. and Kalantzis, M. (2001) Putting 'Multiliteracies' to the Test. *ALEA Today*. Adelaide: Australian Literacy Educators' Association. [On line at http://www.alea.edu.au/multilit.htm]

Council of Europe (1994) *The case for intercultural education*. Strasbourg: Council of Europe.

Crowley, T. (1996) *Language in history*. London: Routledge.

Damhuis, R. (2000) A different teacher role in language arts education: Interaction in a small circle with teacher. In J.K. Hall and L.S. Verplaetse (eds), *Second and foreign language learning through classroom interaction* (pp. 243–64). Mahwah, NJ: Lawrence Erlbaum.

Davies, A. (1999) *An introduction to applied linguistics*. Edinburgh: Edinburgh University Press.

Day, E. (1999) *Identity formation in a kindergarten ESL learner: An ethnographic study*. Paper presented at the American Association for Applied Linguistics Annual Conference, Stamford, Connecticut.

de Certeau, M. (1984) *The practice of everyday life*. Berkeley: University of California Press.

Dien, T. (1998) Language and literacy in Vietnamese American communities. In B. Perez (ed.), *Sociocultural contexts of language and literacy* (pp. 123–62). Mahwah, NJ: Lawrence Erlbaum Associates.

Doughty, C. and Williams, J. (1998) Pedagogical choices in focus on form. In C. Doughty and J. Williams (eds), *Focus on form in classroom second language acquisition* (pp. 197–261). Cambridge: Cambridge University Press.

Duff, P.A. (1995) An ethnography of communication in immersion classrooms in Hungary. *TESOL Quarterly*, 29 (3): 505–37.

Duff, P.A. (2000) Repetition in foreign language classroom interaction. In J.K. Hall and L.S. Verplaetse (eds), *Second and foreign language learning through classroom interaction* (pp. 109–38). Mahwah, NJ: Lawrence Erlbaum.

Duff, P.A. and Uchida, Y. (1997) The negotiation of teachers' sociocultural identities and practices in postsecondary EFL classrooms. *TESOL Quarterly*, 31 (3): 451–86.

Duranti, A. (1997) *Linguistic anthropology*. Cambridge: Cambridge University Press.

Edwards, A.D. and Westgate, D.P. (1994) *Investigating classroom talk*. London: The Falmer Press.

Edwards, D. (1995) Two to tango: Script formulations, dispositions, and rhetorical symmetry in relationship troubles talk. *Research on Language and Social Interaction*, 28 (4): 319–50.

Eggins, S. and Slade, D. (1997) *Analyzing casual conversation*. London: Cassells Academic.

Eisenberg, A. (1986) Teasing: Verbal play in two Mexican homes. In B. Schieffelin and E. Ochs (eds), *Language socialization across cultures*. Cambridge: Cambridge University Press.

Ellis, R. (1994) A theory of instructed second language acquisition. In N. Ellis (ed.), *Implicit and explicit learning of language* (pp. 79–115). London: Academic Press.

Ellis, R. (1997) SLA and language pedagogy. *Studies in Second Language Acquisition*, 19: 69–92.

Elman, J. (1999) The emergence of language: A conspiracy theory. In B. MacWhinney (ed.), *The emergence of language* (pp. 1–28). Mahwah, NJ: Lawrence Erlbaum.

Erickson, E. and Shultz, J. (1982) *The counselor as gatekeeper: Social interaction in interviews*. New York: Academic Press.

Fairclough, N. (1992) *Discourse and social change*. Cambridge: Polity Press.

Fairclough, N. (1995a) *Critical discourse analysis: The critical study of language*. London: Longman.

Fairclough, N. (1995b) *Media discourse*. New York: Edward Arnold.

Fairclough, N. (2000) *New labour, new language?* New York: Routledge.

Field, M. (1998) Participation structure as cultural schema: examples from a Navajo preschool. *Issues in Applied Linguistics*, 9 (2): 123–37.

Field, M. (2001) Triadic directives in Navajo language socialization. *Language in Society*, 30 (2): 249–63.

Fillmore, L.W. and Snow, C. (2000) *What teachers need to know about language*. [On line at: http://www.cal.org/ericcll/teachers.pdf]

Fishman, A. (1991) Because this is who we are: Writing in the Amish community. In Barton, D. and Ivanic, R. (eds), *Writing in the community* (pp. 14–37). Newbury Park: Sage.

Firth, A. and Wagner, J. (1997) On discourse, communication, and (some) fundamental concepts in SLA research. *Modern Language Journal*, 81 (3): 277–300.

Foster, M. (1989) 'It's cooking now': A performance analysis of the speech events of a Black teacher in an urban community college. *Language in Society*, 18: 1–29.

Fotos, S. (1994) Integrating grammar instruction and communicative language use through grammar consciousness-raising tasks. *TESOL Quarterly*, 28 (2): 323–51.

Foucault, M. (1972) *The archaeology of knowledge* (A.M. Sheridan Smith, trans.). New York: Pantheon.

Fowler, R. (1991) *Language in the news: Discourse and ideology in the British press*. New York: Routledge.

Freire, P. (1972) *Pedagogy of the oppressed*. New York: Continuum.

Freire, P. (1973) *Pedagogy for critical consciousness*. New York: Seabury Press.

Gallimore, R., Boggs, J.W. and Jordan, C. (1974) *Culture, behavior, and education: A study of Hawaiian-Americans*. Beverly Hills, CA: Sage.

Garcez, P. (1997) Microethnography. In N. Hornberger and D. Olson (eds), *Encyclopedia of language and education, Volume 8: Research methods in language and education* (pp. 187–96). The Netherlands: Kluwer Academic Publishers.

Gass, S.M. (1997) *Input, interaction, and the second language learner*. Mahwah, NJ: Lawrence Erlbaum Associates.

Gass, S.M. (1998) Apples and oranges: Or, why apples are not orange and don't need to be: A response to Firth and Wagner. *Modern Language Journal*, 82 (1): 83–90.

Gee, J.P. (1996) *Social linguistics and literacies: Ideology in discourses* (2nd edn). London: Taylor & Francis.

Gee, J. and Green, J. (1998) Discourse analysis, learning, and social practice: A methodological study. *Review of Educational Research*, 23: 119–69.

Giddens, A. (1984) *The constitution of society: Outline of the theory of structuration*. Berkeley: University of California Press.

Giddens, A. (1991) *Modernity and self-identity*. Stanford, CA: Stanford University Press.

González, N. and Amanti, C. (1992) *Teaching ethnographic methods to teachers: Successes and pitfalls*. Paper presented at the annual meeting of the American Anthropological Association, San Francisco, CA.

González, N., Moll, L., Floyd-Tenery, M., Rivera, A., Rendon, P., González, R. and Amanti, C. (1993) Teacher research on funds of knowledge: Learning from households. *Educational Practice Report* 6. National Center for Research on Cultural Diversity and Second Language Learning. [On line at: http://www.ncbe.gwu.edu/miscpubs/ncrcdsll/epr6.htm]

González, N., Moll, L., Floyd-Tenery, M., Rivera, A., Rendon, P., González, R. and Amanti, C. (1995) Funds of knowledge for teaching in Latino households. *Urban Education*, 29 (4): 443–70.

Goodenough, W. (1964) Cultural anthropology and linguistics. In D. Hymes (ed.), *Language in culture and society: A reader in linguistics and anthropology* (pp. 36–9). New York: Harper and Row.

Goodwin, C. and Heritage, J. (1990) Conversation analysis. *Annual Review of Anthropology*, 19: 283–307.

Goodwin, C. and Duranti, A. (1992) Rethinking context: An introduction. In A. Duranti and C. Goodwin (eds), *Rethinking context: Language as an interactive phenomenon* (pp. 1–42). Cambridge: Cambridge University Press.

Goodwin, M.H. (1990) *He-said-she said: Talk as social organization among black children*. Bloomington: Indiana University Press.

Goodwin, M.H. (1995) Co-construction in girls' hopscotch. *Research on Language and Social Interaction*, 8 (3): 261–81.

Gumperz, J.J. (1981) The linguistic bases of communicative competence. In D. Tannen (ed.), *Analyzing discourse: Text and talk* (pp. 323–34). Washington, DC: Georgetown University Press.

Gumperz, J.J. (1982a) *Discourse strategies*. Cambridge: Cambridge University Press.

Gumperz, J.J. (ed.) (1982b) *Language and social identity*. Cambridge: Cambridge University Press.

Gumperz, J.J. (1992) Contextualization and understanding. In A. Duranti and C. Goodwin (eds), *Rethinking context* (pp. 229–52). Cambridge: Cambridge University Press.

Gumperz, J.J. (1999) On interactional sociolinguistic method. In S. Sarangi and C. Roberts (eds), *Talk, work and institutional order* (pp. 453–71). Berlin: Mouton de Gruyter.

Gumperz, J., Cook-Gumperz, J. and Szymanski, M. (1999) Collaborative Practices in Bilingual Cooperative Learning Classrooms. Research Report 7. Washington, DC: Center for Research on Education, Diversity and Excellence. [On line at http://www.cal.org/crede/pubs/research/rr7.htm]

Gumperz, J.J., Jupp, T. and Roberts, C. (1979) *Crosstalk: A study of cross-cultural communication*. London: The National Centre for Industrial Language Training.

Gutierrez, K. (1994) How talk, context, and script shape contexts for learning: A cross-case comparison of journal sharing. *Linguistics and Education*, 5: 335–65.

Hajer, M. (2000) Creating a language promoting classroom: Content area teachers at work. In J.K. Hall and L.S. Verplaetse (eds), *Second and foreign language learning through classroom interaction* (pp. 265–86). Mahwah, NJ: Lawrence Erlbaum.

Hall, J.K. (1993a) The role of oral practices in the accomplishment of our everyday lives: The sociocultural dimension of interaction with implications for the learning of another language. *Applied Linguistics*, 14 (2): 145–66.

Hall, J.K. (1993b) Tengo una bomba: The paralinguistic and linguistic conventions of the oral practice *Chismeando*. *Research on Language and Social Interaction*, 26 (1): 57–85.

Hall, J.K. (1993c) Oye, oye lo que ustedes no saben: Creativity, social power and politics in the oral practice of *chismeando*. *Journal of Linguistic Anthropology*, 3 (1): 75–98.

Hall, J.K. (1995) 'Aw, man, where we goin?': Classroom interaction and the development of L2 interactional competence. *Issues in Applied Linguistics*, 6 (2): 37–62.

Hall, J.K. (1998) Differential teacher attention to student utterances: The construction of different opportunities for learning in the IRF. *Linguistics and Education*, 9 (3): 287–311.

Hall, J.K. (2002) *Methods for teaching foreign languages: Creating a community of learners in the classroom*. Columbus, OH: Prentice-Hall.

Halliday, M.A.K. (1973) *Explorations in the functions of language*. London: Edward Arnold.

Halliday, M.A.K. (1975) *Learning how to mean: Explorations in the development of language*. London: Edward Arnold.

Halliday, M.A.K. (1978) *Language as social semiotic: The social interpretation of language and meaning*. London: Edward Arnold.

Halliday, M.A.K. (1985) *An introduction to functional grammar*. London: Edward Arnold.

Halliday, M.A.K. (1993) Toward a language-based theory of learning. *Linguistics and Education*, 5: 93–16. (pp. 93–116)

Halliday, M.A.K., McIntosh, A. and Strevens, P. (1964) *The linguistic sciences and language teaching*. Bloomington: Indiana University Press.

Hanks, W. (1996) *Language and communicative practices*. Boulder: Westview Press.

Harklau, L. (1994) ESL versus mainstream classes: Contrasting L2 learning environments. *TESOL Quarterly*, 28 (2): 241–72.

Harklau, L. (1999) Representing culture in the ESL writing classroom. In E. Hinkel (ed.), *Culture in second language teaching and learning*. Cambridge: Cambridge University Press.

Harkness, S., Super, C.M. and Keefer, C.H. (1992) Learning to be an American parent: How cultural models gain directive force. In R.G. D'Andrade and C. Strauss (eds), *Human motives and cultural models* (pp. 163–78). New York: Cambridge University Press.

Haviland, J.B. (1977) *Gossip, reputation and knowledge in Zinacantan*. Chicago: University of Chicago Press.

He, A.W. (1995) The case of student counselees. *Research on Language and Social Interaction*, 28 (3): 213–31.

Heap, J. (1997) Conversation analysis methods. In N. Hornberger and D. Olson (eds), *Encyclopedia of language and education, Volume 8: Research methods in language and education* (pp. 217–25). The Netherlands: Kluwer Academic Publishers.

Heath, S.B. (1983) *Ways with words*. Cambridge: Cambridge University Press.

Heath, S.B. (2000) Linguistics in the study of language in education. *Harvard Educational Review*, 70 (1): 49–59.

Heath, S.B. and Mangiola, L. (1991) *Children of promise: Literate activity in linguistically and culturally diverse classrooms*. Washington, DC: National Education Association.

Hewstone, M. and Jaspers, J. (1984) Social dimensions of attribution. In H. Tajfel (ed.), *The social dimension: European developments in social psychology, Vol. 2* (pp. 379–404). Cambridge: Cambridge University Press.

Hickmann, M. (2001) Language and cognition in development: Old questions, new directions. *Pragmatics*, 11 (2): 105–26.

Holt, D. (ed.) (1993) *Cooperative learning: A response to linguistic and cultural diversity*. McHenry, IL: Delta Systems.

Hopper, P.J. (1987) Emergent grammar. *Berkeley Linguistics Society*, 13: 139–57.

Hopper, P.J. (1998) Emergent grammar. In M. Tomasello (ed.), *The new psychology of language* (pp. 155–75). Mahwah, NJ: Lawrence Erlbaum Associates.

Hopper, P.J. and Thompson, S. (1993) Language universals, discourse pragmatics and semantics. *Language Sciences*, 15 (4): 357–76.

Hopper, R. and Chen, C.H. (1996) Languages, cultures, relationships: Telephone openings in Taiwan. *Research on Language and Social Interaction*, 29 (4): 291–313.

Hymes, D. (1962) The ethnography of speaking. In T. Gladwin and W.C. Sturtevant (eds), *Anthropology and human behavior* (pp. 13–53). Washington, DC: Anthropology Society of Washington.

Hymes, D. (1964) Formal discussion. In U. Bellugi and R. Brown (eds), *The acquisition of language: Monographs of the society for research in child development*, 29 (1): 107–11.

Hymes, D. (1971) Competence and performance in linguistic theory. In R. Huxley and E. Ingram (eds), *Language acquisition: Models and methods*. London: Academic Press.

Hymes, D. (1972a) Models of the interaction of language and social life. In J.J. Gumperz and D. Hymes (eds), *Directions in Sociolinguistics: The ethnography of communication* (pp. 35–71). New York: Holt, Rinehart & Winston.

Hymes, D. (1972b) On communicative competence. In J.B. Pride and J. Holmes (eds) *Sociolinguistics* (pp. 169–93). Harmondsworth: Penguin.

Hymes, D. (1974) *Foundations in sociolinguistics*. Philadelphia: University of Pennsylvania Press.

Hymes, D. (1980) *Language in education: Ethnolinguistic essays*. Washington, DC: Center for Applied Linguistics.

Hymes, D. (1998) *When is oral narrative poetry? Generative form and its pragmatic conditions*. Paper presented at the International Pragmatics Conference, Reims, France (July).

Ibrahim, A. (1999) Becoming Black: Rap and hip-hop, race, gender, identity, and the politics of ESL learning. *TESOL Quarterly*, 33 (3): 349–69.

Ivanic, R. (1998) *Writing and identity: The discoursal construction of identity in academic writing*. Philadelphia, PA: John Benjamins.

Jacoby, S. and Gonzales, P. (1991) Creation of expert-novice in scientific discourse. *Issues in Applied Linguistics*, 2 (2): 149–81.

Jacoby, S. and Ochs, E. (1995) Co-construction: An introduction. *Research on Language and Social Interaction*, 28 (3): 171–83.

Johnson, D.W. and Johnson F. (1991) Learning together and alone: Cooperation, competition, and individualization (3rd edn). Englewood Cliffs, NJ: Prentice Hall.

Johnson, D.W. and Johnson, F. (1997) *Joining together: Group theory and group skills* (6th edn). Englewood Cliffs, NJ: Prentice Hall.

Johnson, D.W., Johnson, R.T. and Holubec, E.J. (1993) *Cooperation in the classroom* (6th edn). Edina, MN: Interaction Book.

Kandiah, T. (1991) Extenuatory sociolinguistics: Diverting attention from issues to symptoms in cross-cultural communication studies. *Multilingua*, 10 (4): 345–79.

Kasermann, M.-L. (1991) Obstruction and dominance: Uncooperative moves and their effect on the course of conversation. In I. Marková and K. Foppa (eds), *Asymmetries in dialogue* (pp. 101–23). Hertfordshire: Harvester Wheatsheaf.

Katriel, T. (1987) Bexibudim!: Ritualized sharing among Israeli children. *Language in Society*, 16: 305–20.

Kim, D. and Hall, J.K. (2002) The role of an interactive book reading program in the development of L2 pragmatic competence. *Modern Language Journal*, 86 (3).

Kramsch, C. (1993) *Context and culture in language teaching*. Oxford: Oxford University Press.

Kramsch, C. (1995) The cultural component of language teaching. *Language, Culture and Curriculum*, 8 (12): 83–92.

Kramsch, C. (1998) The privilege of the intercultural speaker. In M. Byram and M. Fleming (eds), *Language Learning in Intercultural Perspective* (pp. 16–31). Cambridge: Cambridge University Press.

Krashen, S.D. and Terrell, T.D. (1983) *The natural approach*. Hayward, CA: Alemany Press.

Kwan, M. (2002) *The learning of English vocabulary by local and Chinese immigrant children: A critical and sociocultural analysis*. Unpublished doctoral dissertation, Department of English and Communication, City University of Hong Kong.

Labov, W. (1972) *Language in the inner city: Black English vernacular*. University of Pennsylvania Press.

Lave, J. and Wenger, E. (1991) *Situated learning: Legitimate peripheral participation*. Cambridge, England: Cambridge University Press.

Layder, D. (1993) *New strategies in social research: An introduction and guide*. Cambridge: Polity Press.

Lee, P. (1996) *The Whorf theory complex: A critical reconstruction*. Philadelphia: John Benjamins.

Leeds-Hurwitz, W. (1984) On the relationship of the 'Ethnography of Speaking' to the 'Ethnography of Communication'. *Papers in Linguistics*, 17: 7–32.

Leontiev, A.A. (1981) *Psychology and the language learning process*. Oxford: Pergamon Press.

Leontiev, A.N. (1981) *Problems of the development of the mind*. Moscow: Progress.

Lévi-Strauss, C. (1963) *Structural anthropology*. New York: Basic Books.

Lin, A. (1999a) Resistance and creativity in English reading lessons in Hong Kong. *Language, Culture and Curriculum*, 12 (3): 285–96.

Lin, A. (1999b) Doing-English-Lessons in the reproduction or transformation of social worlds? *TESOL Quarterly*, 33 (3): 393–412.

Lin, A. (2000) Lively children trapped in an island of disadvantage: Verbal play of Cantonese working-class schoolboys in Hong Kong. *International Journal of the Sociology of Language*, 143: 63–83.

Livia, A. and Hall, K. (1997) *Queerly phrased: Language, gender, and sexuality*. Oxford: Oxford University Press.

Long, M. (1997) Construct Validity in SLA Research: A Response to Firth and Wagner. *Modern Language Journal*, 81 (3): 318–23.

Long, M. and Crookes, G. (1993) Units of analysis in syllabus design: The case for task. In G. Crookes and S. Gass (eds), *Tasks in a pedagogical context* (pp. 9–54). Clevedon: Multilingual Matters.

Long, M. and Robinson, P. (1998) Focus on form, theory, research and practice. In C. Doughty and J. Williams (eds), *Focus on form in classroom second language acquisition* (pp. 15–41). Cambridge: Cambridge University Press.

Lotan, R. (1997) Complex instruction: An overview. In E. Cohen and R. Lotan (eds), *Working for equity in heterogeneous classrooms* (pp. 15–30). New York: Teachers College Press.

Luckmann, T. (1995) Interaction planning and intersubjective adjustment of perspectives by communicative genre. In E. Goody (ed.), *Social intelligence and interaction* (pp. 175–86). Cambridge: Cambridge University Press.

Martin-Jones, M. and Bhatt, A. (1998) Literacies in the lives of young Gujarati speakers in Leicester. In L. Verhoeven and A.Y. Durgunoglu (eds), *Literacy development in a multilingual context* (pp. 37–50). Mahwah, NJ: Lawrence Erlbaum Associates.

McCarthy, M. (1991) *Discourse analysis for language teachers*. New York: Cambridge University Press.

McCarty, T.L. (1989) School as community: The Rough Rock demonstration. *Harvard Educational Review*, 59 (4): 484–503.

McCarty, T. and Watahomigie, L. (1998) Language and literacy in American Indian and Alaska native communities. In B. Perez (ed.), *Sociocultural contexts of language and literacy* (pp. 69–98). Mahwah, NJ: Lawrence Erlbaum Associates.

McKay, S. and Wong, S.L. (1996) Multiple discourses, multiple identities: Investment and agency in second-language learning among Chinese adolescent immigrant students. *Harvard Educational Review*, 66 (3): 577–608.

Mehan, H. (1979) *Learning lessons*. Cambridge, MA: Harvard University Press.

Mey, J. (1985) *Whose language: A study in linguistic pragmatics*. Amsterdam: John Benjamins.

Miller, J. (2000) Language use, identity and social interaction: Migrant students in Australia. *Research on Language and Social Interaction*, 33 (1): 69–100.

Mittins, B. (1991) *Language awareness for teachers*. Buckingham: Open University Press.

Moerman, M. (1988) *Talking culture: Ethnography and conversation analysis*. Philadelphia: University of Pennsylvania Press.

Moll, L.C. (1992) Bilingual classroom studies and community analysis: Some recent trends. *Educational Researcher*, 21 (3): 20–4.

Moll, L. (2000) Inspired by Vygotsky: Ethnographic experiments in education. In C. Lee and P. Smagorinsky (eds), *Vygotskian perspectives on literacy research* (pp. 256–268). Cambridge: Cambridge University Press.

Moll, L.C. and Greenberg, J. (1990) Creating zones of possibilities: Combining social contexts for instruction. In L.C. Moll (ed.), *Vygotsky and education* (pp. 319–48). Cambridge: Cambridge University Press.

Moll, L.C., Amanti, C., Neff, D. and González, N. (1992) Funds of knowledge for teaching: Using a qualitative approach to connect homes and classrooms. *Theory into Practice*, 31 (2): 132–41.

Morson, G. and Emerson, C. (1990) *Mikhail Bakhtin: Creation of a prosaics*. Stanford: Stanford University Press.

Nassaji, H. and Wells, G. (2000) What's the use of 'traidic dialogue'? An investigation of teacher-student interaction. *Applied Linguistics*, 21 (3): 376–406.

National Research Council (1999) *How people learn: Brain, mind, experience, and school*. Washington, DC: National Academy Press.

New London Group (1996) A pedagogy of multiliteracies: Designing social futures. *Harvard Educational Review*, 66: 60–92.

New London Group (2000) A pedagogy of multiliteracies: Designing social futures. In B. Cope and M. Kalantzis (eds), *Multiliteracies: Literacy learning and the design of social futures* (pp. 9–38). London: Routledge.

Ninio, A. and Snow, C. (1996) *Pragmatic development*. Colorado: Westview Press.

Norton, B. (2000) *Identity and language learning*. Harlow, England: Pearson Education.

Nunan, D. (1995) Closing the gap between learning and instruction. *TESOL Quarterly*, 29 (1): 133–58.

Nystrand, M., Gamoran, A., Kachur, R. and Pendergast, C. (1997) *Opening dialogue: Understanding the dynamics of language and learning in the English classroom*. New York: Teachers' College Press.

Ochs, E. (1979) Transcription as theory. In E. Ochs and B.B. Schieffelin (eds), *Developmental pragmatics* (pp. 43–72). New York: Academic Press.

Ochs, E. (1988) *Culture and language development: Language acquisition and language socialization in a Samoan village*. Cambridge: Cambridge University Press.

Ochs, E. (1993) Constructing social identity: A language socialization perspective. *Research on Language and Social Interaction*, 26 (3): 287–306.

Ochs, E. (1996) Linguistic resources for socializing humanity. In J. Gumperz and S. Levinson (eds), *Rethinking linguistic relativity* (pp. 407–37). Cambridge: Cambridge University Press.

Ochs, E. and Schieffelin, B. (1982) Language acquisition and socialization: Three developmental stories and their implications. *Sociolinguistic Working Paper no.* 105. Austin, TX: Southwest Educational Developmental Laboratory.

Ochs, E. and Schieffelin, B. (1995) The impact of language socialization on grammatical development. In P. Fletcher and B. MacWhinney (eds), *The handbook of child language* (pp. 73–94). Oxford: Blackwell.

Ortner, S. (1989) *High religion: A cultural and political history of Sherpa Buddhism.* Princeton, NJ: Princeton University Press.

Ortner, S. (1996) *Making gender: The politics and erotics of culture.* Boston: Beacon Press.

Pennycook, A. (1994) *The cultural politics of English as an international language.* London: Longman.

Pennycook, A. (1998) *English and the discourses of colonialism.* New York: Routledge.

Pennycook, A. (2001) *Critical applied linguistics: A critical introduction.* Mahwah, NJ: Lawrence Erlbaum Associates.

Penuel, W. and Wertsch, J. (1995) Vygotsky and identity formation: A sociocultural approach. *Educational Psychologist*, 30: 83–92.

Peters, A. and Boggs, S. (1986) Interactional routines as cultural influences upon language acquisition. In B. Schieffelin and E. Ochs (eds), *Language socialization across cultures* (pp. 80–96). New York: Cambridge University Press.

Phillips, S. (1983) *The invisible culture: Communication in classroom and community in the Warm Springs Indian Reservation.* White Plains, NY: Longman.

Phillipsen, G. (1975) Speaking like a man in Teamsterville: Cultural patterns of role enactment in an urban neighborhood. *Quarterly Journal of Speech*, 61: 13–22.

Phillipson, R. (1992) *Linguistic imperialism.* Oxford: Oxford University Press.

Phillipson, R. (2000) English in the new world order: Variations on a theme of linguistic imperialism and 'world' English. In T. Ricento (ed.), *Ideology, politics and language policies: Focus on English* (pp. 87–106). Amsterdam: John Benjamins.

Pierce, B.N. (1995) Social identity, investment and language learning. *TESOL Quarterly*, 29 (1): 9–31.

Pine, J. (1994a) The language of primary caregivers. In C. Gallaway and B. Richards (eds), *Input and interaction in language acquisition* (pp. 15–37). Cambridge: Cambridge University Press.

Pine, J. (1994b) Environmental correlates of variation in lexical style: Interactional style and the structure of input. *Applied Psycholinguistics*, 15: 355–70.

Potter, J.W. (1996) *An analysis of thinking and research about qualitative methods.* Mahwah, NJ: Lawrence Erlbaum.

Pratt, M.L. (1987) Linguistic utopias. In N. Fabb, D. Attridge, A. Durant and C. McCabe (eds), *The linguistics of writing* (pp. 48–66). New York: Metheun.

Psathas, G. (1995) *Conversation analysis: The study of talk-in-interaction.* Thousand Oaks, CA: Sage.

Radway, J. (1984) *Reading the romance: Women, patriarchy, and popular literature.* Chapel Hill, NC: University of North Carolina Press.

Ramirez, A. and Hall, J.K. (1990) Language and culture in secondary-level Spanish textbooks. *Modern Language Journal*, 74: 48–65.

Rampton, B. (1995) *Crossing: Language and ethnicity among adolescents.* London: Longman.

Reed, E. (1996) *Encountering the world: Toward an ecological psychology.* New York: Oxford University Press.

Reisigl, M. and Wodak, R. (2001) *Discourse and discrimination: Rhetorics of racism and anti-Semitism.* New York: Routledge.

Reisman, K. (1974) Contrapuntal conversations in an Antigual village. In R. Bauman and J. Sherzer (eds), *Explorations in the Ethnography of Speaking*. Cambridge: Cambridge University Press.

Rogoff, R. (1984) Developing understanding of the idea of communities of learners. *Mind, Culture and Activity*, 1 (4): 209–29.

Rogoff, B., Matusov, E. and White, C. (1996) Models of teaching and learning: Participation in a community of learners. In D. Olson and N. Torrance (eds), *The handbook of education and human development: New models of learning, teaching, and schooling* (pp. 388–415). Cambridge, UK: Basil Blackwell.

Sanders, R. (1999) The impossibility of a culturally contexted conversation analysis: On simultaneous, distinct types of pragmatic meaning. *Research on Language and Social Interaction*, 31 (1–2): 129–440.

Sapir, E. (1929/1949) In D.G. Mandelbaum (ed.), *The selected writings of Edward Sapir in language, culture, and personality* (pp. 160–6). Berkeley: University of California Press.

Sarangi, S. (1994) Intercultural or not? Beyond celebration of cultural differences in miscommunication analysis. *Pragmatics*, 4 (3): 409–27.

Sarangi, S. and Roberts, C. (1999) The dynamics of interactional and institutional orders in work-related settings. In S. Sarangi and C. Roberts (eds), *Talk, work and institutional order* (pp. 1–57). Berlin: Mouton de Gruyter.

Saville-Troike, M. (1987) Dilingual discourse: The negotiation of meaning without a common code. *Linguistics*, 25: 81–109.

Saville-Troike, M. and Kleifgen, J. (1986) Scripts for school: Cross-cultural communication in elementary classrooms. *Text*, 6 (2): 207–2l.

Schecter, S. and Bayley, R. (1997) Language socialization practices and cultural identity: Case studies of Mexican-descent families in California and Texas. *TESOL Quarterly*, 31 (3): 513–41.

Schieffelin, B. (1990) *The give and take of everyday life: Language socialization of Kaluli children*. Cambridge: Cambridge University Press.

Schieffelin, B. and Ochs, E. (eds) (1986) *Language socialization across cultures*. Cambridge: Cambridge University Press.

Schultz, E. (1990) *Dialogue at the margins: Whorf, Bakhtin and linguistic relativity*. Madison: University of Wisconsin Press.

Schutz, P., Cambless, C. and DeCuir, J. (in press) Multimethods research. In K.B. deMarrais and S.D. Lapan (eds), *Foundations of research: Methods of inquiry in education and the social sciences*. Hillsdale, NJ: Lawrence Erlbaum.

Scollon, R. and Scollon, S. (1981) *Narrative, literacy and face in interethnic communication*. Norwood, NJ: Ablex.

Scribner, S. (1997a) A sociocultural approach to the study of mind. In E. Tobach, R.J. Falmagne, M. Parlee, L. Martin and A.S. Kapelman (eds), *Mind and social practice: Selected writings of Sylvia Scribner* (pp. 266–80). Cambridge, UK: Cambridge University Press.

Scribner, S. (1997b) Thinking in action: Some characteristics of practical thought. In E. Tobach, R.J. Falmagne, M. Parlee, L. Martin and A.S. Kapelman (eds), *Mind and social practice: Selected writings of Sylvia Scribner* (pp. 319–37). Cambridge, UK: Cambridge University Press.

Sercu, L. (2000) *Acquiring intercultural communicative competence from textbooks*. Leuven, Belgium: Leuven University Press.

Sharan, S. (1980) Cooperative learning in small groups: Recent methods and effects on achievement, attitudes and ethnic relations. *Review of Educational Research*, 50: 241–71.

Sharan, S. (1984) *Cooperative learning in the classroom: Research in desegregated schools.* Hillsdale, NJ: Lawrence Erlbaum Associates.

Shea, D. (1994) *Incorporating ideology and structuring mismatch in cross cultural discourse.* Paper presented at the 1994 AAAL Conference, Baltimore, MD.

Shor, I. (1992) *Empowering education: Critical teaching for social change.* Chicago: The University of Chicago Press.

Shotter, J. (1993) Harre, Vygotsky, Bakhtin, Vico, Wittgenstein: Academic discourses and conversational realities. *Journal for the Theory of Social Behaviour*, 23 (4): 459–82.

Shotter, J. (1996) Living in a Wittgensteinian world: Beyond theory to a poetics of practices. *Journal for the Theory of Social Behaviour*, 26 (3): 292–311.

Shotter, J. (1997) Dialogical realities: the ordinary, the everyday and other strange new worlds. *Journal for The Theory of Social Behaviour*, 27 (2): 245–357.

Sherzer, J. (1983) *Kuna ways of speaking: An ethnographic perspective.* Austin: University of Texas Press.

Siegler, R.S. and Crowley, K. (1991) The microgenetic method: A direct means for studying cognitive development. *American Psychologist*, 46 (6): 606–20.

Sims-Holt, G. (1972) Stylin' outta the black pulpit. In T. Kochman (ed.), *Rappin and stylin' out.* Urbana: University of Illinois Press.

Sinclair, J. and Coulthard, M. (1975) *Towards an analysis of discourse: The English used by teachers and pupils.* London: Oxford University Press.

Skutnabb-Kangas, T. (1999) Linguistic human rights – are you naive or what? *TESOL Journal*, 8 (3): 6–12.

Skutnabb-Kangas, T. (2001) Linguistic human rights in education for language maintenance. In Maffi, Luisa (ed.), *On biocultural diversity: Linking language, knowledge and the environment* (pp. 397–411). Washington, DC: The Smithsonian Institute Press.

Slavin, R.E. (1980) Cooperative learning in teams: State of the art. *Educational Psychologist*, 15: 93–111.

Slavin, R.E. (1988) Cooperative learning and student achievement. In R.E. Slavin (ed.), *School and classroom organization.* Hillsdale, NJ: Lawrence Erlbaum.

Slavin, R.E. (1989/1990) Research on cooperative learning: Consensus and controversy. *Educational Leadership*, 47 (4): 52–5.

Slavin, R.E. (1995) *Cooperative learning: Theory, research and practice* (2nd edn). Boston: Allyn & Bacon.

Slobin, D. (1996) From 'thought' and 'language' to 'thinking for speaking'. In J. Gumperz and S. Levinson (eds), *Rethinking linguistic relativity* (pp. 70–96). Cambridge: Cambridge University Press.

Slobin, D. (ed.) (1997) *The crosslinguistic study of language acquisition: Expanding the contexts.* Mahwah, NJ: Lawrence Erlbaum Associates.

Smagorinsky, P. and Fly, P. (1993) The social environment of the classroom: A Vygotskyan perspective on small group process. *Communication Education*, 42 (2): 159–71.

Smitherman, G. (1994) *Black talk: Words and phrases from the hood to the amen corner.* New York: Houghton Mifflin.

Snow, C., Cancino, H., de Temple, J. and Schley, S. (1991) Giving formal definitions: A linguistic or metalinguistic skill? In E. Bialystok (ed.), *Language processing in bilingual children* (pp. 90–112). Cambridge: Cambridge University Press.

Spack, R. (1998) The author responds to Nelson. *TESOL Quarterly*, 32 (4): 732–5.

Stanley, W. (1992) *Curriculum utopia*. Albany: SUNY Press.

Street, B. (1993a) *Cross-cultural approaches to literacy*. Cambridge, UK: Cambridge University Press.

Street, B. (1993b) Culture is a verb: Anthropological aspects of language and cultural process. In D. Graddol, L. Thompson and M. Byram (eds), *Language and culture* (pp. 23–43). Clevedon: Multilingual Matters.

Tajfel, H. and Turner, J. (1986) The social identity theory of intergroup behavior. In S. Worchel and W. Austin (eds), *Psychology of intergroup relations*. Chicago: Nelson-Hall.

Taylor, C. (1995) 'You think it was a *fight*?': Co-constructing (the struggle for) meaning, face, and family in everyday narrative activity. *Research on Language and Social Interaction*, 28 (3): 283–317.

Tharp, R.G., Feathers, M., Bird, C., Epaloose, G. and Hilberg, R. (1998) *A report to Zuni*. University of California, Santa Cruz: Center for Research on Education, Diversity and Excellence .
[On line at: http://crede.ucsc.edu/Reports/5.6doc1.html]

Tollefson, J.W. (1991) *Planning language, planning inequality: Language policy in the community*. London: Longman.

Tollefson, J. (ed.) (2002) *Language policies in education: Critical issues*. Mahwah, NJ: Lawrence Erlbaum.

Tomasello, M. (1998) Introduction: A cognitive-functional perspective on language structure. In M. Tomasello (eds), *The New Psychology of Language* (pp. vii–xxiii). Mahwah, NJ: Lawrence Erlbaum Associates.

Tomasello, M. (1999) *The cultural origins of human cognition*. Cambridge: Harvard University Press.

Tomasello, M. (2000) Culture and cognitive development. *Current Directions in Psychological Science*, 9 (2): 37–40.

Tomasello, M. (2001) Perceiving intentions and learning words in the second year of life. In M. Bowerman and S. Levinson (eds), *Language acquisition and conceptual development* (pp. 132–58). Cambridge: Cambridge University Press.

Tomasello, M. and Barton, M. (1994) Learning words in non-ostensive contexts. *Developmental Psychology*, 30 (5): 639–50.

Tomasello, M., Conti-Ramsden, G. and Ewert, B. (1990) Young children's conversations with their mothers and fathers: Differences in breakdown and repair. *Journal of Child Language*, 17: 115–30.

Toohey, K. (1998) 'Breaking them up, taking them away': ESL students in Grade 1. *TESOL Quarterly*, 32 (1): 61–84.

Toohey, K. (2000) *Learning English at school*. Clevedon: Multilingual Matters.

Torres, L. (1997) *Puerto Rican discourse: A sociolinguistic study of a New York suburb*. Mahwah, NJ: Lawrence Erlbaum Associates.

Torres-Guzman, M. (1998) Language, culture and literacy in Puerto Rican communities. In B. Perez (ed.), *Sociocultural contexts of language and literacy* (pp. 99–122). Mahwah, NJ: Lawrence Erlbaum Associates.

Tyler, A. and Davies, C. (1990) Cross-linguistic communication missteps. *Text*, 10 (4): 385–411.

Urciuoli, B. (1996) *Exposing prejudice: Puerto Rican experiences of language, race, and class.* Boulder, CO: Westview Press.

Valdes, G. (1998) The construct of the near-native speaker in the foreign language profession: Perspectives on ideologies about language. *ADFL Bulletin*, 29 (30): 4–8.

van Dijk, T. (1993) Editor's forward to critical discourse analysis. *Discourse and Society*, 4: 131–2.

van Dijk, T. (1993) *Discourse and elite racism.* London: Sage.

van Patten, B. (1990) Attending to form and content in the input. *Studies in Second Language Acquisition*, 12: 287–301.

van Patten, B. and Cadierno, T. (1993) Explicit instruction and input processing. *Studies in Second Language Acquisition*, 15: 225–41.

Verplaetse, L.S. (2000) Mr. Wonder-ful: Portrait of a dialogic teacher. In J.K. Hall and L.S. Verplaetse (eds), *Second and foreign language learning through classroom interaction* (pp. 221–42). Mahwah, NJ: Lawrence Erlbaum Associates.

Verschueren, J. (1999) *Understanding pragmatics.* New York: Oxford University Press.

Vygotsky, L.S. (1978) *Mind in society: The development of higher psychological process.* Cambridge, MA: Harvard University Press.

Vygotsky, L.S. (1981) The genesis of higher mental functions. In J.V. Wertsch (ed. and trans.), *The concept of activity in Soviet psychology.* Armonk, NY: M.E. Sharpe.

Vygotsky, L.S. (1986) *Thought and language.* Cambridge, MA: MIT Press.

Vygotsky, L.S. (1994) The problem of the environment. In R. van der Veer and J. Valsiner (eds), *The Vygotsky reader* (pp. 338–54). Oxford: Blackwell.

Villegas, A.M. (1991) *Culturally responsive pedagogy for the 1990s and beyond.* Princeton, NY: Educational Testing Service.

Wallace, M. (1998) *Action research for language teachers.* Cambridge: Cambridge University Press.

Wallerstein, N. (1983) *Language and culture in conflict: Problem posing in the ESL classroom.* Reading, MA: Addison-Wesley.

Watson-Gegeo, K.A. and Boggs, S.T. (1977) From verbal play to talk story: The role of routine in speech events among Hawaiian children. In S. Ervin-Trip and C. Mitchell-Kernan (eds), *Child Discourse* (pp. 67–90). New York: Academic Press.

Watson-Gegeo, K.A. (1997) Classroom ethnography. In N. Hornberger and D. Olson (eds), *Encyclopedia of language and education, Volume 8: Research methods in language and education* (pp. 135–44). The Netherlands: Kluwer Academic Publishers.

Weedon, C. (1997) *Feminist practice and poststructuralist theory.* Cambridge, MA: Blackwell.

Weedon, C. (1999) *Feminism, theory, and the politics of difference.* Oxford: Blackwell Publishers.

Weigel, R., Wiser, P. and Cook, S. (1975) Impact of cooperative learning experiences on cross-ethnic relations and attitudes. *Journal of Social Issues*, 31 (1): 219–45.

Wells, G. (1993) Reevaluating the IRF sequence: a proposal for the articulation of theories of activity and discourse for the analysis of teaching and learning in the classroom. *Linguistics and Education*, 5: 1–17.

Wells, G. (1994) The complementary contributions of Halliday and Vygotsky to a 'language-based theory of learning'. *Linguistics and Education*, 6: 41–90.

Wells, G. (1996) Using the tool-kit of discourse in the activity of learning and teaching. *Mind, Culture and Activity*, 3 (2): 74–101.

Wells, G. (1999) *Dialogic inquiry: Toward a sociocultural practice and theory of education.* Cambridge: Cambridge University Press.

Well, G. (2000) Dialogic inquiry in education: Building on the legacy of Vygotsky. In C. Lee and P. Smagorinsky (eds), *Vygotskian perspectives on literacy research* (pp. 51–85). Cambridge: Cambridge University Press.

Wenger, E. (1998) *Communities of practice: Learning, meaning, and identity.* Cambridge, UK: Cambridge University Press.

Wertsch, J. (1991) *Voices of the mind.* Cambridge, MA: Harvard University Press.

Wertsch, J. (1994) The primacy of mediated action in sociocultural studies. *Mind, Culture, and Activity,* 1 (4): 202–8.

Wertsch, J. (1998) *Mind as action.* New York: Oxford University Press.

Wertsch, J.V. and Stone, C.A. (1978) Microgenesis as a tool for developmental analysis. *Quarterly Newsletter of the Laboratory of Comparative Human Cognition,* 9 (8): 8–10.

Wertsch, J.V. and Bivens, J. (1992) The social origins of individual mental functioning: Alternatives and perspectives. *Quarterly Newsletter of the Laboratory of Comparative Human Cognition,* 14 (2): 35–44.

Wertsch, J.V., del Rio, P. and Alvarez, A. (1995) Sociocultural studies: History, action and mediation. In J.V. Wertsch, P. del Rio and A. Alvarez (eds), *Sociocultural studies of mind* (pp. 1–34). New York: Cambridge University Press.

Whorf, B.L. (1940/1956) Science and linguistics. In J.K. Carroll (ed.), *Language thought and reality. Selected writings of Benjamin Lee Whorf* (pp. 207–19). Cambridge, MA: MIT Press.

Widdowson, H.G. (1989) Knowledge of language and ability for use. *Applied Linguistics,* 10 (2): 128–37.

Widdowson, H.G. (1998a) The ownership of English. In V. Zamel and R. Spack (eds), *Negotiating Academic Literacies* (pp. 237–48). Mahwah, NJ: Lawrence Erlbaum Associates.

Widdowson, H.G. (1998b) Skills, abilities, and contexts of reality. *Annual Review of Applied Linguistics,* 18: 323–33.

Widdowson, H. (2000) On the limitations of linguistics applied. *Applied Linguistics,* 21 (1): 3–25.

Willett, J. (1995) Becoming first graders in an L2: An ethnographic study of L2 socialization. *TESOL Quarterly,* 29 (3): 473–503.

Williams, G. (1992) *Sociolinguistics: A sociological critique.* London: Routledge.

Williams, R. (1977) *Marxism and literature.* Oxford: Oxford University Press.

Willis, J. (1996) *A framework for task-based learning.* Essex: Longman.

Wittgenstein, L. (1963) *Philosophical investigations* (G.E.M. Anscombe, trans.). Oxford: Basil Blackwell.

Wittgenstein, L. (1980) *Remarks on the philosophy of psychology. Vol.* 2. Oxford: Basil Blackwell.

Wodak, R. (ed.) (1997) *Gender and discourse.* London: Sage .

Wodak, R. (1999) Critical discourse analysis at the end of the 20th century. *Research on Language and Social Interaction,* 32 (1–2):

Wodak, R., de Cillia, R., Reisigl, M. and Liebhart, K. (1999) *The discursive construction of national identity.* Edinburgh: Edinburgh University Press.

Wolfram, W. (1974) *Sociolinguistic aspects of assimilation: Puerto Rican English in New York City.* Arlington, VA: Center for Applied Linguistics.

Wolfram, W. and Christian, D. (1976) *Appalachian Speech.* Arlington, VA: Center for Applied Linguistics.

Wolfram, W., Adger, C. and Christian, D. (1999) *Dialects in schools and communities*. Mahwah, NJ: Lawrence Erlbaum Associates.

Wong, J. (2000a) Delayed next turn repair initiation in native/nonnative speaker English conversation. *Applied Linguistics*, 21: 244–67.

Wong, J. (2000b) The token 'yeah' in nonnative speaker English conversation. *Research on Language and Social Interaction*, 33: 39–67.

Wong, S. (2000) Transforming the politics of schooling in the US: A model for successful academic achievement for language minority students. In J.K. Hall and W. Eggington (eds), *The sociopolitics of English language teaching* (pp. 117–36). Clevedon: Multilingual Matters.

Wortham, S. (2001) *Narratives in action: A strategy for research and analysis*. New York: Teachers College Press.

Wu, H.-F., De Temple, J., Herman, J. and Snow, C. (1994) 'L'animal qui fait oink!oink!': Bilingual children's oral and written picture descriptions in English and French under varying conditions. *Discourse Processes*, 18: 141–64.

Zentella, A.C. (1997) *Growing up bilingual*. Oxford: Blackwell.

Author Index

Abrahams, R., 22
Adger, C., 80, 82
Ahearn, L., 3, 35, 38
Allport, G., 98
Altieri, C., 35, 36
Alvarez, A., 8, 29, 175
Amanti, C., 77, 78, 79
Andrade, R., 80
Andrews, L., 80, 82
Aronson, E., 99, 100
Au, K.H., 76
Auerbach, E.R., 113, 114, 115, 116, 117

Bachman, L.F., 107
Bakhtin, M.M., 11, 13, 14, 16, 17, 37
Barnes, D., 63, 89, 90
Barton, D., 23, 73
Barton, M., 57
Baugh, J., 75
Bauman, R., 35
Bayley, R., 83
Begay, S., 77
Bergvall, V.L., 43
Berkowitz, S., 135
Berman, R., 57
Bhabha, H., 19
Bhatt, A., 74
Bing, J.M., 43
Bird, C., 77
Bivens, J., 64
Bixler-Márquez, D.J., 75
Boggs, J.W., 76
Boggs, S.T., 54
Bourdieu, P., 33, 37, 38, 42
Bowerman, M., 60, 61
Boxer, D., 93, 150
Boyd, M., 93
Bryman, M., 134
Bucholtz, M., 43
Byram, M., 109

Cadierno, T., 104
Calderon, M., 98
Cambless, C., 134
Canagarajah, A.S., 45, 87
Canale, M., 105, 106, 107
Cancino, H., 59
Candlin, C.N., 151, 152
Capps, L., 43, 188
Cazden, C., 63, 83, 89, 90, 106
Celce-Murcia, M., 107, 123
Chaiklin, S., 94
Chapelle, C., 26
Chen, C.H., 44
Chomsky, N., 21, 105
Christian, D., 75, 80, 82
Christie, F., 26
Choi, S., 60, 61
Civil, M., 80
Cohen, E., 98
Cole, M., 8, 155
Collins, C., 177
Consolo, D., 93
Conti-Ramsden, G., 57, 59
Cook, S., 98
Cook, V., 111
Cook-Gumperz, J., 101
Cope, B., 118, 121
Cortés-Conde, F., 93
Council of Europe, 110
Coulthard, M., 89
Crookes, G., 86, 104, 105
Crowley, K., 156
Crowley, T., 27

Damhuis, R., 93
Davies, A., 130
Davies, C., 40
Day, E., 45
de Certeau, M., 42, 131
de Cillia, R., 44, 154
DeCuir, J., 134
De Temple, J., 59

del Rio, P., 8, 29, 175
Dick, G.S., 77
Dien, T., 23, 74
Dornyei, Z., 107
Doughty, C., 104
Dube, N., 75
Duff, P.A., 22, 87, 88, 93
Duranti, A., 15, 18, 36, 46, 135, 136, 150

Edwards, A.D., 135, 136
Edwards, D., 9
Eggins, S., 27
Eisenberg, A., 54
Ellis, R., 62, 104
Elman, J., 58
Emerson, C., 14
Epaloose, G., 77
Erickson, E., 39
Estell, D.W., 77
Estell, J., 77
Ewert, B., 57, 59

Fairclough, N., 154, 176
Feathers, M., 77
Field, M., 40, 44
Fillmore, L.W., 82
Fishman, A., 74
Firth, A., 110
Fleming, M., 109
Floyd-Tenery, M., 77
Foster, M., 22, 87
Fotos, S., 104
Foucault, M., 42
Fowler, R., 176
Freed, A.F., 43
Freire, P., 113
Fly, P., 63

Gallimore, R., 76
Gamoran, A., 63, 89, 91, 92
Garcez, P., 149
Gass, S.M., 86
Gee, J.P., 33, 66
Giddens, A., 36, 37, 42
González, N., 77, 78, 79, 80
Gonzales, P., 43, 188
González, R., 77, 78, 79
Goodenough, W., 18
Goodwin, C., 149, 150
Goodwin, M.H., 24
Green, J., 66
Gumperz, J.J., 9, 38, 39, 40, 100, 146, 147, 148
Gutierrez, K., 63, 89, 90

Hajer, M., 93
Hall, J.K., 13, 22, 24, 91, 93, 101, 111, 156, 193, 194

Hall, K., 43
Halliday, M.A.K., 9, 25, 26, 56, 57, 96
Hamilton, M., 23
Hanks, W., 46
Harklau, L., 45, 87
Harkness, S.M., 35
Haviland, J.B., 22
He, A.W., 24
Heap, J., 149
Heath, S.B., 35, 54, 72–3, 117, 134
Heritage, J., 149
Herman, J., 59
Hertz-Lazarowitz, R., 98
Hewstone M., 33
Hickmann, M., 61
Hilberg, R., 77
Holt, D., 101
Holubec, E.J., 98
Hopper, P.J., 10, 11, 15
Hopper, R., 44
Hymes, D., 9, 14, 21, 22, 25, 105, 106, 142, 143, 148, 183, 198

Ibrahim, A., 45
Ivanic, R., 23

Jacoby, S., 24, 43, 150, 188
Jaspers, J., 33
Johnson, D.W., 98, 99
Johnson, F., 98
Johnson, R.T., 98, 99
Jordan, C., 76
Jupp, T., 40

Kachur, R., 63, 89, 91, 92
Kalantzis, M., 118, 121
Kandiah, T., 40, 41
Kasermann, M-L., 167
Katriel, T., 22
Keefer, C.H., 35
Kim, D., 156, 194
Kleifgen, J., 87
Kramsch, C., 110
Krashen, S.D., 104
Kwan, M., 101

Labov, W., 75
Lave, J., 94, 95, 131, 132
Layder, D., 133, 173, 176, 193
Lee, P., 20
Leeds-Hurwitz, W., 22
Leontiev, A.A., 49, 50, 132
Leontiev, A.N., 49, 50, 52, 61
Levinson, S., 61
Levi-Strauss, C., 18
Liang, A.C., 43
Liebhart, K., 44, 154
Lin, A., 91, 177

Livia, A., 43
Long, M., 86, 104, 105
Lotan, R., 98
Luckmann, T., 9

Maloof, V.M., 93
Mangiola, L., 117
Martin-Jones, M., 74
Mason, J.M., 76
Matusov, E., 95, 96
McCarthy, M., 82
McCarty, T.L., 23, 74, 77
McIntosh, A., 56
McKay, S., 44, 48
Mehan, H., 63, 89
Mey, J., 154
Miller, J., 43
Mittins, B., 82
Moerman, M., 24
Moll, L.C., 77, 79
Morson, G., 14

Nassaji, H., 92
National Research Council, 111, 112, 156
Neff, D., 79
New London Group, 118, 120, 122
Ninio, A., 57
Norton, B., 44, 65, 117
Nunan, D., 111
Nystrand, M., 63, 89, 91, 92

Ochs, E., 10, 24, 33, 43, 46, 53, 54, 55, 56, 72, 135, 150, 188
Ornstein-Galacia, J., 75
Ortner, S., 45, 47

Palmer, A.S., 107
Patnoe, S., 99, 100
Pennycook, A., 7, 114, 176
Pendergast, C., 63, 89, 91, 92
Penuel, W., 158
Peters, A., 54
Phillips, S., 54, 72–3
Phillipsen, G., 34
Phillipson, R., 176
Pierce, B.N., 44, 117
Pine, J., 57, 59
Poole, D., 189
Potter, J.W., 134
Pratt, M.L., 40, 42, 45
Psathas, G., 24

Radway, J., 23
Ramirez, A., 111
Rampton, B., 45, 193
Reed, E., 130
Rendon, P., 77, 78, 79
Reisigl, M., 44, 154, 176

Reisman, K., 14
Rivera, A, 77, 78, 79
Roberts, C., 40, 42
Robinson, P., 86, 104
Rogoff, R., 94, 95, 96
Rymes, B., 195

Sanders, R., 149
Sapir, E., 19, 20
Sarangi, S., 18, 40, 42
Saville-Troike, M., 86
Schecter, S., 83
Schley, S., 59
Schieffelin, B., 10, 53, 54, 72
Schultz, E., 14
Schutz, P., 134
Scollon, R, 40
Scollon, S., 40
Scribner, S., 49, 53, 94
Sells, A., 77
Sercu, L., 110
Sharan, S., 98
Shea, D., 41, 193
Shor, I., 115
Shotter, J., 9, 28, 29, 131
Sherzer, J., 22
Shultz, J., 39
Siegler, R.S., 156
Sims-Holt, G., 14
Sinclair, J., 89
Skutnabb-Kangas, T., 176
Slade, D., 27
Slavin, R.E., 98, 99
Slobin, D., 57, 61
Smagorinsky, P., 63
Smitherman, G., 75
Snow, C., 57, 59, 82
Spack, R., 42
Stanley, W., 114
Street, B., 19
Strevens, P., 56
Stone, C.A., 156
Super, C., 35
Sutton, L.A., 43
Swain, M., 105, 106, 107
Szymanski, M., 101

Tajfel, H., 33
Taylor, C., 44, 82
Taylor, O., 82
Terrell, T.D., 104
Tharp, R.G., 77
Thibodeau, R., 100
Thompson, S., 10
Thurrell, S., 107
Tollefson, J.W., 176
Tomasello, M., 9, 50, 57, 58, 59, 60, 62, 155

Toohey, K., 45, 87, 184
Torres, L., 75
Torres-Guzman, M., 23
Turner, J., 33
Tyler, A., 40

Uchida, Y., 88
Unsworth, L., 26
Urciuoli, B., 75

Valdes, G., 110
van Dijk, T., 176
van Patten, B., 104
Verplaetse, L.S., 93
Verschueren, J., 42
Vygotsky, L.S., 49, 50, 51, 52, 56, 61, 64, 155, 175
Villegas, A.M., 76

Wagner, J., 100
Wallace, M., 138
Wallerstein, N., 113, 114, 115, 116
Watahomigie, L., 23, 74
Watson-Gegeo, K.A., 149, 150
Weedon, C., 36, 42, 46
Weigel, R., 98
Wells, G., 64, 91, 92, 94, 96, 97

Wenger, E., 94, 95, 131, 132
Wertsch, J., 8, 29, 49, 51, 53, 61, 64, 111, 155, 156, 158, 175
Westgate, D.P., 135, 136
White, C., 95, 96
Whorf, B.L., 19, 20, 25, 61
Widdowson, H.G., 7, 109, 111, 112, 130, 133, 151, 177
Willett, J., 87
Williams, G., 18, 83
Williams, J., 104
Williams, R., 13, 50, 66
Willis, J., 105
Wiser, P., 98
Wittgenstein, L., 9, 10, 17
Wodak, R., 44, 154, 176
Wolfram, W., 75, 80
Wong, J., 44
Wong, S., 113
Wong, S.L., 44, 48
Wortham, S., 151, 152
Wu, H-F., 59

Yates, S., 100

Zarate, G., 109
Zentella, A.C., 75

Subject Index

agency, 35–6
  agent, cooperative, 39
archives *see* research, data sources

classroom-based social research *see*
    participatory pedagogy
classroom discourse, 63–4, 89–93
  IRE, 89–91
  IRF, 91–3
co-construction, 43
competence
  communicative, 105–108
  linguistic, 105
communicative activity *see* communicative
    event, *see also* research contexts
communicative event, 22–4, 142–3
  oral, 22
  literacy, 23
communicative plans, 9
communities
  inquiry, of, 97
  learners, of, 94–6
  practice, of, 94–5
contextualization cues, 38–9, 42, 55
conversation analysis, 23–4, 148–50
cooperative learning, 98–100
  Student-team learning, 99–100
  Jigsaw, 100
critical discourse analysis *see* discourse
    analysis
critical framing *see* multiliteracies
    pedagogy
critical pedagogy *see* participatory
    pedagogy
culturally responsive pedagogy, 76–7
  KEEP, 76–7
  Rough Rock, 77

dialect education *see* language awareness
    curricula
dialogue, 11–13
dialogicality, 12

discourse analysis, 151–3
  critical, 154–5
  explanatory, 151–2
  narrative, 151–2
discourse-historical methodology, 154
discourse-historical methodology *see* discourse
    analysis

emergent grammar, 10–11
ethnography of communication, 22–3, 142–6
  SPEAKING model, 142–3, 167
ethnography of speaking *see* ethnography of
    communication
explanatory discourse analysis *see* discourse
    analysis

field notes *see* research, data sources
funds of knowledge, 77–80

habitus, 33, 37–8

indexicality, 55
indexicals, linguistic, 55
interactional sociolinguistics, 38–40, 146–8
intercultural communicative competence,
    109–10
interviews *see* research, data sources
IRE *see* classroom discourse
IRF *see* classroom discourse

language awareness curricula, 80
  dialect education, 80
language games, 9–10, 17, 130–1
language socialization, 54–6
  home versus school practices, 72–4
  literacy practices, 73–4
language variation, 74–5
legitimate peripheral participation, 95
linguistics applied approach, 7, 17–18, 31–2,
    48–9, 65, 128–30
linguistic relativity, 19–20, 25, 61
literacy, definition of, 23

mediated action, 51
mediational means, 51–2
microgenetic approach, 155–8
micro-ethnography, 149–50
multiliteracies pedagogy, 118–22
  critical framing, 120–2
  overt instruction, 119–20
  situated practice, 119
  transformed practice, 122

narrative analysis *see* discourse analysis

overt instruction *see* multiliteracies pedagogy

participant observation *see* research, data
    sources
participatory pedagogy, 113–17
  classroom-based social research, 117
  critical pedagogy, 114
  problem-posing approach, 114–17
personal reflection journals *see* research, data
    sources

questionnaires *see* research, data sources

research
  contexts, 175–98
    communicative activities, 187–92
    individual experiences, 193–8
    institutional, 182–7
    sociocultural structures, 175–82
  cycle, 160–1
  data sources, 163–5
    archives, 165
    field notes, 164

    interviews and questionnaires, 163
    participant-observation, 164
    personal reflection journals, 165
    think-aloud protocols, 163–4
    video-recordings, 164–5
  ethics, 137–9
  guidelines, 169
  methods, 132–5

situated practice *see* multiliteracies pedagogy
social identity, 32–35
socially constituted linguistics, 21–2
social practice, theory of, 130–2
sociolinguistic relativity, 25
SPEAKING *see* ethnography of
    communication
structuration, theory of, 36–7
Systemic functional linguistics, 25–6

think-aloud protocols *see* research, data
    sources
transformed practice *see* multiliteracies
    pedagogy
translinguistics, 12
turn-taking patterns, 14

utterance, 11, 14–16
  double-voiced, 15–16
    active, 15–16
    passive, 15
  single-voiced, 14–15

video-recordings *see* research, data sources

zone of proximal development, 49–50